THE RED HAND

———

Protestant Paramilitaries
in Northern Ireland

STEVE BRUCE

Oxford   New York

OXFORD UNIVERSITY PRESS

Oxford University Press, Walton Street, Oxford OX2 6DP

Oxford New York Toronto
Delhi Bombay Calcutta Madras Karachi
Kuala Lumpur Singapore Hong Kong Tokyo
Nairobi Dar es Salaam Cape Town
Melbourne Auckland Madrid

and associated companies in
Berlin Ibadan

Oxford is a trade mark of Oxford University Press

British Library Cataloguing in Publication Data
Data available

Library of Congress Cataloging in Publication Data
Bruce, Steve, 1954-
The red hand: Protestant paramilitaries in Northern Ireland /
Steve Bruce.
p. cm.
Includes bibliographical references.
1. Northern Ireland—History—1969- . 2. Paramilitary forces—
Northern Ireland—History. 3. Protestants—Northern Ireland—
History. 4. Terrorism—Northern Ireland—History. 5. Violence—
Northern Ireland—History. I. Title.
941.60824—dc20 DA990.U46B678 1992 91-46663
ISBN 0-19-215961-5
ISBN 0-19-285256-6 (pbk)

3 5 7 9 10 8 6 4

Printed in Great Britain by
Biddles Ltd
Guildford and King's Lynn

For Roy Wallis

ACKNOWLEDGEMENTS

Any major piece of research overdraws on the goodwill of a large number of institutions and individuals and I would like to thank a number of them. In the thirteen years I was on its staff, the Queen's University of Belfast was extremely generous with its resources. The Economic and Social Research Council gave a grant which allowed me to buy myself out of teaching and thus work full time on the book for three months. Sam Porter saved me a great deal of time by ploughing through local newspapers looking for relevant stories. My colleague Steven Yearley kindly allowed me to talk some of my ideas at him and made many constructive comments on an early draft of the book. A number of journalists, particularly David McKittrick, helped me by answering my endless questions about their published reports. Harry Reid, deputy editor of the *Glasgow Herald*, allowed me to consult that paper's news-cuttings archives, as did the BBC in Northern Ireland. An obvious (and insufficiently used) technique for improving the accuracy of description is to allow the people one is writing about to read what one has written and comment on it. Although no one has been given a veto on this text, a number of well-informed loyalists have read the draft and made helpful suggestions.

My wife has been more than helpful in compensating for my many hours shut away in the office. On a number of occasions Mr and Mrs Hill of the Gowk Inn, Gartocharn, kindly lent me their house near Loch Lomond for some quiet writing, away from a telephone and university business.

On 1 April 1991 I moved to the University of Aberdeen, and did so with considerable sadness. My years in Belfast have been very enjoyable and rewarding ones and, despite my lack of personal attachment to the causes that so motivate them, I feel privileged to have met so many pleasant people in the course of my research in Northern Ireland.

Finally, I would like to acknowledge my enduring and enormous intellectual debt to Professor Roy Wallis, who died suddenly in May 1990. Roy taught me as an undergraduate and postgraduate student and gave me my first lecturing job. In the twelve years we worked together at Queen's he was a constant source of inspiration and instruction, so much so that I feel everything I now write should appear under both our names. I know I will miss his guidance as much as I miss his friendship, but I hope that the good parts of this book will serve as a very small memorial to his talents.

CONTENTS

LIST OF ABBREVIATIONS, WITH GLOSSARY

CESA   Catholic Ex-Servicemen's Association: *nationalist vigilante group of the early Troubles*

DOW   Down Orange Welfare: *paramilitary organization of County Down farmers founded in 1972 by retired Col. Peter 'Basil' Brush; most respectable and law-abiding of the organizations*

DUP   Democratic Unionist Party: *formed by Ian Paisley in 1971 as successor to his Protestant Unionist Party*

EOKA   Greek Cypriot terror organization

GOC   General Officer Commanding

IIP   Irish Independence Party: *small constitutional nationalist party formed in 1977*

IIP   Irish Information Partnership: *an independent collector and publisher of information relating to the Troubles*

INLA   Irish National Liberation Army: *military wing of the IRSP set up in 1975; murdered Airey Neave; in 1976 and 1977 involved in murderous feud with its breakaway IPLO*

IPLO   Irish People's Liberation Organization: *splinter from INLA in 1976*

IRA   Irish Republican Army: *oldest of armed republican organizations; ran not very successful campaign against the Ulster state in the 1950s; split into OIRA and PIRA in late 1969*

IRSP   Irish Republican Socialist Party: *formed in 1974 from Official Sinn Fein and PIRA dissidents*

LAW   Loyalist Association of Workers

LDV   Loyalist Defence Volunteers: *short-lived Fermanagh-based grouping of OVs, UVSC, and USCA around early 1974; members committed a number of murders in Fermanagh and Tyrone*

LPA   Loyalist Prisoners' Aid: *UDA prisoners' support organization*

LPWA   Loyalist Prisoners' Welfare Association: *UVF prisoners' support organization*

NF   National Front: *largest of British fascist and racist movements*

	of the 1970s; tried with no great success to recruit Ulster loyalists and use Ulster conflict to broaden support base
NICRA	Northern Ireland Civil Rights Association: *formed in January 1967; spearheaded civil-rights agitations*
NILP	Northern Ireland Labour Party: *founded in 1924 and folded in 1987; was moderately successful in Belfast when the border was not threatened*
NUP	National Union of Protestants: *British anti-Catholic and anti-ritualist religious ginger group of the late 1950s and early 1960s; Paisley was active in NI branch*
NUPRG	New Ulster Political Research Group: *UDA think tank led by Glen Barr from 1978 to 1981; produced* Beyond the Religious Divide, *a blueprint for negotiated independence*
OC	Orange Cross: *precursor of LPWA; produced magazine of same name in early 1970s and ran Orange Cross club on the Shankill*
OIRA	Official IRA: *declared a cease-fire in May 1972 and gradually turned itself into non-military left-wing Workers Party*
OUP	'Official' Unionist Party: *name by which the anti-power-sharing part of the Ulster Unionist Party was known when Faulkner took liberal unionists into power-sharing executive*
OV	Orange Volunteers: *formed in 1972 as paramilitary organization for Orange Order members; bombed a pub in Belfast in 1973 but otherwise did little illegal other than collect the considerable bodies of arms found in Belfast Orange Halls in the early 1970s; active in 1974 strike*
PAF	Protestant Action Force: nom de guerre *of UVF used generally by south-east Antrim and mid-Ulster groups and by others during UVF cease-fires*
PAG	Protestant Action Group: *as for PAF*
PIRA	Provisional IRA: *the mainly northern and more militant wing of the IRA that split from the IRA in late 1969 and continued the armed struggle*
PUP	Progressive Unionist Party: *Hugh Smyth's Shankill Road-based party formed in 1979*
PUP	Protestant Unionist Party: *Paisley's first political party; replaced by DUP*
RHC	Red Hand Commando: *loyalist paramilitary organization founded in 1972 by John McKeague after he was pushed out of*

	the SDA; *mostly very close to the UVF, but sometimes feuding with that body*
RIC	Royal Irish Constabulary: *the pre-partition Irish police force*
RUC	Royal Ulster Constabulary: *the police force of Northern Ireland*
RUCR	Royal Ulster Constabulary Reserve: *reserve of RUC; has full-time and part-time members*
SAS	Special Air Service: *élite and secretive unit of British Army*
SDA	Shankill Defence Association: *loyalist vigilante group led by John McKeague which was one of main components of the UDA; active in early communal violence*
SDLP	Social Democratic and Labour Party: *constitutional nationalist party formed in 1970 by Gerry Fitt, John Hume, and others*
TA	Territorial Army: *British army reserve units; recruits in Northern Ireland but is not deployed there*
Tara	*paramilitary organization formed by William McGrath in 1966; alone of the paramilitaries, it promoted a religious anti-Catholicism; infiltrated by UVF men, it collected weapons but took little aggressive action*
Third Force	*term used to describe Paisley's periodic attempts to recruit a mass defensive militia; most commonly used for the one paraded in 1981*
UAC	Ulster Army Council: *talking shop from 1973 until late 1974 for the loyalist paramilitary organizations*
UCA	Ulster Citizens' Army: *completely fictitious left-wing loyalist paramilitary organization invented by British army intelligence as a device for stirring up inter-paramilitary suspicion and hostility*
UCAG	Ulster Community Action Group: *UDA-backed community group association*
UCCL	Ulster Citizens' Civil Liberties: *UDA-backed legal representation group led by Sammy Smyth and Harry Chicken; produced Bill of Rights which formed part of NUPRG's* Beyond the Religious Divide *proposals*
UCDC	Ulster Constitution Defence Committee: *vehicle for organizing Paisley's demonstrations against O'Neill in late 1960s*
UDA	Ulster Defence Association: *largest loyalist paramilitary*

organization; formed in September 1971 as a union of the district vigilante groups

UDR   Ulster Defence Regiment: *locally recruited and often part-time British army regiment formed in 1970 to replace USC*

UFF   Ulster Freedom Fighters: nom de guerre *of UDA men; first used to claim pub bomb in Belfast in June 1973*

ULCCC   Ulster Loyalist Central Co-ordinating Committee: *umbrella for paramilitaries; successor to UAC; UDA withdrew in 1976 over claimed ULCCC–PIRA contacts; revived in 1991 as co-ordinator of paramilitary response to Brooke political talks*

ULDP   Ulster Loyalist Democratic Party: *formed by UDA in June 1981 to succeed NUPRG; led by John McMichael, it produced* Common Sense

ULF   Ulster Loyalist Front: *very short-lived 1972 combination of Shankill Road loyalist politicians and paramilitaries*

UPA   Ulster Protestant Action: *unionist ginger group of the late 1950s and early 1960s*

UPV   Ulster Protestant Volunteers: *Paisleyite 'mass membership' counterpart to the UCDC, 1967–9; many members were also in the UVF*

UPNI   Unionist Party of Northern Ireland: *formed by Brian Faulkner for his liberal 'power-sharing' wing of the Unionist Party*

UR   Ulster Resistance: *small rural organization formed in 1986 in opposition to Anglo-Irish accord; raised money illegally and joined UDA and UVF in arms purchase, but took no hostile action*

USC   Ulster Special Constabulary: *raised as an anti-IRA paramilitary police force in 1920; initially in three sections—A, B, and C—the A and C parts were stood down, leaving the B Specials as a part-time force; replaced in April 1970 by UDR*

USC   Ulster Service Corps: *largest of the small paramilitary organizations in the mid-1970s; formed by ex-Specials; retained structure and popular in rural areas but did little*

USCA   Ulster Special Constabulary Association: *semi-paramilitary organization of ex-B Specials*

UUAC   United Unionist Action Council: *formed in March 1976 when Convention steering group of unionist parties fell apart; umbrella for DUP, UDA, and other groups supporting 1977 strike*

UUP	Ulster Unionist Party: *the main unionist party, governed the province from partition to the closing of Stormont in 1972; also known as the 'Official' UP*
UUUC	United Ulster Unionist Council: *coalition of anti-power sharing unionists (DUP, OUP, and VUP) from April 1974 to 1977 strike when OUP withdrew*
UUUM	United Ulster Unionist Movement: *rump of Vanguard party after split over voluntary coalition proposals; led by Ernest Baird; supported DUP in 1977 strike*
UV	Ulster Vanguard: *William Craig's ginger group within the Unionist Party from 1972 to 1973*
UVF	Ulster Volunteer Force: *1912 force formed by Carson and Craig to oppose Irish independence plans; incorporated in 1914 British army as 36th (Ulster) Division; also 1966 paramilitary organization formed by Shankill Road loyalists; banned in June 1966; legalized in April 1974; banned again in October 1975*
UVSC	Ulster Volunteer Service Corps: *formed in 1973 as successor to VSC*
UWC	Ulster Workers' Council: *successor to LAW and forum for workers' representatives who helped organize 1974 strike*
VPP	Volunteer Political Party: *short-lived 1974 political experiment of the UVF; led by Ken Gibson*
VSC	Vanguard Service Corps: *paramilitary wing of the Vanguard movement and Craig's bodyguard; led by Hugh Petrie, wore uniform but did little else; changed name to UVSC when Vanguard became a party*
VUPP	Vanguard Unionist Progressive Party: *Ulster Vanguard became a political party in 1973*
WDA	Woodvale Defence Association: *most influential constituent part of UDA*
YCV	Young Citizens' Volunteers: *in 1912 a separate 'élite' unit which became part of Carson's UVF; used by present UVF to designate 'juvenile' unit*
YM	Young Militants: *cover name used in UDA murders in mid-1970s and also youth wing, analogous to UVF's YCV*

Introduction: Researching a Grey World

THIS book was written because I wanted to read it or something like it. While researching *God Save Ulster!: The Religion and Politics of Paisleyism*, I wanted to check some details of the early history of the Ulster Defence Association (UDA) and discovered that very little had been written about loyalist paramilitaries and most of it was fanciful. The neglect is even more noticeable when one considers the extensive literature on the Irish Republican Army (IRA), some of which is well researched.

The lack of serious interest in Protestant terrorist organizations cannot be explained by their insignificance. Put very crudely, they have been responsible for just under half the civilian deaths during the present unrest in Ulster. They have also brought down a government. My guess is that loyalists are neglected because few academics and serious journalists are unionists. The university-educated middle classes have difficulty understanding why anyone would fight for something as insubstantial as patriotism. They can almost understand Irish nationalism, because the geography of the place would suggest that everyone here ought to 'live together'. If, as many are, they are also left-leaning, they will sympathize with what can be portrayed as an anti-imperialist movement. But when the patriotism is something as unfashionable as a desire to remain part of the United Kingdom, comprehension fails completely, and most people fall back on imputing alternative motives to Ulster loyalists. So it is supposed that they are not really fighting to keep Ulster British but to keep their economic and political privileges. In an extreme example of the genre, Lebow explains loyalist sectarian murder as stemming from a desire to keep Catholics out of Protestant workplaces and preserve 'Protestant' jobs.[1] Can we imagine an academic suggesting that the IRA kills Protestants to create job vacancies for Catholics?

---

[1] N. Lebow, 'The Origins of Sectarian Assassination: The Case of Belfast', in A. D. Buckley and D. D. Olson (eds.), *International Terrorism* (Wayne, NJ, 1980), 41–53.

Researching paramilitary organizations is difficult and time consuming. People will readily invest great effort in writing about causes with which they sympathize. They may invest a smaller amount of effort in writing ill-informed books about things they do not like. They are not likely to sink three years of their lives in researching the beliefs and behaviour of those they view with either loathing or incredulity. Hence, to put it simply, the lack of serious books about the UDA and the Ulster Volunteer Force (UVF) is probably explained by the unpopularity of their cause among the writing classes.

This book aims to be two things: a work of record and, where possible, an explanation. It is not a work of moral judgement. There is already quite enough of that about and there is nothing in the professional training of sociologists that gives me any greater insight into how the world should be than has the layman. The more dreadful the subject-matter, the more important it is to concentrate on describing and explaining. It is not my job to tell people how they ought to feel about the people and organizations herein described.

How does one know when a writer has got it right? With research such as opinion polling, which is based on administering standard questionnaires to samples of people and then statistically analysing the responses, we can get some idea of whether we should believe the conclusions from examining the research procedures: is the sample representative; have appropriate tests been performed on the results? With the sort of research reported here such tests are not possible. It is important, therefore, that I give the reader some idea of my sources so that the quality of my information and the conclusions drawn from it can be judged.

Unlike Martin Dillon, whose three books about the troubles— *Political Murder in Northern Ireland*, *The Shankill Butchers*, and *The Dirty War*—are all written with the certainty of a man 'discovering' the truth, I doubt if I have discovered anything except what people, for reasons often too complex even to begin to unpack, wanted to tell me. To report the stories that are told here as if there were no doubts about their accuracy would be deceit. In the course of my research I have frequently had to change my mind as one version of events which I had accepted at face value was challenged by another quite different but plausible account. People I had taken to be honest I later came to see as crooks;

people I had summed up as self-interested villains turned out much-maligned saints. Like a set of Russian dolls, every layer which I took to be the final definitive version was peeled away to reveal yet another possible interpretation.

Accounts are the major source of information. First there are the 'hearsay' accounts of some people telling us what *others* have done. These are obviously fallible, in that the teller may not be as well informed as he or she thinks. Even if well informed, he or she may have a wide variety of reasons for distorting and dissembling. But even when one is dealing with first-hand accounts—the stories told by people about their own activities—there are still a number of reasons why they cannot be accepted at face value. In the case of statements made to the police and in court testimony, we readily appreciate that the stories told are more than simple attempts to describe the past correctly. Often the speaker will be trying to win some sort of advantage or favourable outcome from the encounter. For example, it is a common feature of statements made in connection with serious crimes that those making the statements minimize their own part. If one took any number of those at face value, one would have to conclude that everybody was just 'holding the coats', 'just driving the car', or just giving the victim a 'wee kicking'; nobody actually did the killing.

Were it always the case that people played down their involvement in crimes or tried to present themselves as more 'respectable', one could compensate for the bias, but it is not unknown for people to build a heroic image for themselves and to claim responsibility for crimes they almost certainly did not commit and a degree of involvement they did not have. For example, it has been suggested by some people who might be in a position to know that the Milltown cemetery killer Michael Stone did not commit the other murders which he claimed and for which he was convicted.

Put bluntly, there are an enormous number of reasons why people might distort, embellish, prevaricate, disguise, and plain lie in their evidence. And the problem is further compounded by a lack of perfect recall and perfect knowledge. These are not just problems of interpreting accounts given in such formal settings as interrogations and courtroom testimonies. They are also part of the everyday life of conversation. When people tell me about what they did and why they did it, they are always doing more than exercising their fallible recall; they are trying to make particular impressions on me and on themselves. They may wish to appear more insightful, honest, courageous, or principled than they really believe themselves to be.

These problems with 'accounts' infect history and social science and everyday life. Contrary to the impression given by some research-methods textbooks, there are no techniques or procedures that definitively resolve them. One can only hope that the diligence and common sense of researchers allow them to penetrate the most obvious smokescreens. I only raise the issue at the start because this book is concerned almost entirely with activities that are illegal or that offend against the simplest ethical codes. Whatever its long-term goal and its procedural niceties, paramilitary activity involves killing people, conspiring to kill people, and preparing to kill people. More than any field of human endeavour which a social scientist is liable to research, this area is one of lies, deception, and self-deception. A general weakness of the work of such journalists as Martin Dillon is that it does not often enough and explicitly enough admit the weakness of its sources and the likelihood that much of it is little more than plausible speculation.

My major second-hand sources have been the local and Dublin newspapers and magazines: *Irish News*, *Irish Times*, *Newsletter*, *Belfast Telegraph*, *Fortnight*, *Magill*, and *Hibernia*. In particular, the work of David McKittrick for the *Irish Times* and (since 1987) the *Independent* and of Kevin Myers of *Hibernia* was informative and insightful. The publications of various parties to the conflict— *Republican News*, *Ulster*, *Combat*, *Loyalist News*, and *Protestant Telegraph*, as well as a host of many shorter-lived periodicals— have been examined.

But the main source of information has been interviews with a large number of loyalist paramilitaries (retired and still active). For obvious reasons, I cannot be more specific and indeed have taken some trouble to disguise the identity of sources. The only way the sceptical reader can be assured that the right people have been consulted is to note that, between fifty-eight of them, they have served well over two hundred years' imprisonment or internment.

In his famous study of suicide, Emile Durkheim defended his use of suspect official statistics with the argument that, while such figures may be riddled with errors, in any long series of statistics the errors will cancel out, leaving reliable overall patterns.[2] Although most of us are trained to see through that defence, I would like to offer a version of it for the validity of this study. The details of this or that event may well be wrong; some are certain to be wrong and no amount of additional research would have altered that fact. So we should never construct an explanation that needs to rest, like an inverted pyramid, on just one event or one source. I hope that the general story, the big picture, is right more often than not, but I can only remind the reader that this account of the UDA and UVF, although it represents the best I can do, is still often little more than plausible speculation.

Finally, a word must be said about British libel laws and their impact on authors. In the United States it is possible to say damaging things about a person provided one has good reason to believe them to be true and does so without 'malice afterthought'. In British law, the odds are stacked the other way; absence of malice and good reason are not enough to prevent an erroneous accusation being libellous. Most British book-publishing contracts make the author solely liable for any legal costs incurred. This naturally makes authors very cautious of saying even those things of which they are confident. This is one reason why many opinions and actions are attributed to such anonymous characters as 'senior UDA men' and 'a UVF leader'. One cannot say 'the cat sat on the mat', if the cat has not been convicted of this offence. Often I have had to say 'It was believed by many people that the cat sat on the mat', but even this is no sure protection, and so sometimes the cautious writer has to say 'The mat was sat upon by some small animal' or 'Something sat on the mat'.

There are other reasons for such cautions. Not being in the game of moral judgement, I have no desire to 'finger' individuals, except where establishing the identity of an agent is crucial to understanding some important event in the history of the paramilitary organizations. Given the habit of the IRA and the Irish National Liberation Army (INLA) of trying to murder the loyalists named in the 'supergrass' trials of the early 1980s, such reticence seems appropriate. I also have no desire to spend the rest of my life looking over my shoulder for offended loyalist gunmen. Friendly as they have been on many occasions, I am well aware

[2] E. Durkheim, *Suicide* (London, 1968).

that the people I have interviewed either have guns or have friends with guns.

Fortunately, I am more interested in describing and explaining the general developments of loyalist paramilitarism than I am in attributing blame for particular actions, and the frequent absence of names should not undermine that exercise.

I

Ulster and the First Ulster Volunteer Force

LIKE the half-full glass, the history of most societies can be described in two ways: a story of peace occasionally disrupted, or a series of wars linked by temporary truces. Which of the two versions one favours can rarely be settled by the historical record; one is as reasonable a version as the other. Which is the abnormal and which the normal state of a society is rarely a matter of fact; more often it is a question of perspective. It would be possible to write the history of Ulster as one of peaceful progress and gradual enlightenment, interrupted by the odd unfortunate incident. However, my interests cause me to concentrate on those aspects of the past which show the constant tension towards violence in Ulster.

Ulster Protestants are predominantly descendants of the Scots (and some English) who settled in the north-east of Ireland in the sixteenth and seventeenth centuries.[1] That the settlers were of a different 'race', were of a different religion, and were in economic competition with the native Irish meant that relations between the two groups were generally distant and periodically degenerated into open warfare. Little or nothing that has happened in the history of Ireland since settlement has brought the two populations any closer together. For a very brief period in 1798, when the inspiration of the French Revolution produced the radical United Irishmen movement, there seemed some hope of an alliance of Ulster Presbyterians and Irish Catholics against the English, but a common religion and shared status interests made the other alignment—the two Protestant groups versus the Catholics—the one that prevailed.[2]

An important part in bringing the two Protestant populations together was played by the Orange Order. Ireland in the eighteenth

---

[1] W. Macafee and V. Morgan, 'Population in Ulster, 1660–1760', in P. Roebuck (ed.), *Plantation to Partition* (Belfast, 1981), 47.

[2] On the United Irishmen, see A. T. Q. Stewart, *The Narrow Ground* (London, 1977), 101–10.

century was littered with secret societies and informal militias. These were largely agrarian movements; Protestant and Catholic small farmers and peasants banded together against each other in such movements as the Defenders and the Peep O'Day Boys. The Orange Order (named after the Dutch territories of King William III, the Protestant monarch who ousted Catholic James VII in 1690) was founded after a battle at the Diamond in 1795 by Protestants who expected it to be the first of many skirmishes with their Catholic neighbours.[3] Like so many associations of the time, the Order was modelled on the Freemasons. At first the Episcopalian gentry were ambivalent about the Order. It had the right religion, but there was always the danger that it might move from destroying and expropriating Catholic property to stealing from the aristocracy. It was only when the United Irishmen seemed an even greater threat that the gentry entered the Order. In the relative peace of the first two decades of the nineteenth century the movement declined and there was considerable internal dissension. It revived in the 1820s as a vehicle for popular opposition to Daniel O'Connell and then faded again before the Irish home-rule agitations of the late nineteenth century gave it a new salience. Now professional and urban Ulster Presbyterians joined the rural Anglican gentry and their peasants.

The Original UVF

Pressure for home rule for Ireland mounted through the last half of the nineteenth century. Two home-rule bills were defeated— the first in the Commons, the second in the Lords—but in 1910 a Liberal government came to power, dependent on the votes of the Irish Parliamentary Party, which meant that it could not be long before the third such bill. Furthermore, a vital obstacle to home rule had been removed in 1911 when the power of the House of Lords to veto major pieces of Commons legislation was removed. Autonomy for an Ireland that had a majority Catholic population looked extremely likely, and Ulster Protestants responded with popular mobilization. After a series of extremely well-organized

---

[3] On secret societies and early Orangeism, see T. D. Williams (ed.), _Secret Societies in Ireland_ (Dublin, 1973), and E. McFarland, _Protestants First: Orangeism in 19th Century Scotland_ (Edinburgh, 1990).

public meetings and rallies, Edward Carson led the signing in September 1912 of the Solemn League and Covenant. The 470,000 people in the nine Ulster counties who signed the Covenant committed themselves to use 'all means which may be found necessary to defeat the present conspiracy to set up a Home Rule Parliament in Ireland'.[4] One of the means was the formation of the UVF.

Groups of Volunteers had played a part in the rallies which led up to Covenant Day. At the first meeting, in Enniskillen, Carson found himself accompanied by two squadrons of mounted Fermanagh farmers to Portora Hill, where forty thousand men of the Ulster Unionist Clubs marched past. In early January 1912 some Unionist local leaders had begun to raise and drill troops of volunteers, which was quite legal provided one applied for a licence from two magistrates and claimed to be preparing to defend the realm. At the end of the year the executive of the Ulster Unionist Council, which was co-ordinating the campaign against home rule, decided to bring together the various teams of volunteers into a single force, to be known as the UVF. Lt.-Gen. Sir George Richardson, a retired and distinguished Indian Army general, was appointed commander after Lord Roberts had declined because of frail health. Led by a small but extremely experienced staff, the UVF grew to some ninety thousand well-trained and well-organized men.

In view of the narrow working-class base of the present-day UVF, it is worth remembering the universal appeal of the 1912 Volunteer movement. The Duke of Abercorn's estate at Baronscourt, Co. Tyrone, and Shane's Castle, the seat of the O'Neills, were used as training grounds for the militias of farmers and labourers.

A fairly typical situation developed at Springhill House, near Moneymore, Co. Derry; not only did the owner, William Lenox-Conyngham help to raise two battalions of the UVF's South Derry regiment but his wife was closely involved in the UVF Nursing Corps, arranging for eleven hospital centres in the area.[5]

---

[4] P. Buckland, *James Craig: Lord Craigavon* (Dublin, 1980), 27. For an excellent illustrated account of the build-up to the signing of the Covenant, see G. Lucy, *The Ulster Covenant: A Pictorial History of the 1912 Home Rule Crisis* (Lurgan, 1989).

[5] P. Orr, *The Road to the Somme: Men of the Ulster Division Tell their Story* (Belfast, 1987), 7.

A major problem for the UVF was a lack of arms. After a few months of drilling, Volunteers became frustrated that their training seemed like mere ritual. They even joined their enemies in making fun of their efforts, as we can see in this captain's account of a weekend exercise:

Lord Clanwilliam took the company out for exercise and extended them from Montalto gardens past Drumaness to the Spaw Road. We advanced on the far wood. We leap-frogged across the field and when we came close enough to the wood, Lord Clanwilliam lead the charge, and we took the wood without casualty.[6]

Major Frederick Crawford, a Belfast businessman and former artillery officer, proposed to the small committee that was organizing the resistance a plan for the purchase in Germany of twenty thousand guns and their shipment direct to Ulster. The committee had doubts, not only about the adventurer Crawford but also about the wisdom of fully arming the UVF, but James Craig, the administrative counterpart to Carson in the unionist leadership, strongly supported the scheme and, despite some close calls during the gun-running, it worked. On 24 April 1914 the UVF completely took over the port town of Larne. At the same time, a large UVF contingent was very publicly marched down to the Belfast docks, where it met and appeared to protect the decoy SS *Balmerino*. Crawford steamed the *Clyde Valley* with its cargo of thirty-five thousand rifles and two million rounds of ammunition into Larne. Five hundred UVF cars collected the weapons and distributed them to units around the province. The UVF had suddenly become a real army.

The First World War and After

Armed rebellion was pre-empted by the collapse of Europe into what became the First World War. Less than four months after Crawford's gun-running escapade gave the UVF the power to take on the British government, Britain declared war on the source of the weapons. Secretary for War Lord Kitchener wanted the UVF to enlist in his army. To ensure he got it, he had to promise to keep the men together and to prevent the provisions of the home-rule bill (which would be passed on 18 September) becoming effective until after the war. The 36th (Ulster) Division was formed, and Carson encouraged the UVF men to enlist in it. Throughout the war, but especially in the battle of the Somme, the division acquitted itself heroically. On 1 July twenty-one thousand British soldiers died or were mortally wounded. Of all the divisions, the 36th's losses ranked fourth; at least two thousand men died on that day alone.

That sacrifice and the continued threat of Ulster unionist resistance were rewarded by the Government of Ireland Act of 1920, which gave the Irish home rule for twenty-six counties but exempted a six-county Ulster with its own parliament. In the spate of confusion before the partition compromise was agreed, Carson had threatened to reform the UVF. At a Twelfth of July Orange parade in 1920 he said, 'I tell the British people . . . if there is any attempt to take away one jot or tittle of your rights as British citizens . . . I will call out the Ulster Volunteers.'[7]

Fear of the IRA and concern that the Royal Irish Constabulary (RIC) was impotent in the country areas led local unionist leaders to mobilize vigilante groups. One of the most active was that raised by Sir Basil Brooke (later Lord Brookeborough and Prime Minister of Northern Ireland) in Fermanagh. In Tyrone, General Ricardo also organized companies of volunteers. Frederick Crawford, now a lieutenant-colonel, was promoting the idea of re-forming the UVF in Belfast. As IRA violence and loyalist retaliation increased, the Ulster unionist leadership approved the re-launch. Lieut.-Col. William Spender, who had been active in the first UVF, left his job with the Ministry of Pensions to take charge, and on 23 July unionist newspapers carried advertisements calling all members and former members of the UVF to report for duty.[8]

As with the 1912 formation, it is worth noting the élite support for the 1920 UVF; the commanders were lords, knights, and very senior army officers. It is also worth noting that, for an entirely unofficial (and possibly illegal) organization, the 1920 UVF had an extremely privileged relationship with the police and the army. Spender was able to send Colonel George Moore Irvine (recently

---

[7] M. Farrell, *Arming the Protestants: The Formation of the Ulster Special Constabulary and the Royal Ulster Constabulary, 1920–27* (London, 1983), 9.
[8] Ibid. 21.

retired from charge of the British army's ordnance depot at
Carrickfergus) to Londonderry as the UVF's full-time organizer.
Crawford reported that Irvine had so impressed the army's GOC
with the object and aims of the UVF (and with its intelligence on
the IRA) that he became *de facto* governor of Derry, though he had
no official status.[9]

Not surprisingly when many Protestants and Catholics found
themselves on the wrong side of the proposed border, the partition
of Ireland was not achieved without bloodshed. There was considerable unrest in the summer and autumn of 1920. IRA attacks
on RIC men and buildings were invariably followed by Protestant
attacks on Catholics. After the RIC divisional commander for
Munster (an Ulsterman) was murdered by the IRA, there was
rioting in Banbridge and Belfast. Catholics who lived in small
pockets within otherwise Protestant areas were driven out of their
houses. Catholic workers in predominantly Protestant workplaces
(the shipyards were the most important case) were forced out of
their jobs. As Farrell correctly points out, these expulsions had
two purposes: in addition to punishing Catholics for the acts of
the IRA, they created vacancies for unemployed Protestants.
Unemployment was an emotive issue. Protestants who had fought
in the war to defend their country could not see why they should
be out of work while Catholics (whose southern brethren had
staged a rebellion in Dublin in 1916, when Britain was fighting in
France) had jobs. That many Catholics had also fought for Britain
was forgotten as stereotypes took over.

Unionist leaders saw a clear need for some sort of auxiliary
police force, organized on military lines, to put down and keep
down the 'rebels', and persuaded the British government to
authorize (and fund) the Ulster Special Constabulary (USC),
which was in effect the UVF. The IRA was beaten by 1921
but it was 1925 before two of the three categories of Special
Constables—the A and C—were stood down. The B Specials
continued as a locally recruited part-time Protestant militia.
Whether it could have been any different is unlikely, but Sir James
Craig's commitment to reforming the UVF and turning it into an
official state militia ensured that the state's security forces would
be explicitly Protestant.

It is a common but mistaken view that Northern Ireland was at

[9] Ibid. 23.

peace from the mid-1920s to the start of the present 'Troubles'. In fact, the fundamental divisions persisted and periodically erupted in violence. There were sectarian riots in Belfast in the 1930s. In 1942 the IRA Northern Command launched a new campaign. In April of that year an officer of the Royal Ulster Constabulary (RUC) was shot dead in Dungannon, Co. Tyrone. Three days later IRA men fired on an RUC patrol car in Kashmir Road in Belfast and killed one officer. Another RUC officer was shot and wounded in Strabane. When an IRA man was executed for his part in the Kashmir Road shooting, the IRA threw everything it had at Northern Ireland; an RUC officer and two B Specials were killed. Internment was used both in Ulster and in the Irish Free State (where the government which had accepted the partition settlement was itself at war with the IRA), and IRA activity 'tailed off'.[10]

It revived again in 1956 when, on the night of 11 December, 150 IRA men attacked ten targets in Ulster. In the next year there were over three hundred incidents. Three RUC officers were killed, as were seven republicans, five of them by their own bomb. Even faster than the previous one, this campaign petered out, although an RUC man was blown up in South Armagh in November 1961. When the campaign was formally stood down in the following February, eleven republicans and six RUC men had been killed.[11]

These details have been given to make it clear that the threat to the Ulster state and to Ulster Protestants from militant 'physical force' republicanism did not end in 1921. Although not very successful, the IRA actions were enough to remind Ulster loyalists that they had an enemy to the south and an enemy within. However, there was reassurance to be had in the extensive police powers held by the Stormont government and in the effectiveness of the B Specials and, despite these periodic bouts of disorder, the UVF was not again mobilized. The state had become sufficiently stable not to need the assistance of a popular militia, the important functions of which had been subsumed in the B Specials.[12]

[10] M. Farrell, *Northern Ireland: The Orange State* (London, 1980), 167.
[11] Ibid. 21.
[12] A. Hezlet, *The 'B' Specials: A History of the Ulster Special Constabulary* (London, 1972).

The 1966 Volunteers

On 4 May 1966 a member of the Northern Ireland parliament at Stormont asked the Minister for Home Affairs if he knew anything about a new organization which was rumoured to be drilling with automatic weapons somewhere near the border. Brian McConnell said that the suggestion was hair-raising, though he knew nothing about it.

On the 27th of the month a group of Shankill Road loyalists went out to find and kill Leo Martin, a well-known Republican connected to the Belfast brigade of the IRA. Driving through the Clonard area and failing to find Martin, they came across John Scullion, a young labourer who had the misfortune to be drunk and singing Republican songs. He was shot and left for dead. An anonymous phone call to the *Belfast Telegraph* claimed the attack in the name of the UVF. Scullion died on 11 June.

A month after that attack, in the very small hours of 26 June, four young Catholic barmen who had been drinking after hours were shot at as they left the Malvern Arms in Malvern Street, just off Belfast's Shankill Road. One, Peter Ward, died; two others were seriously wounded. A party of off-duty RUC men had also been drinking late in the pub and, within hours of the shootings, three Protestants were arrested and questioned. Two days later, Augustus 'Gusty' Spence, Bobby Williamson, and Hugh McClean were charged with the murder.

In the Stormont House of Commons two days later, Prime Minister Terence O'Neill briefly described the successful RUC operation to arrest the loyalists and went on to announce the banning of the UVF:

As honourable members may know, I flew back last night from France. The purpose of my visit there was to honour the men of the 36th (Ulster) Division, many of whom were members of the authentic and original UVF. Let no one imagine there is any connection whatever between the two bodies; between men who were ready to die for their country on the fields of France, and a sordid conspiracy of criminals prepared to take up arms against unprotected fellow citizens. No, this organization now takes its proper place alongside the IRA in the schedule of illegal bodies.[13]

[13] Northern Ireland *Hansard*, 28 June 1966.

Almost all Ulster Protestants were unionists. Most were deliberately and self-consciously so, willing to go to various lengths to defend the union with Britain and to counter the threat of being forced into a united Catholic Ireland. Many were members of the Orange Order. Some working-class unionists—loyalists, as they are more often known—were willing to go further than others and believed it both necessary and right to use violence (or at least prepare to be in a position to use violence) to defeat nationalism. In relatively tranquil and prosperous times, the number of men (they were mostly men) who were willing to kill, go to prison, and die for their unionism was very small. They did, however, share a large number of common biographical features and I will briefly describe a number of fairly typical early activists.

Gusty Spence came from a staunch Orange Order family, well known and well connected on the Shankill Road. His brother, William Spence, was a major figure in the local Unionist Party and was election agent for James Kilfedder, who won the West Belfast Westminster seat in 1964. Gusty Spence was an ex-soldier who had served in Cyprus as a military police sergeant. On his return to Belfast he worked as a stager in Harland and Wolff, the famous shipyard firm which made the *Titanic*. Stagers built the scaffolding inside which ships were constructed. The demands of strength and nerve of the job meant that stagers had traditionally occupied a position of prestige among the shipyard work-force, which was in turn an élite within the Protestant working class. Shipwrights formed an 'aristocracy' of labour—better paid, housed, fed, and dressed than those who lived around them—and they were expected to give a lead in protecting the interests of their community. In the Belfast riots of the late nineteenth century they played a very active part, and they were described in a contemporary report as being 'the strongest, healthiest and most highly intelligent and highly paid body of men in the whole of Belfast'.[14] In addition to the Order, Gusty Spence was involved in Ulster Protestant Action (UPA)—a populist grouping which argued for preferential treatment in employment for loyalists—and other loyalist movements. His occupation, his army service, the standing of his family, and

---

[14] P. Gibbon, *The Origins of Ulster Unionism: The Formation of Popular Protestant Politics and Ideology in Nineteenth-Century Ireland* (Manchester, 1975), 81–2.

his activities in the Order and UPA would all have made him an ideal candidate for a major part in any paramilitary activity.

'Frank' grew up in the Old Lodge Road area of north Belfast in a thoroughly Orange family. In adolescence his main interest was following Linfield football club—the Blues. Mainly because it was the centre of social life for young boys, he joined a junior Orange Lodge. On leaving school he served his apprenticeship as a fitter and then joined the army, which took him to the trouble spots of Suez and Cyprus. In Cyprus, he fought EOKA and learnt to hate 'freedom fighters'. This experience was added to his childhood memories—he had grown up in the war—of stories of disloyal IRA men on roof-tops with torches, directing the German bombers to their targets in Belfast.

When he left the army, he returned to Belfast with a reputation as a 'bit of a hard man' and with his views of nationalists and the IRA confirmed by his army experience. He joined the same Lodge as Gusty Spence—the Prince Albert Temperance—but he did not know Spence well. His involvement in the UVF came from a whispered invitation from a man he didn't know who approached him in a bar and asked if he would 'do a job'. He didn't say 'no'.

Although he now finds it hard to reconstruct his feelings at the time and refuses to produce a neat retrospective explanation, it is clear that he believed that there was threat to Ulster from a resurgent IRA, and he willingly got involved in what he saw as necessary preventative action.

'Sammy' was raised in a church-going Baptist family in Glengormley, the area into which north Belfast sprawled in the 1950s and 1960s. Although not personally religious enough to have undergone a distinct conversion experience, he had been surrounded by the common elements of Protestant culture. Among the books in his house were *Scots Worthies* (a collection of biographies of the Covenanters) and a book about the Huguenots, the staples of Sunday School prize-giving. His grandfather had been active in the 1912 UVF and involved in the famous gun-running episode in Larne; his father was an Orangemen. He remembers the 1959 IRA campaign:

It wasn't really something that touched our area, although the politicians would use it as propaganda in their speeches so you were hearing about it all the time. And there would be gossip that this fella or that fella were

IRA men. There was the odd thing around North Antrim—a bomb up in Toome, I remember—but there was never anything near us.[15]

However, like many working-class Protestants, he had a close family connection with the campaign in that an uncle was in the B Special Constabulary and was mobilized.

Like many a young Protestant, much of Sammy's social life was built around the Orange Order and the flute bands that led the Lodges on their parades. His hobbies brought him into contact with the young Ian Paisley, who was making himself a reputation as a fiery anti-Catholic speaker: 'I was in a band then and some of the fellas took me to hear Paisley speak after he came back from that trip to Rome . . . our band became a Paisley band and I knocked around with Noel Doherty [the organizer of Paisley's rank-and-file support].' His involvement with Doherty led him first to attend various political and religious meetings and then to help form Ulster Protestant Volunteer (UPV) units (as the Paisley groups were known) in various parts of the province. His frequent appearance on marches and at meetings brought him to the attention of another ex-serviceman, who was a leading UVF man: 'Bo says to me "Are you in the Order?" and I said I was and he said "There's this wee thing going on in the Order. Do you want to come down to a meeting?"' The 'wee thing' was an organization called Tara, of which more later.

Of the four activists, 'David' is the youngest. He grew up in a Belfast street that runs from the Catholic lower Falls, along the bottom end of the Shankill Road area to the Catholic Unity Flats. Before the communal violence of 1969 forced many people to move house and clarified boundaries, a few working-class areas were thoroughly mixed, but mostly mixed streets represented borders, with each side clustered at the end nearest its heartland. David was raised in such a street, close to but having little friendly contact with the Catholics at the far end. Contrary to the myth of pre-Troubles communal harmony, such proximity reinforced the sense of distinctiveness. David remembers the stark difference in culture. 'Them' with their strange dress for Irish dancing and

[15] Except where otherwise stated, all quotations that do not have a cited source are from interviews conducted between 1989 and 1991.

ceilidhs; his friends with their junior teddy boy outfits and Buddy Holly records. 'Them' playing in the playground on Sundays, even though the council had chained up the swings and rides for the preservation of the sabbath; his friends confined and cramped by the Presbyterian sabbatarian ethos of Protestant Belfast.

His father, who worked in the shipyards all his life, was not an active Orangeman, although he was keen on the flute bands; like many working-class unionists, he was an admirer of the trade unionist and Labour man Billy Boyd. But David grew up with a strong sense of Protestant identity, channelled through the Orange Order, the flute bands, the football, and support for the Unionist Party.

To the three working-class loyalists just described, Spence was a hero, a man willing to fight for his country and his convictions. To the middle classes, Gusty Spence was inexplicable, a throw-back to a past which they hoped to forget. With Spence's Standard Bar UVF—most paramilitary groups were organized around the pub where they drank—in prison, the minor crisis seemed over. The Malvern Street verdicts were not followed by any surge in loyalist activity and, although a small number of sympathizers tried to create the impression that the UVF was unaffected by the imprisonments by sending threats and issuing press releases under the UVF code name 'Captain William Johnston', there was little enduring organization and surprisingly little organized support.[16] One man who was active in protests outside Crumlin Road prison told me: 'When Gusty was in prison, you only had half a dozen people picketing the place.'

However, a small number of men, almost all ex-servicemen, were determined to continue the work. They met and plotted and recruited their close friends and picked up others who by their frequent appearance at marches and political rallies made it clear that they shared a strong concern for the Protestant struggle. There was some arms training. Money was collected for guns. There were even 'stand to's', in which the hard core of regulars would practise 'defending' an area against republican attack.

---

[16] However, Dillon is exaggerating slightly when he says 'the life sentence given to Spence was greeted with relief' (M. Dillon, *The Shankill Butchers: A Case Study of Mass Murder* (London, 1989), p. xxx).

Paisley and the UPV

The large and loud figure of the Reverend Ian Paisley has already been mentioned. Since the Northern Ireland parliament had been opened, it had been dominated by the Ulster Unionist Party (UUP), which at the first elections had won forty seats to the twelve of the Nationalist Party and Sinn Fein. Over the years the number varied slightly, with the occasional promise of a threat from the Labour Party, but Ulster was effectively a one-party state. Furthermore, it was a one-party state with a popular mass organization—the Orange Order—to link working-class Protestants to their social betters. While there was, until 1969, very little effective opposition outside the Unionist Party, there were two internal factions which were a constant irritant: working-class populists and evangelical revivalists. The former tried to ensure that the working-class Protestant got his just deserts (that is, larger deserts than the rebels). The latter tried to ensure that the unionist leadership's periodic invocation of religious symbolism was turned into a reality of state support for the 'true religion'. Paisley was vocal in both groups.

Ian Paisley was the son of an independent fundamentalist Baptist preacher from Ballymena, the market town of the rich farming area of North Antrim, Ulster's 'bible belt'.[17] He learnt theology at the Reformed Presbyterian College in Belfast and preaching at an evangelistic college in Wales. His forceful personality and preaching skills soon made him a figure on Belfast's independent evangelical preaching circuit and in 1945 he was invited to pastor a small dissident Presbyterian congregation in east Belfast. Over the next decade Paisley worked the province, acquiring a reputation as a great revival preacher and a fierce opponent of Romanism, apostasy, liberal Protestantism, and ecumenism. He also became active in such populist political movements as the UPA, which described itself as follows:

Its basis and union is Protestantism, the Protestantism of the Bible. It unflinchingly maintains the cardinal doctrines of Christianity as set forth in the Apostle's Creed and uncompromisingly denounces all forms of

[17] On Paisley's early career, see S. Bruce, *God save Ulster!: The Religion and Politics of Paisleyism* (Oxford, 1986). For a hostile account, see A. Pollak and E. Moloney, *Paisley* (Dublin, 1986).

popery.... Its purpose is to permeate all activities social and cultural with Protestant ideals and in the accomplishment of this end it is primarily dedicated to immediate action in the sphere of employment.[18]

As an aside, and because critics miss the point, it is worth noting that the UPA modelled itself on the far more efficiently exclusivist Catholic Action movement which had become popular in a number of European countries and in Australia.

Until the 1960s Paisley was a voice crying in the wilderness. What turned his constant doom-saying into popular analysis was the liberalization of Ulster religion and politics. Although well protected against modernizing influences by its geographical location, Ulster was not immune. The urban and middle-class sections of the main Irish Presbyterian Church gradually shifted from anti-Catholicism to a more liberal Protestant faith and a tentative ecumenism. The change in politics was even more dramatic. Ulster's leaders lived a long time. Sir James Craig (later Lord Craigavon) was Prime Minister from 1921 to his death in 1940. The short-lived premiership of his deputy J. M. Andrews was followed by the twenty-year rule of Sir Basil Brooke (later Lord Brookeborough). Like Craig, Brooke had been active in the first UVF and in its 1920 revival. Against the more liberal policies of many of his fellow landowners, Brooke was thoroughly opposed to hiring Catholics when there were 'good Protestant lads and lassies' needing work.

Like Craigavon, Brookeborough did not want to exercise power. His generation of unionists wanted to be ruled from Westminster like the rest of the Union and was reluctant to have Stormont do more than protect the security of Northern Ireland and shadow Westminster legislation. Brookeborough liked very long holidays. When he eventually resigned in 1963, he nominated as his replacement Captain Terence O'Neill. Analysts will argue about how significantly O'Neillism departed from the exclusivist unionism of earlier regimes, but there is no doubt that O'Neill was less of an Ulsterman and far more cosmopolitan than his predecessors. Although he joined the Orange Order and the Apprentice Boys of Derry (the other major fraternal organization for loyalists), he did so late in life, reluctantly, and held no major office. He had little

[18] K. J. Kelley, *The Longest War: Northern Ireland and the IRA* (London, 1988), 75.

or no sympathy for anti-Catholicism, which he viewed as a point-less diversion from the government's task of rationally managing economic growth. Development, infrastructure, improved labour relations—these were O'Neill's concerns. Why anyone should want to remember 1690 was not at all clear to him.

The extent of real change under O'Neill—it was not enough to make Catholics active supporters of the state—is not too important for understanding responses to his premiership. People respond to symbols and perceptions, and O'Neill broke new symbolic ground. He visited a Catholic school and allowed himself to be photographed smiling with nuns and priests. He met a cardinal. Most dramatically, without consulting his cabinet colleagues, he invited Irish premier Sean Lemass to Stormont and accepted a return invitation.

Ian Paisley built a career on denouncing O'Neillism in politics, and its equivalent, ecumenism, in religion. When O'Neill sent a telegram of condolence to Cardinal Conway on the death of Pope John XXIII, Paisley led a march to the city hall to denounce 'the lying eulogies now being paid to the Roman antichrist'.[19] During the 1964 Westminster elections, he provoked the worst rioting in Belfast since 1935 by insisting that the RUC remove an Irish Republic tricolour from a Sinn Fein election office in Divis Street.

Although there had been almost no IRA activity since 1961, Paisley was convinced that any sign of weakness from the government would simply encourage the rebels to rise again. As he put it in 1966:

Captain Terence O'Neill ... will soon have to make up his mind whether he intends to appease the republican minority or serve the vast so-called extremist majority. Surely he does not seriously think that appeasement will stop the IRA attacks or the cries of discrimination. Or is he secretly selling us to the South?[20]

Although Paisley had been a significant figure in the UPA and in the National Union of Protestants (NUP) (a religious pressure group), the first political organization which was solely his vehicle was the Ulster Constitution Defence Committee (UCDC), which organized rallies and marches to provide regular platforms for

[19] Bruce, *God Save Ulster*, 73.
[20] Ibid. 77.

Paisley's combination of evangelical religion and right-wing union-ism. The original thirteen-man committee had a popular base provided for it by Noel Doherty, a young Belfast printer and fervent supporter of Paisley who organized small groups of loyalists into divisions of the UPV. Although the term 'division' was later explained as referring not to army units but to Stormont parlia-mentary constituencies, there is no doubt that the name and structure of the UPV were chosen to signal continuity with the old UVF. However, the UPV constitution provided that 'any member associated with, or giving support to, any subversive or lawless activities whatsoever shall be expelled from the body. The chair-man of the UCDC has vested in him full authority to act in such cases.'[21] That Paisley as chairman should insist on reserving such a power suggests that he had a strong suspicion of what sort of person the UPV might attract. To put it at its simplest, many active UPV members were also UVF men and, as subsequent actions were to prove, a core of UPV men was quite willing to use explosives to imitate the IRA and hence dramatize the claim that O'Neillism would encourage physical force nationalism. The claim of Paisley's *Protestant Telegraph*, that 'the UPV ... has proved over and over again that it is a constitutional organization working within the framework of the law for the preservation of our Prot-estant heritage',[22] could only be true if the organization had no responsibility for the actions of some of its members.

This is not to say that Paisley either knew of or encouraged illegal acts of violence. Despite the considerable interest of such anti-Paisley writers as Boulton, and Pollak and Moloney, in claim-ing that the present troubles are largely his fault, the only evidence that Paisley had any involvement in serious illegal acts came in the trial testimony of a UPV informer whose evidence was rejected by the jury.[23]

---

[21] D. Boulton, *The UVF, 1966–73: An Anatomy of Loyalist Rebellion* (Dublin, 1973), 28. For an authoritative and detailed account of this period, see the report of the Cameron Commission, *Disturbances in Northern Ireland*, Cmnd 532 (Belfast, 1969).

[22] *Protestant Telegraph*, 27 Apr. 1968.

[23] The involvement of UVF–UPV men in a series of explosions at public utilities is described in detail in the Cameron Commission report and by Boulton, whose conclusion that the RUC had the right men but charged them with the wrong things is not far from the mark.

Tara

Another organization which came from the same milieu as Paisley's
UCDC–UPV was Tara, a strange body founded by William
McGrath, who was later disgraced when he was convicted of
repeated sexual abuse of residents of a boys' home where he
worked. Tara combined a number of themes in an interesting
alternative to mainstream unionism. McGrath was a British Israelite
who believed the original Ulster people were one of the lost
tribes of Israel. There was an interest in Irish pre-history,
which McGrath used to argue that the Protestants were the
original people of Ireland, driven out to Scotland by the later
Celtic invaders. He resented the usurpation of Irish language and
culture by the Catholics, named the Orange Lodge he founded
'Ireland's Heritage', and gave it a Gaelic motto, yet he was fiercely
anti-Catholic.

Initially a secretive ginger group within the Orange Order, Tara
became a paramilitary organization. As in the case of the UPV,
many of the most committed Tara people were closet UVF men. A
Woodvale UVF man explained: 'When Tara was started a number
of our people were invited to go along. We asked [the UVF chief
of staff] what we should do and were instructed that we should go,
get involved, take rank and then report back.'

Sammy, who attended all the early Tara meetings, was convinced by the apparent political sophistication of the speakers that
it really had the backing of the Orange Order hierarchy, 'although
they couldn't come out and say it'.

McGrath and the other Tara leaders were articulate proponents
of the view that the Union was being subverted by a conspiracy
of liberal unionists, communists, and Irish republicans, but the
harder men of the UVF were not impressed: 'They talked a good
line, had a good spiel, like, but we wanted to know where the arms
training was, where the guns was, and it wasn't there. They
weren't going to do anything.'

Tara had a good line in martial rhetoric but even its claims to
be ready for armed defence rang hollow. The UVF men who
attended its meetings rather cynically used them to identify and
recruit potential supporters, people who might become thoroughly
committed to the struggle.

The UVF and Unionist Élites

Nationalist and left-wing critics of unionism tend to portray loyalist political violence as no more than one would expect from such people, or from such a class, or from the underclass of an imperialist power (depending on the implied explanation of unionism). Spence and the UVF are presented as being only the most stark expression of what the bankrupt political philosophy of unionism has to offer; the UVF is the RUC without the pretence of legality. A close link between loyalist paramilitaries and more respectable politicians is taken for granted. In one version, the connections between the UVF and Paisley are stressed. One of the most commonly repeated evidences of such links—the statement to the effect that he wished he had never heard of that man Paisley made by Hugh McClean during his trial for his part in the Shankill Road UVF—is frequently repeated as a way of blaming Paisley for the UVF without any recognition that McClean's counsel denied in court that he ever made such a statement to the police.

In a second version, the terrorists are linked to more mainstream political figures in the Unionist Party. There were certainly shared interests. Many people in the Unionist Party (and many members of O'Neill's own cabinet) thoroughly disapproved of his liberal rhetoric and thought it profoundly dangerous. The leadership of the Orange Order shared much of Paisley's analysis of O'Neillism as rebel appeasement. However, that both gunmen and politicians shared the same goals does not mean that the latter supported, encouraged, or organized the former.

What makes it difficult to evaluate the claims for covert élite support for the UVF is the fact that loyalists have their own reasons for claiming it. UVF men want to point to the continuity between their activities and those of the Ulster aristocracy and middle classes who founded the Unionist Party and formed the first UVF in 1912. The leader of the Standard Bar UVF, Gusty Spence, himself claims that he was only a part of a larger movement which had élite unionist backing:

The UVF had been reformed in 1965. I was approached and asked, because of my political involvement and expertise as a soldier to become an active service unit commander on the Shankill.

[Q: You mean you were not responsible for setting up the modern-day UVF?]

By no means. I was responsible for reforming it on the Shankill but the old UVF was originally reformed by none other than Sir Basil Brooke, who was to become Prime Minister. It existed mainly on border areas. . . . There is a thread which runs right through from 1921. Anyway the re-emergence of the UVF in 1965 was actively encouraged by members of the Unionist party who wanted rid of O'Neill.[24]

In another interview he said that he was recruited by a Unionist Party politician and that orders were regularly transmitted from top unionist politicians in Stormont to the Shankill Road UVF active service unit.[25] Martin Dillon asserts that the UVF was re-formed by 'three prominent Unionists'.[26]

Members and associates of Spence's UVF are not so certain. All of those I talked to said something similar to the views of this member of the early UVF: 'Gusty always liked to make out there was some Mister Big behind the organization who would look after us if we got into trouble but I think that was just talk. I certainly don't know of anyone and I've spent a lot of time thinking about that.' Certainly Gusty and others had good reason to want to think of themselves simply as recruits to an existing organization. For the 'UVF' to have a continuous history back to the 1920s would give it the legitimacy of tradition. To claim respectable political figures (even anonymous ones) as leaders allowed Spence to deflect the criticism that he and his men were just thugs by showing that they were every bit as good as middle-class unionists, and better because they had the courage of their convictions. One sees the same desire in the belief of many Tara members that the Orange hierarchy 'really' approved of them. One UDA man, in talking about his impressions of the organization before he joined it, said: 'You know, we'd see all these guys in camouflage jackets and masks talking real well on the TV and we were sure they were big Unionist politicians. We used to try and guess who was who, you know. Which one was Craig?' The truth of Dillon's bold assertion of Unionist party leadership may rest on what is meant by 'prominent' in the phrase 'prominent Unionist

[24] *Shankill Bulletin*, 31 May 1985.
[25] *Sunday World*, 15 Sept. 1985.
[26] Dillon, *The Shankill Butchers*, p. xxxix.

politicians'. If it means top party officials or members of the Stormont parliament, then it is unlikely to be true. In the twenty-five years since, no names and no evidence have come to light and, in a world that leaks gossip, this almost certainly means no story. A second way of evaluating Dillon's proposition is to run through the senior Unionist politicians to search for someone with the right politics and character. David McKittrick, the experienced *Irish Times* and *Independent* journalist, and I spent some time musing on likely candidates and failed to find anyone who combined right-wing populism, working-class connections, status, and a ruthless character in the right mixture. One name that was suggested by a UVF source fitted the bill in terms of status and location (he had a shop on the Shankill Road) but was on the liberal wing of unionism. Another person mentioned was a member of the Senate but a marginal and insignificant character.

My tentative conclusion (and like much in this story it is tentative) is that there was no élite unionist conspiracy behind the UVF. The early paramilitaries may have been supported by an isolated Tyrone farmer of some substance, but they were essentially a self-recruiting, working-class movement.

Civil Rights and Protestant Backlash

If the reforming policies of Premier Terence O'Neill had been opposed only by right-wing unionists, he would have survived. His major problem has not yet been mentioned, and that was the 'civil-rights' movement. Fortunately, there are now a number of excellent histories of the civil-rights movement and its evolution into armed republicanism, and this résumé can be kept brief.[27]

For Catholics, the O'Neill years were ones of growing frustration:

the post-war free education system and increase in university scholarships was creating a much larger, better-educated Catholic middle class, ambitious, anxious to participate in politics and to end their second class status. Free education and the welfare state also made them less anxious

[27] P. Arthur, *The People's Democracy, 1968–73* (Belfast, 1974); B. Purdie, *Politics in the Streets: The Origins of the Civil Rights Movement in Northern Ireland* (Belfast, 1990).

for immediate unity with the South with its inadequate social services, and more willing to work within the Northern system.[28]

The O'Neill reforms increased expectations but failed to deliver enough to satisfy them. Heavily influenced by the black civil-rights campaigns and the student anti-war movement in the United States and major European capitals, a new generation of Catholics created a number of organizations to protest against unionist discrimination in housing and employment, council boundary gerrymandering, and security policy. Paisley and other right-wing unionists organized counter-demonstrations and blocked marches. The police and the B Specials alternated sloppy policing of potentially dangerous situations with uncontrolled over-reaction, and thus further alienated Catholic opinion.

The civil-rights slogan 'One Man—One Vote' was extremely powerful. Although it referred strictly only to a property qualification which stopped some Catholics (and more Protestants!) voting in local government elections, it conveyed the impression that Catholics could not vote in major elections and suggested a society as radically discriminatory as the one in South Africa. As rhetoric it worked extremely well and there was considerable pressure from the Labour government at Westminster on the Stormont administration to reform its attitude to its Catholic minority.

Very quickly civil rights became old-fashioned nationalism. The claim for fair treatment within Northern Ireland became the old rebel demand of a united Ireland. Much of that change can be seen as a response to the intransigence of the government in its unwillingness to face down its own right wing. O'Neill did not deliver enough soon enough. But too many accounts of this period have accepted too readily the anti-unionist view that politically active Catholics initially wanted only a fair deal within the North and became anti-state nationalists only when their reasonable demands were met with violence. There is plenty of evidence in the accounts of civil-rights activists that many of them were thoroughly cynical in their claim for equal treatment within the Ulster state; they saw civil rights as another stick with which to

[28] Farrell, *Northern Ireland*, 238.

beat the Prods, another device to destabilize Stormont.[29] There is
also plenty of evidence of involvement of committed republicans
and nationalists in the civil-rights movement. Dillon believes that a
very prominent member of the Northern Ireland Civil Rights
Association (NICRA)

did provide NICRA funds for the Republican movement just prior to
August 1969 in the belief that guns might be needed to protect Catholic
areas, and it must be said that he was later involved with the defence
organisations which also sought guns from the Dublin government.[30]

Furthermore, it is clear that many of those involved in the civil-
rights protests were every bit as 'sectarian' as their Protestant
opponents. For many, civil-rights marches were deliberate exercises in coat-trailing. The supposedly non-sectarian People's
Democracy deliberately chose a route for the Belfast–Derry
march that went through staunchly loyalist areas.

It is worth adding an important reason why some loyalists
reacted to the civil-rights movement with so much hostility: they
were as poor as the Catholics who were doing all the complaining.
Like Catholics, many of them lived in squalid terraced houses with
no inside toilet. Like Catholics, they had rising expectations that
were not being met.

What chance did we have? With us, you got bucked out of school at
fifteen and into the shipyards and that was you. They used to walk past
our house every day in their nice uniforms going to their good school up
the Antrim road and getting a better education than us and suddenly they
are going on about civil rights.

Sarah Nelson, whose *Ulster's Uncertain Defenders* offers considerable insight into the world of the Shankill Road, got it right when
she wrote:

Divis flats may actually be hell to live in but to the Prod watching them
being built from his rat-infested house, they may seem proof positive to
him that his traditional leaders are not even sharing out their new found
wealth evenly but are giving it all to his traditional enemy.[31]

[29] See the Adams and Devlin contributions to M. Farrell, *Twenty Years On*
(Dingle, 1988); Purdie, *Politics in the Streets*.

[30] M. Dillon, *The Dirty War* (London, 1990), 6.

[31] S. Nelson, *Ulster's Uncertain Defenders: Loyalists and the Northern Ireland
Conflict* (Belfast, 1984), 207.

Crossroads, Burntollet, and Bombs

The civil-rights marches and the Protestant counter-demonstrations were bringing the tensions which had existed since 1921 to a head. In December 1968 O'Neill sacked his Minister for Home Affairs, William Craig, for heavy-handed policing and for criticizing the government's reformist policies. On 9 December he went on television to deliver his famous 'Ulster stands at the crossroads' speech. After promising that the civil-rights concessions already made—the abolition of the Londonderry Corporation, the appointment of an Ombudsman, and the creation of a fair system of housing allocation—would not be withdrawn, he asked: 'What kind of Ulster do you want? A happy and respected province, in good standing with the rest of the United Kingdom? Or a place continually torn apart by riots and demonstrations, and regarded by the rest of Britain as a political outcast.'[32] Although NICRA called off its demonstrations, People's Democracy went ahead with a plan to march from Belfast to Londonderry. Setting off on the morning of New Year's Day, forty or so marchers reached Antrim town in the afternoon, where there were scuffles as police tried to escort them through a crowd of angry loyalists. Eventually they accepted the police offer of transport in police vehicles to their night's destination. This set the pattern for the next two days, with loyalist protests forcing reroutings and the marchers being well received in such Catholic strongholds as Toomebridge. On the last day, the march was met at the junction of the main Dungiven–Derry road by a crowd of some 150 loyalists, who threw stones and bottles at the marchers.[33] Just further along, at Burntollet Bridge,

two groups of attackers, armed with cudgels, lengths of lead piping, crowbars and iron bars, were concealed. . . . Since the police were grouped at the head of the march, they offered little or no protection when these attackers leaped out and assaulted the marchers. The attack was brutal and relentless; the unresisting marchers were beaten, knocked down and kicked, prevented from seeking shelter, pursued and further assaulted. There was at least one near fatality when a girl was knocked unconscious and left lying face down in a stream.[34]

[32] T. O'Neill, *The Autobiography of Terence O'Neill* (London, 1972), 149.
[33] B. Egan and V. McCormack, *Burntollet* (London, 1969).
[34] Purdie, *Politics in the Streets*, 214.

There was further violence when the marchers reached Derry, and, as Purdie notes, there was an ominous development in that a number of policemen ran amuck in the city centre, attacked shoppers, broke windows, and sang sectarian songs in Catholic areas late into the night. This, added to the evidence of reporters that some policemen at Burntollet Bridge had done nothing to prevent (and something to encourage) the attacks, confirmed the views of many Catholics that the security forces were fundamentally anti-Catholic, fuelled criticism of the police, and reinforced unionist views that the civil-rights movement was simply a cover for republican provocation.

With the security situation deteriorating, O'Neill called an election in February and failed to get the clear mandate he wanted. His own party divided, with some Unionist candidates supporting him and others campaigning against him. In his own seat of Bannside in North Antrim he was opposed by Ian Paisley and only narrowly won.

With the anti-O'Neill campaign within the Unionist Party developing momentum, the hard men in the UPV decided to increase the pressure. In the absence of any effective IRA to be encouraged by weak appeasing government, the UPV played the IRA's role and over the next two months organized a series of explosions at public-utility installations. If not Paisley himself, at least some people connected with his *Protestant Telegraph* must have known the real identity of the bombers. None the less, the paper hailed the explosions as proof of the IRA's potential and intent:

This is the first act of sabotage perpetrated by the IRA since the murderous campaign of 1956. . . . Suggestions have been made that an IRA splinter-group—Saor Uladh—was responsible for the blast, but the sheer professionalism of the act indicates the work of a well-equipped IRA. . . . this latest act of IRA terrorism is an ominous indication of what lies ahead for Ulster.[35]

Actually, the blast was the work of a not-very-well-equipped UPV, as was made clear on 19 October when Thomas McDowell, a Free Presbyterian and member of the South Down UPV (he was also claimed by the UVF), fatally injured himself while trying to

[35] *Protestant Telegraph*, 5 Apr. 1969.

blow up an electricity substation at Ballyshannon, just over the border in Co. Donegal.

The UPV–UVF was more successful in another operation. It blew up the pipes that brought water to Belfast from the Silent Valley reservoir in the Mournes, and parts of Belfast were without water for three days.

Retaliation

The above account gives us some idea of how things stood at the start of the present Troubles and introduces the major players. It also allows us to consider what at first sight appears to be a major inconsistency in loyalist explanations of their use of violence for political ends. Both in terms of the individual decision to get involved and in the general accounts of how the UVF and later the UDA came into being, the strongest theme is retaliation and defence. Almost every Volunteer I have interviewed has expressed a view which could be summarized as 'If there was no IRA, there would be no UVF or UDA.' Yet this is not easily reconciled with the strong sense of pride which the pre-1969 UVF men have in their early involvement and the awe in which many of them are held by younger men. To most outsiders, the IRA was of little or no consequence until 1970. The first explosions of the Troubles were set by UPV and UVF men pretending to be the IRA.

I do not mean to be facetious in suggesting that this apparent paradox can be understood if one recalls the football manager who recommended that his players got their retaliation in first. For most of their history, but especially since the home-rule crisis at the start of the century, Ulster Protestants have felt threatened by Irish nationalists. Although it was not very successful, the IRA campaign of the 1950s did enough to remind Protestants of their beleaguered position and to confirm the views of those loyalists who believed that one could never trust Catholics to accept the Northern Ireland state. In those circumstances, even extended periods of peace could never be anything other than a ploy to lull loyalists into a false sense of security. An absence of IRA activity did not signal a change in Catholic attitudes; it only meant that the IRA was regrouping. And such views were not entirely groundless. It was only eight years earlier that the IRA had murdered an RUC officer and the IRA still existed. A September 1969 *World in Action* documentary showed film footage of IRA units drilling.

In the period leading up to the outbreak of civil unrest, only a small core of men was prepared to be involved in paramilitary activity. The early UVF had three questions which it asked of potential recruits: were they ready to kill, were they ready to go to prison, and were they ready to be killed to preserve Ulster from a united Ireland? The numbers they found to answer in the affirmative were small, but they continued as 'wee teams', committing the occasional fund-raising robbery and armoury raid and representing a particular virulent version of a fear of republicanism that was widely shared among Protestants. Which particular organization the 'operators' belonged to at this or that time is of little importance. There were just individuals and 'wee teams' circulating in a small world of militant Protestant organizations with overlapping memberships. Then, as later, the UVF title was the most evocative, the one with the strongest historical resonances, and it was the one which was to emerge from the mishmash of small groups when the predicted civil unrest finally occurred.

From Civil Rights to Civil Strife

THE situation in May 1969, when Terence O'Neill resigned to be replaced by his cousin Major Chichester-Clark, can be neatly summarized by saying that the Catholics would no longer settle for any concession Stormont was likely to make and the Protestants would no longer tolerate any being made. Through the summer months small incident was added to small incident in a gradual escalation of violence. RUC intervention in a brawl in a pub on the Crumlin Road triggered several weekends of rioting in the republican Ardoyne area. The unrest there gave an important spur to a movement that was mobilizing on the other side of the Crumlin Road: the Shankill Defence Association (SDA).

John McKeague and the SDA

John McKeague was a committed Free Presbyterian and supporter of Ian Paisley who had a small stationer's and printer's shop on the Albertbridge Road in east Belfast. He had associated with the Shankill UVF men and was active in the Willowfield 'division' of Paisley's UPV. He was also involved with the UPV bombing campaign of 1969. A man who could only be a part of a movement if he led it, his career took in the early days of all the paramilitary organizations.

Curiously his greatest fame came not from the UPV bombing campaign but from his involvement in what was very briefly an innocent 'community-action' group. A week after O'Neill's resignation, a group of Shankill community leaders called a meeting in the Tennent Street Hall to launch a 'community association'. The enemy against which the SDA expected to fight was the town hall and the urban planner. The housing in the Shankill area was appalling, every bit as bad as that found in any Catholic part of the city, and was scheduled for redevelopment. Anyone who suspected that the planners would destroy a community with ugly, soulless, and quickly dilapidating modern housing would have been right.

Wiener's *Rape and Plunder of the Shankill*[1] is sufficient testimony to the need for a 'defence association' but, with the rioting in the Ardoyne, the SDA quickly became something much more traditional.

Although he lived in the east of city, McKeague was very friendly with Mina Browne, a militant Protestant 'character'. Mina was a middle-aged part-time cleaner who had attained local fame in 1963 by leading a march of cleaners to protest against the corporation's decision to include Catholics on the rolls of school cleaners. She was a member of UPA and attended Paisley's church. Mina Browne was also a strong supporter of Spence's UVF and, after Stormont MP Nat Minford had publicly called Paisley a 'bloated bull frog', Browne had sent an anonymous telegram to Minford threatening him: 'The officers and members of the 1st Shankill division UVF will not tolerate your lies and duplicity no longer stop hundred percent behind Ian Paisley.'[2]

Although sent anonymously, the clerk had recorded the address of the sender on the reverse. The Stormont committee set up to investigate the intimidation of an MP thus had no trouble in finding Mrs Browne.

Mina Browne got McKeague to the first SDA meeting, and his contacts and manner got him elected chairman. The SDA did hold one or two meetings to protest against redevelopment, but the bulk of its energies went into a more traditional form of 'defence'.

An important part of that was competition to dominate territory symbolically. Superiority was asserted by marching through the territory of the other side and by preventing the other side from marching. Early on in his leadership of the SDA, McKeague won an important contest by having a James Connolly commemoration march to the city centre banned and himself leading an anti-Connolly parade. Standing on the steps of the Linenhall Library, McKeague triumphantly announced: 'Loyalists of the Shankill, we have won a victory here today. We have prevented the Connolly

---

[1] R. Wiener, *The Rape and Plunder of the Shankill: Community Action: The Belfast Experience* (Belfast, 1980).

[2] D. Boulton, *The UVF, 1966–73: An Anatomy of Loyalist Rebellion* (Dublin, 1973), 44–5.

Association from holding a parade past the unholy ground where James Connolly spoke from, many years ago.'[3]

The Fighting Begins

The symbolic contests of parades and demonstrations turned to actual violence in August. A series of minor incidents through June and July—which included the death of an elderly Catholic man during an RUC baton charge in Dungiven—culminated in serious disorder in Londonderry on 12 August. The occasion was the annual assembly of the Apprentice Boys of Derry, a Protestant fraternal organization which celebrates the actions of Apprentice Boys in sealing the city against the army of King James in 1689. As Farrell describes the Catholic view of the assembly: 'It was virtually a direct celebration of the plantation and the Protestant ascendancy and served as a yearly reminder to the Catholic population of who was master even in this Catholic city.'[4]

Knowing that the Protestants would not tolerate a ban on the Apprentice Boys parade and that trouble would follow it, the Prime Minister and the Minister for Home Affairs had seen the British Home Secretary in London on 8 August to ask for British troops. Their prognosis was correct. The Boys marched, the Catholic Bogsiders stoned them, the RUC baton-charged the Bogside, the Bogside Defence Association erected barricades, and the RUC laid siege.[5]

To stretch further the police, who had seven hundred of their complement of three thousand in Derry, NICRA and the People's Democracy (PD) arranged confrontational marches in twelve other centres. In Belfast several buildings on the Falls Road were burnt. On the night of 13 August a crowd in west Belfast petrol-bombed a police station, a grenade was thrown at a police car, and shots were fired at its occupants. A car showroom on the Falls was burnt

---

[3] R. Deutsch and V. Magowan, *Northern Ireland, 1968–74: A Chronology of Events*, ii (Belfast, 1975), 30.

[4] M. Farrell, *Northern Ireland: The Orange State* (London, 1980), 259. Describing Derry as a 'Catholic city' neatly and inadvertently illustrates the ground for the Protestant concern that the only alternative to loyalist domination of Catholics is the reverse.

[5] M. Farrell, *Twenty Years On* (Dingle, 1988), 59, forgets to mention the stoning part, and thus implies that the RUC started the fighting.

out and a fire officer's car was torched. Shots were fired at the Springfield Road police station. The Protestants of Cupar Street, North Howard Street, and Third Street observed this commotion and prepared for the worst.

Rather than pull back the RUC from the Bogside, the government mobilized the B Special Constabulary. There was talk in the Dublin government of invading the North, and troops were sent to the border in the guise of field hospitals for those injured in the rioting. Although Dublin did not follow through, Premier Lynch's promise that 'the Irish government can no longer stand by and see innocent people injured and perhaps worse'[6] was taken by the Catholic minority as an encouragement to further resistance. On the 14th British troops moved in to replace the RUC in the Bogside.

The fighting in Londonderry, a more radically segregated city than Belfast, had been between Catholics and the security forces. In Belfast, the violence of the evenings of the 14th and the 15th was communal, with Protestants and Catholics attacking each other at the many interfaces.

The Catholic crowd, like footsoldiers in a Homeric skirmish, formed up behind sheets of corrugated iron fencing and drove the Protestants back up Dover Street only to be halted and pushed back themselves. Petrol bombs and dustbin lids flew between both sides.... Police reinforcements arrived in armoured vehicles and broke through the Catholics' by now battered mobile barricade and the B Specials swarmed into the breach followed by the Protestant crowd. The street was full of writhing, punching bodies, dramatically illuminated by the light for the burning buildings.[7]

That night in Cupar Street the IRA fired at the RUC. There was also heavy IRA firing from St Comgall's primary school at a mob of Protestants throwing petrol bombs in Divis Street.

As the army moved in to separate the two sides in one area, the violence moved to another. Once the divide between the Shankill and the Falls was sealed, a loyalist mob burnt down most of Bombay Street and houses on the Catholic side of Kashmir and Cupar Streets in the Clonard area. A Protestant participant described the night in his diary:

---

[6] Farrell, *Northern Ireland*, 261.
[7] P. Bishop and E. Mallie, *The Provisional IRA* (London, 1988), 106.

About 500 yards away the lights were being extinguished in Catholic homes in the street. The gas lamps had been smashed and the whole place was in darkness. The invisible barrier that was no-mans-land had not yet been breached by either side. Each was hesitant, as if afraid of the blackness. Suddenly flames appeared from behind the 'enemy' lines and Big Thompson shouted in awe: 'The bastards are fleeing their homes. They are putting them to the torch!' It was the signal for attack. The rest of the night was spent burning rows of terraced houses in Cupar Street, Bombay Street and the surrounding areas. The police were powerless to prevent the raging mass's rampage of burning and destruction. I saw one young fellow smash the front windows of a tiny kitchen-house with a flag pole and light the billowing curtains. Soon the place was ablaze.[8]

Protestants followed Catholics in shifting from petrol bombs to guns. On the afternoon of 15 August a member of the IRA's youth wing was shot dead while helping to evacuate a house in Bombay Street. When the troops moved into Clonard, the fighting shifted to the Ardoyne, where one Protestant was shot dead and Catholic Brookfield was burnt out.

In all these disturbances McKeague's SDA was to the fore, and he began to acquire among Catholics almost bogeyman status. From a small office above the Bricklayer's Arms in Wilton Street, McKeague orchestrated pressure, much of it directed at the small Catholic enclave of Unity flats at the bottom of the Shankill and the Ardoyne, which bordered on the north side of the Shankill Road area.

According to the Scarman report into the disturbances, the SDA 'was active in assisting Protestant families to move out of Hooker St, and there is evidence, which we accept, that it encouraged Catholic families to move out of Protestant streets south of the Ardoyne.'[9] Far from denying his part in 'encouraging' Catholics to move, McKeague boasted of his role and revelled in the notoriety. '48 hours' became a slogan to be used either boastfully or wistfully in Shankill Road pubs to express loyalist confidence that, had the troops taken just forty-eight hours longer to get in position, the Catholics would have been burnt out of Belfast.

Although McKeague could muster a hard core of two or three

---

[8] This is an excerpt from a typescript composed by a middle-ranking UDA man.
[9] W. D. Flackes and S. Elliott, *Northern Ireland: A Political Directory, 1968–88* (Belfast, 1989), 249.

hundred young men for impromptu rioting, he was not terribly popular. His militancy had already led Paisley to criticize him. Many Shankill leaders resented an outsider 'coming on to the Road and telling us what to do'. Partly because they wanted to distance themselves from his activities, and partly because they wanted to retain control of the Protestant working class themselves, the Orange Order, the Unionist Party in west Belfast, and Paisley's UCDC unusually sank their differences and went on the record to denounce McKeague. A spokesmen said the three organizations

want to make it clear that none of their associations have any connection with the Shankill Defence Association and that any public statement made in the past or in the future by any of this body doesn't represent the views or opinions of the above associations or any loyalists or Protestants in this area.[10]

This was curiously both entirely true and totally misleading. As an interloper, McKeague was not well liked and his life-style was not likely to endear him to either the hard man of the working class nor the lay preacher of the gospel hall: he was a homosexual who was regularly accompanied by young men. Even those who did not know of his homosexuality thought him a little odd. One man described him as a 'figure of fun'. However, to have read his personal unpopularity as a sign of the popularity of the militant Protestant 'defence' which he advocated would have been a big mistake.[11] Looking back on over a year of civil-rights marches and disturbances, government compromises to accommodate the protesters, and then just more protests and further demands, many working-class loyalists were perfectly happy to see the 'rebels' getting their come-uppance. As developments elsewhere were to demonstrate, the SDA would be superseded by the same thing writ large.

McKeague was removed from the streets on 10 December 1969 to be charged in relation to the UPV explosions. But the riots continued. On 13 January some minor boundary was crossed with the first bomb to be directed at private property and at a Catholic

[10] Statement phoned to BBC Belfast, 26 Aug. 1969.
[11] As *The Times* did at the time.

target when a bomb damaged a shop in the Catholic Ardoyne district of Belfast.

In March Paisley moved to distance himself from his more militant supporters, now an embarrassment in the courts on explosives charges; he had McKeague expelled from the Willowfield division of the UPV.

By the early summer of 1970 McKeague was back out and making an unsuccessful bid to take over the other embryonic 'defence committees'. The Donegal Road Defence Committee (DRDC) decided to

disassociate the DRDC from John McKeague and the Shankill Road Defence Association. Mr McKeague, we feel, has tried to involve the defence associations in general and the DRDC in particular with his intention to run for North Belfast in the forthcoming general election. The DRDC is non-political and will not be drawn into any political arena.[12]

Billy Dickson, the secretary of the DRDC, was active in Paisley's Protestant Unionist movement and hence hardly disinterested. Paisley's candidate for north Belfast in the June general election—Revd William Beattie—took 11,173 votes. The Northern Ireland Labour Party (NILP) got 18,894. The sitting Unionist MP was returned with 28,668. John McKeague, despite being well known, polled only 441 votes. The working-class loyalist who advocated violence drew hardly any support, but the large vote for an unknown clergyman showed the depth of Protestant unhappiness with the government.

Bombs, Internment, and Flight

The last months of 1969 were unhappy ones for unionists. Behind their barricades, Catholics maintained 'no-go' areas, parts of Ulster that had effectively seceded. The presence of the British army curtailed the power of Stormont. The Cameron Commission, appointed by O'Neill to investigate Catholic grievances, published its report, which documented evidence of considerable anti-Catholic discrimination.[13] The working party on the police chaired

[12] Press statement, 21 May 1970.
[13] Cameron Commission, *Disturbances in Northern Ireland*, Cmnd 532 (Belfast, 1969).

by Lord Hunt reported and recommended the disarming of the
RUC and the disbanding of the B Specials. The RUC Inspector
General was replaced by an English Chief Constable.

Dismayed by their poor showing in the August disturbances,
many IRA members became vocally critical of the left-wing
direction of the movement, and the IRA split, with the northern
militants forming the 'Provisional' IRA (PIRA). Free to recruit
behind the barricades, PIRA set about building an organization. At
the same time, right-wing unionists were pressing the government
for a tougher line against republicans and an end to appeasement.

Initially Catholics had seen the British army as a counter to the
security policies of the Stormont government, but, as the honey-
moon months passed and the government of Northern Ireland was
not radically reformed, the initiative passed more and more to the
spokesmen for old-fashioned 'physical-force' republicanism which
saw Britain as the prime enemy and killing the British as the major
strategy for achieving national unity and independence. It could
not have done anything else, given that it could hardly refuse to
support the elected government, but the army became drawn into
the conflict on the government side, which to Catholics meant the
Protestant side. On 31 March Catholic youths from Clonard and
Ballymurphy attacked an Orange lodge as it marched out of the
Protestant New Barnsley estate and down the Springfield Road.[14]
That evening, when the Orangemen returned from Bangor, the
Springfield Road was crowded with Catholics, who attacked the
bandsmen. The Royal Scots 'immediately turned on Ballymurphy
and the first major engagement between the British army and Irish
nationalists for two generations was under way'.[15]

The rioters appear to have got the better of the army on the first
night, but on the second night of rioting the army fired cartridge
after cartridge of CS gas into the estate: 'it caused havoc and
terror as people fainted and retched and tried to protect their
children. The young people in the streets replied with stones and
petrol bombs, and an even fiercer determination than the night
before.'[16] The British GOC threatened to shoot petrol-bombers.
The Provies threatened to shoot soldiers if they shot Irishmen.

[14] C. De Baróid, *Ballymurphy and the Irish War* (Dublin, 1989), 12–15.
[15] Ibid. 12.
[16] Ibid.

The UVF threatened to shoot Catholics if the IRA shot any soldiers.

And that is exactly what everybody did, although not quite in that order. On 27 June Provisionals from the Ardoyne fired on an Orange parade. There was rioting and a gun-battle, and three Protestants were killed. In east Belfast fire was exchanged between the Short Strand, a ghetto of about six thousand Catholics, and the surrounding Protestant streets. Two Protestants were shot dead and two fatally wounded. One IRA man was shot dead, and Billy McKee, the Belfast commander of PIRA, was seriously wounded by a member of the Young Citizens' Volunteers (YCV), the junior wing of the UVF.

Two weeks later the army imposed a curfew on the lower Falls and for two days searched house by house, allowing people out of their houses for only an hour to collect food. The weapons find was significant—52 pistols, 35 rifles, 6 automatics, 14 shotguns, 100 home-made bombs, a grenade, 250 lb. of explosives, and 21,000 rounds of ammunition—but the alienation of the Catholics of the lower Falls was even more so. The next month the IRA blew up two RUC men near Crossmaglen in the border area.

In 1969 the Troubles had claimed thirteen lives: one RUC officer and twelve civilians. In 1970 there were twenty-five violent deaths: two RUC men, the rest civilians, many killed in the inter-communal violence. But the following year there were 174 deaths. Of these, 11 were RUC men, 115 were civilians, and 43 were soldiers. Much of this escalation was the work of the Provies. Although many of the killings were memorable—violent death was not yet so common as to be easily forgotten—the IRA murder of the three young Highland Fusiliers in March 1971 was a new landmark. They were not shot by snipers in the heat of battle but were befriended in a pub by people who bought them drinks, offered them a lift (probably to a promised party), stopped the car to let them get out to urinate, and then shot them in the back of the head.

In 1971 the Provisionals broadened their operations by adding, to their campaign against security-force personnel, attacks on the economic fabric of Northern Ireland: shops and factories were to be blasted out of business. There were thirty-seven serious explosions in April, forty-seven in May, and fifty in June. And those were just the ones that went off. The bomb disposal teams dismantled between 200 and 600 lb. of explosives every month of 1971.[17] As the level of violence increased, new targets were added when the IRA began to bomb Protestant pubs. In May drinkers in the Mountainview Tavern on the Shankill were seriously injured by a bomb. On 29 September a bomb at the Four Step Inn on the Shankill killed two people and injured twenty. One of the dead— 'Joker' Andrews—was laid out in the Orange Hall and guarded by a UVF 'honour party' while Protestants filed by the coffin throughout the night to pay their respects.

Through the summer of 1971 Brian Faulkner (who had succeeded Chichester-Clark as Prime Minister) had been arguing for the return of the favoured weapon of Protestant crisis policing: internment. Senior army officers were extremely reluctant and resisted as long as they could. As a compromise, the GOC suggested a co-ordinated arrest of a hundred republicans to collect information and to show the Provisionals that 'the hairs on their heads were numbered'.[18] It was not a great success. Only twenty people were charged, few arms were found, and the main effect was to provoke further Catholic hostility. Under pressure from right and left, Faulkner insisted on the double strategy of a ban on marches (to keep Catholics happy) and internment (to do likewise for Protestants).

The original intention was to lift 520 suspects on 10 August. However, the numbers of troops needed for such a number of arrests forced the number down to 450 and, because the Commander Land Forces was sure that the date would be leaked, the real date was moved forward from Tuesday to Monday. At 4.30 a.m. on 9 August, army units, each accompanied by a police officer to make the identification, moved in.

The poor quality of the intelligence provided by the RUC was apparent almost immediately. Soldiers found they were arresting old men and veterans of the IRA campaigns of the 1940s and 1950s.[19]

---

[17] See G. Styles, *Bombs Have No Pity: My War Against Terrorism* (London, 1975), for a detailed account of the bombing campaign of the early 1970s, and the Statistical Appendix for figures on the scale of the problem.

[18] D. Hamill, *Pig in the Middle: The Army in Northern Ireland, 1969–1984* (London, 1985).

[19] For a nationalist view of internment, see J. McGuffin, *Internment* (Tralee, 1973).

There was an immediate upsurge of Catholic violence, directed not only at the security forces, but at Protestants. Protestants retaliated and the result was, in this second major wave of inter-communal violence, an unprecedented flight of people. In the space of just three weeks, over two thousand families left their homes. One whole estate in the New Ardoyne area was razed; 240 houses in Farringdon Gardens, Velsheda Park, and Cranbrook Park were burnt out.

The basic pattern of movement is what one would have expected. People on interfaces moved in the direction of the nearest large concentration of their own people. The Protestants from the New Ardoyne moved outward, north-west, to the Ballysillan and Glencairn estates. Catholics in Ballysillan moved down to the New Ardoyne and their houses were taken over by Protestants.

In the Oldpark Road area there was a general 'shaking out'. Catholics left the south-east of the area—Louisa Street, Manor Street, and Rosapenna Street—and Protestants left the Ballynure part in the centre.[20] Suffolk was a new housing estate in the west of Belfast with a large Protestant population, but in the last three weeks of August there was considerable movement out of the area and 80 per cent of the migrants were Protestant. Because they were largely surrounded by Catholic west Belfast, the Suffolk Protestants could not follow the common pattern of moving only a few streets and most found their way across Belfast to Dundonald.[21]

Rumours and Myths

When people badly want to know what is going on and hard information is in short supply, the 'bad coin' of rumour takes the place of knowledge, and rumours build into myths. Everyone saw the intimidation directed at them as concerted. Catholics believed

---

[20] Community Relations Commission Research Unit, *Flight: A Report on Population Movement in Belfast during August 1971* (Belfast, 1971); J. Darby, *Intimidation and the Control of Conflict in Northern Ireland* (New York, 1986).

[21] For a personal account of the situation in Suffolk at this time, see N. Bradford, *A Sword Bathed in Heaven: The Life, Faith and Cruel Death of Robert Bradford MP* (Basingstoke, 1984). Robert Bradford was a young Methodist minister in the estate before he became a politician.

that John McKeague had planned and orchestrated the evacuation of Protestants and that the UVF deliberately fired the houses being vacated. Both beliefs were inaccurate, as it happens. It is probable that many of the fires were accidentally caused by people stealing gas meters. But McKeague's demon status was understandable given his quite open role in promoting such movements in the 1969 violence.

With justification, Catholics believed that they suffered considerably more than Protestants. However, there was a tendency to exaggerate. Despite the press photographs of panicking Protestants trying to save their possessions, it was widely claimed on the Catholic side that the Protestants had already moved all their possessions out before the torching started. For their part, the Protestants believed that the intimidation was premeditated and all part of the IRA plot. It was claimed that Catholics had been seen in those streets from which Protestants were chased, picking out the houses they wanted. While exaggerating the degree of organization in the intimidation they suffered, members of each side down-played their intimidation of the other side and suggested that 'they' had left 'voluntarily' or had over-reacted, while 'we' had been driven out.

Darby notes an interesting feature of the stories he heard:

There was an almost universal contention that all personal acts of intimidation were carried out by outsiders to the area. Victims often recounted how local people had pleaded with them to remain, arguing that the threats came from a few agitators from outside the district.[22]

There may have been an element of truth in this. If it is easier to threaten strangers than acquaintances, the heavies will work some area other than their own. But another appeal of the outsider myth was that it allowed those who had been scared out of their homes to reconcile what had happened with their previous 'good' relations with their neighbours of the opposite persuasion.

We had Catholics living in our street and I got on with them fine. They had a wee laddie about the same age as mine and they played together. My lad was always in their house and they would come in to us. When the trouble started, they got a couple of bricks through their windows and there was a mob gathering outside. I didn't recognize them. I went to get

[22] Darby, *Intimidation*, 83.

John [McKeague] and said 'You've got to come up. There's a house with kids in it that's going to get burnt out.' And he came up and talked to the men and we stopped them burning it. They moved of course, but they didn't get hurt.

Despite his good relations with his Catholic neighbour that man went on to become a leading loyalist paramilitary. This highlights an important paradox in sectarian relationships: most Protestants and Catholics, even those who got involved in the UDA and UVF, got on well with the other side. One needs to understand that the conflict was not a result of bad manners or social awkwardness writ large. It was the result of rational competition over resources and goals, and there is no reason why that sort of conflict should be incompatible with previously friendly everyday interaction.

It is also the case that most people were forced out of their houses not by violence so much as by the fear of violence. Irrespective of how they got on with their neighbours, they followed the news reports of what was happening in Londonderry or in other parts of Belfast and concluded that what was happening elsewhere could soon be happening to them unless they moved to secure areas.

3

Vigilantes and the Ulster Defence Association

THE Catholic response to the internment swoop 'Operation Demetrius' raised the tension levels and boosted recruitment to the Protestant street vigilante groups which had been formed two years earlier but were now fading. Three days after internment, a leaflet was widely circulated around loyalist areas of Belfast:

Being convinced that the enemies of the Faith and Freedom are determined to destroy the State of Northern Ireland and thereby enslave the people of God, we call on all members of our loyalist institutions, and other responsible citizens, to organize themselves *immediately* into platoons of twenty under the command of someone capable of acting as sergeant. Every effort must be made to arm these platoons, with whatever weapons are available. The first duty of each platoon will be to formulate a plan for the defence of its own street or road in cooperation with platoons in adjoining areas. A structure of command is already in existence and the various platoons will eventually be linked in a coordinated effort.[1]

Although many readers would have been unmoved by the claims of threats to 'the people of God', more and more Protestants were coming to agree with the basic point. Journalists working in the city were being introduced to vigilante group leaders. Under the headline 'The voices and guns of loyalist backlash', Robert Chesshyre reported the eagerness of Protestants to sign up for the 'third force' which Ian Paisley was then promoting.[2] Ex-members of the B Special Constabulary (which had been stood down the previous April) formed networks of contact which were eventually formalized in the Ulster Special Constabulary Association (USCA). A vigilante leader in east Belfast said: 'I went round to all the houses and asked the men if they wanted to guard their homes against the Roman Catholics and there was a great response . . . I

---

[1] M. Dillon and D. Lehane, *Political Murder in Northern Ireland* (Harmondsworth, 1973), 51.
[2] *Observer*, 12 Sept. 1971. It is worth noting that Paisley was promoting the idea of a 'third force' to complement police and army as early as this.

have no love for them. What I cannot understand is that they just will not accept this country.'[3] The need for vigilante groups was felt most by people living in areas such as Woodvale, Oldpark, and the Shankill, where there were communal interfaces, but it was not confined to those with personal experience of violence and intimidation. The people who were intimidated out of a trouble spot to Rathcoole, Glengormley, east Belfast, and Dundonald took with them their own experiences, which they shared with their new neighbours. Secondly, IRA violence—especially the bombs which were running at around three a day—had the potential to make everyone feel threatened. To quote from the front page of the first edition of a newsletter produced by the Dundonald UDA:

The Mountain View, The Blue Bell, The Four Step Inn, where will it happen next? We ask you, will it be Glengormley, Ormeau, Castlereagh, Albertbridge or Newtownards Road, or will it be the Dundonald area? We are concerned for our Protestant people and the protection of our homes and local shopping centres, the loss of life, the maiming of men, women and children for life. Collection boxes have been put around the Dundonald area and we do hope, and request that you will make a voluntary subscription which will enable us to make the Dundonald area as safe as possible within the laws of our beloved Province. We are dedicated and pledged to uphold the Constitution of our beloved Ulster, to honour the forces of our beloved Majesty the Queen.

This we will maintain, if the force of law and order cannot give or afford us immediate protection, we the Protestant people of Dundonald area, will defend to our utmost our Protestant heritage and we will never surrender to the murdering scum, the rebels.[4]

The relationships between the army and the vigilante groups patrolling loyalist areas were generally amicable. The army was fully occupied with its worsening relationships with Catholics and with the IRA campaign and did not want to have to fight on two fronts. In east Belfast, vigilantes had been patrolling since mid-August when Protestants were fired on from the Catholic enclave of the Short Strand. An army officer said of the patrols:

A lot of what they do is illegal, of course, and if they so much as pointed a gun at anyone in anger we'd shoot them. They all know that. They also know it's illegal to block off roads and stop traffic and most of them only

[3] *This Week*, 17 Feb. 1972, p. 28.
[4] *Dundonald District UDA*, 16 Oct. 1971.

slow cars down. But since they took over there hasn't been a single bomb at all in their area. Tension is down and the people inside feel they can sleep through the night safely.[5]

An RUC officer also approved of the vigilantes: 'These Protestants found out last Easter that it's not worth rioting. Organising themselves like this seems a far more responsible way of reacting to the troubles.'[6] There was also élite support. Desmond Boal QC, the Stormont MP for Shankill, said on 15 December that he intended to set up an unarmed body of citizens in his constituency and challenged the government that, if they 'did not agree with the general tenor of his scheme it was their bounded duty to provide a scheme which they did regard as viable'. Even the Prime Minister was found giving legitimacy to the vigilante groups. Faulkner was talking about a code of practice for such groups, although he was clear that they would have 'no legal right other than those attaching to the ordinary citizen and . . . must in no circumstances be armed'.[7]

Increasingly, armed is what they were. A member of a vigilante group in north Belfast wrote the following description of his group's first encounter with weapons:

We piled into the hut. Women were not allowed to be present and there was a terrible air of expectancy at the meeting. At the head of the table sat a fit-looking man, dressed in a paratrooper's jacket which displayed the rank of Colonel. He was introduced as 'John from the Shankill' by the chairman of our Tenant's Committee. Without further ado, John addressed the company. He identified himself as a Colonel in the newly-formed Ulster Defence Association and went on to explain that the UDA had already secured the services of 100,000 Ulstermen who were prepared to defend our country with their very lives, if need be. He stressed that unarmed vigilantes were purely 'sitting ducks' for travelling gunmen, that they were only risking life and limb, and had no means of returning fire. The company was in total agreement with these sentiments. John went on to relate his military experience with the British Army paratroopers and shocked the entire assembly by suddenly producing a Sterling sub-machine gun from below the Union Jack draped table. One poor fellow fainted and had to be carried out of the hall on a wooden plank. John then appealed for volunteers for this new 'army' and I think that even he was surprised by this show of hands. He then went into detail regarding

[5] *Guardian*, 27 Sept. 1971.
[6] Ibid.
[7] *Guardian*, 17 Dec. 1971.

weaponry, petrol bombs and other counter-guerilla 'aids' which were needed to arm the new group. After a period of two hours had elapsed, those considered too old or infirm were asked to leave the room, and the remainder—all 51 of us—took an oath. The ceremony meant approaching the table, putting the left hand on the Bible and repeating the following lines: 'I . . . being convinced that republican enemies of our country are hell-bent on creating an all-Ireland Republic against the express wishes of the Protestant majority, do solemnly swear that I will defend my area and my country with all and every means possible. I further swear that in joining the Ulster Defence Association, I hold no dual membership of any other paramilitary body, that I am a Protestant and a true subject of Her Majesty the Queen. I further acknowledge that I will never divulge to friend or foe or to any member of the security forces, any information detrimental to the well-being of my fellow soldiers in the organization, neither will I reveal any knowledge of the workings of the UDA in the event of capture by the security forces or by Republican enemies. I take this oath of my own free will, with full knowledge that if I am found guilty of breach of any part of this oath, that I can expect no mercy from my superiors.' We were IN![8]

Forming the UDA

The UDA grew out of a number of initiatives, and its fragmented origins are reflected in the confusing accounts of its formation. In the background were the remnants of the 'wee teams' of UVF men to be found in Tara. In the foreground were the vigilante groups that had formed in frontline streets.

One element began in Woodvale, which lies in west Belfast at the top of the Shankill and Crumlin Roads. A Protestant area, it is bordered by the nationalist Ardoyne and by the western Catholic estates. The Woodvale Defence Association (WDA) grew out of a number of street vigilante groups and for a few months met in a small pigeon club in Leopold Street. Around the same time, groups of vigilantes from different interface areas came together at a meeting in Aberdeen Street primary school addressed by Alan Moon, an ex-lorry-driver who briefly led the movement, and by Sammy Smyth, who became its spokesman.

The Woodvale group lost some of its initial impetus because of dissatisfaction with its leader. A problem for the UDA in its early days was the random nature of its growth and evolution from lots

[8] Unpublished typescript of UDA activist.

of separate groups, each of which had haphazardly promoted its own leaders. The chairman made himself unpopular by turning up for meetings late and sometimes drunk, by threatening members, and by insulting other senior people in the WDA. There was also suspicion of money going missing. The chairman began a credit union, which was an excellent way of storing and 'laundering' donations, but it was robbed in circumstances that led some people to suspect inside collusion. The regulars at the pigeon club meetings were also unhappy that not enough was being done to provide loyalists with weapons for protection.

There was real atmosphere there at that time, that something was going to happen and we wanted the gear to defend ourselves. The boss kept saying it was stashed and when the time came, it would be there and we were saying 'Let's see the weapons'. Eventually he brought some stuff up in the boot of his car and it was nothing. A couple of old rusty pieces. He was collecting money all over the city and I reckon he just had this wee stash in his boot which he showed to all the groups he had taken money from.

The first 'UDA' meeting in the early summer of 1971 attracted about eighteen people, the second more than a hundred, and the third about three thousand. Moon was already getting cold feet. Billy Hull, a leading Protestant trade unionist, was elected chairman and Moon vice-chairman. When he was eased out by Jim Anderson, a glazier who was prominent in the vigilantes in the Woodvale area, Moon was privately pleased and from September had nothing more to do with the movement. His departure coincided with the organization's take-off, as the nationalist reaction to internment raised the temperature.

When the Troubles started I helped form a vigilante group that became the Oldpark DA [OPDA]. It took in Tyndale, Benview, Silverstream and the 'River' streets. Then we got armed and started shooting back. Mostly Steyrs, the odd Webley or Martini-Henry; a lot of the lads had been in the army and had hung on to something. Within eighteen months the attacks by the IRA had stopped and we had no trouble in our area for four years. There had been meetings in various places with Moon and Hull but they didn't really have any clout. The first UDA meeting proper was in the band hall in Northland Street and it was chaired by Ingram Beckitt.[9] There was the WDA, the OPDA, the EBDA [East Belfast Defence Association], Tigers Bay and SDA.

[9] In March 1972 Beckitt was shot dead by Protestants during an after-hours fight. Dillon and Lehane, *Political Murder*, 63–5, offer a misleading version of the events that tries too hard to find a big explanation for a sordid tussle.

McGurk's Bar

The history of communal violence in Ireland had well established the principle that the best form of defence is attack. Simon Winchester wondered if the vigilantes might be plotting to go on the offensive.[10] The word 'plotting' might suggest a degree of central organization and premeditation which did not obtain, but there were working-class loyalists who were prepared to take the fight to the enemy.

Largely dormant since 1966, the UVF was beginning to come back to life in 1971, as the political instability added plausibility to the analyses of 'mainstream' right-wing unionist politicians such as Bill Craig and Ian Paisley and of working-class militants. The slogan 'Gusty was right' began to appear on walls. At work and in pubs and in clubs, loyalists 'complained about the effin IRA and demanded to know what our people were going to do about it, when was "our side" going to effin do something'. 'Our side' started to do two things: pub bombings and sectarian murders.

On 14 December 1971 a bomb wrecked McGurk's Bar in North Queen Street, Belfast, killing fifteen people, all of them Catholics. Three were women and two were children. Despite the claims of a boy selling papers outside the pub that he saw a man get out of a car and plant the bomb, and an anonymous phone call claiming that the 'Empire Loyalists' were responsible, the army and police decided that the IRA had scored an own goal.[11] *The Times* ran the official version:

Police and Army intelligence officers believe that Ulster's worst outrage, the killing of 15 people, including two children and three women, in an explosion in a Belfast bar last night was caused by an IRA plan that went wrong...

The Army's theory is that the bomb in McGurk's Bar was 'in transit', that it had been left there, probably without the knowledge of any of the people who were killed or injured, by a 'carrier' for another person to pick up, and that the second person was unable to keep his rendezvous because of the security operation.[12]

[10] *Guardian*, 27 Sept. 1971.

[11] The official version derived some plausibility from the frequency of 'own goals'; of 106 IRA men and women who died between 1969 and 1973, 43 were blown up by their own bombs, but in all cases they were being either constructed or moved at the time (P. Bishop and E. Mallie, *The Provisional IRA* (London, 1988), 193). The bomb was actually the work of the UVF.

[12] *The Times*, 6 Dec. 1971. L. Curtis, *Ireland: The Propaganda War* (London, 1984), 91–2, makes much of this as evidence for the right-wing bias of the British

Not surprisingly, given its source and its confirmation of their stereotypes of the IRA, many Protestants believed this version of events. However, John McKeague, who was well connected in UVF circles, certainly knew better when he repeated it in his *Loyalist News*:

Now to the truth about McGurk's pub. What terms can we use . . . . poetic justice? Yes . . . . . a bomb in transit, meant for another building, and we believe it was for the Co-op in York street. Over the past weeks we have had the sneers and gibs from Republican elements, in reference to the fact that business will be brought to a stand still before Christmas, and when it happens to themselves they don't like their own medicine . . . . . . the blast at McGurk's need not have happened, if the 'slugs' responsible for the bomb, had not called for a wee something to boast their moral.

IRA CAUGHT IN THEIR OWN TRAP.[13]

The important point to note in this account is the elision of Catholics and IRA men. Republican elements who threatened a bombing campaign do not like a touch of their own medicine. With no discussion of or justification for it (in fact in the whole article those who died are never referred to as Catholics but just as 'people'), the victims are assumed to be identical to Republicans and the 'slugs' responsible for planting the bomb.

The report in the *WDA News* was significantly different:

Many lies, and much IRA propaganda, have been circulated since the explosion at McGurk's bar, where fifteen people, some of whom were innocent, and probably had no connection with the IRA, died. But, what many people outside Belfast, and all outside the province, do not know, this bar, on numerous occasions, was a meeting place for terrorists. It was also situated in the centre, and surrounded by an IRA fortress, particularly Artillery Flats, where IRA Snipers and machine gunners have reigned terror on Army patrols.

It continues to give reasons why it was hardly likely to be a Protestant bomb and it repeats the army and police theory. It then goes on:

media and misses the point that the official version was as consistent with the facts as any other then available and was given additional plausibility precisely because it was the *official* version.

[13] *Loyalist News*, 11 Dec. 1971. Except where it would have made the text incomprehensible, the spellings and punctuations of extracts from these roneoed news-sheets have been left as they were in the original.

We would wish it to be known, while sympathy is extended to the families of those killed, it should be noted that these people have never once condemned the IRA. In fact, they claim the IRA would have given a warning. Let us remind those people the IRA gave no warning at the Springfield Road Police Station, where a 30 lb bomb was placed just one foot from children standing in the hallway. . . . Is it possible that the Roman Catholics believe that the IRA only give warnings when they, the Roman Catholics, are in danger? This is possible, for the hatred they possess for the Protestant Community leaves them blind to anything else, and they will at all times support any organization or army whose sole purpose is to destroy anything or anyone who is Protestant.[14]

The Woodvale version is more explicit in its view that at least some of those who died deserved it. Only some are 'completely innocent'. It is also more specific in linking the clientele of McGurk's with the IRA and thus justifying the death of at least some of those who died. But then it offers another principle which almost undermines the distinction between deserved and undeserved dead: all Catholics hate Protestants.

The bomb was in fact the work of a UVF team who for this occasion called themselves 'Empire Loyalists'. It is worth mentioning here the general issue of 'claiming jobs', which was hotly debated within the organizations then and periodically thereafter:

If a job took place in a certain area and an organization claimed it, you were just making the police's job easier for them, narrowing down the field. A lot of us thought you should just get on with it and leaving the security forces to sort out who was doing what.

The problem with remaining anonymous was that it weakened the terror impact of any killing. For one's name to strike fear into those who heard it, they had to know the name of those who struck.

While those were considerations for the perpetrators and planners of political murder, there was an obvious value in denying 'military' actions: a lot of ordinary Protestants did not want to believe that their people bombed pubs and killed innocent Catholics. As we have already seen and will see repeatedly, the loyalist paramilitary self-image was based on an explicit contrast with republicans. They were aggressors; loyalists were defenders. They were criminal; loyalists were law-abiding. They were

[14] *WDA News*, 20 Dec. 1971.

murdering scum who killed women and children; loyalists were decent family men who could never do such a thing. Which brings me to the sectarian murder campaign.

Stiffing a Taig

In February 1971 two senior Scotland Yard detectives were seconded to the RUC in Belfast to assist the detective squad working on twenty murders committed in the previous six months: the fifteen victims of the McGurk's bomb and six others, almost certainly all victims of the IRA. In his analysis of fatalities attributable to the civil disturbances, McKeown divides the Troubles into four periods.[15] In the first, from July 1969 to July 1973, 857 people died. Of these the largest number—498—were victims of the battle between the IRA and the troops. They included members of each side, accidental casualties of attacks by one side on the other, and own goals. But in the second half of this first period there was a marked change, with what McKeown classifies as 'sectarianism' becoming more important. In 1972 and 1973 there were 213 fatalities that were the result of republican attacks on loyalists, loyalist attacks on republicans, and the mistakes of loyalist attacks that produced Protestant fatalities.

Loyalist attacks on Catholics varied considerably in the amount of planning involved. Generally it was very little. There was certainly no design formulated among the leadership of the UVF or the embryonic UDA teams and no point at which leaders instructed their people 'now' to kill Catholics. One man who led a vigilante group told me:

We never planned to go on the kill. There was no time that we sat down and said 'That's it. Stiff a Taig'. Mind, we planned doing something to the Ardoyne after the three Scots boys were killed but for some reason it never came off. No, it was ground up. One or two volunteers just started doing it.

There was little or no central control over the murder campaign. Separate teams of Ulster Freedom Fighters (UFF)[16] did what they

---

[15] M. McKeown, *Two Seven Six Three: An Analysis of Fatalities Attributable to Civil Disturbances in Northern Ireland in the Twenty Years between July 13, 1969 and July 12, 1989* (Lucan, 1989).

[16] The name 'Ulster Freedom Fighters', with its anti-colonial struggle

liked and then claimed it using code names (which were modelled on those of the eighteenth-century agrarian secret societies). For a while, different teams used different colours in their 'Captain' tags; the team operating from the Shankill which killed Senator Paddy Wilson claimed responsibility using the name 'Captain Black'. There were also 'Captain Red' and 'Captain White' teams. There was so little co-ordination that, even on major policy matters, teams might differ. In September 1973 'Captain Black' phoned the BBC to announce a UFF cease-fire; 'Captain White' phoned in with a threat to continue bombings!

The mention of the failure of a plan to revenge the three Fusiliers reminds us of one considerable difficulty in trying to date and chart the loyalist murder campaign: not all murder bids succeed. Probably the first loyalist attack on an individual Catholic chosen at random (as distinct from those killed in gun battles) was in April 1970, when an Ardoyne Catholic was shot and wounded on his way home from the pub. Three days later a man was shot and wounded just after leaving the Celtic Bar in the Falls Road area.[17] By good fortune both survived. The first such fatality was Bernard Rice, a 60-year-old member of the Catholic Ex-Servicemen's Association (CESA), who was shot dead on the Crumlin Road on 8 February 1972. In the next eighteen months over two hundred others were to follow.

The RUC chose politically unfortunate terms in referring to these incidents as 'random' or 'motiveless' killings. They were random in the sense that the particular victim was not especially selected, but there were two clear purposes to the murders: to revenge IRA attacks on the state and on individual Protestants, and to deter further attacks: 'If we hadn't done something, they'd have been all over us. We had to stop them. Tribal survival. We had to hit back.' The history of most incidents was similar. A group of loyalists would be sitting drinking in a pub and ruminating on the latest republican outrage. They would decide to even the score, collect a car and weapons, and go out to look for a

connotations, was first suggested as a joke by one of the UDA 'operators'. Although it was not officially used until the following year, it is convenient to bring it forward to identify the group to which that man belonged. I have consistently used 'UFF' to identify the 'operators' within the UDA, even when the group simply called itself 'UDA'.

[17] C. De Baróid, *Ballymurphy and the Irish War* (Dublin, 1989), 62.

victim. There would be varying degrees of premeditation. Many of
the victims were taxi-drivers, people whose occupations identified
their religion and made them available late at night. The murder
of Gerald Patrick Donnelly on 20 April 1972 was typical. Two
men went into the office of Arkle taxis in Clifton Street and asked
for a cab to the Ardoyne. From the location of the company and
the stated destination, they could be sure their driver was a
Catholic. They forced him to stop in Harrybrook Street and shot
him in the head.

Catholic vigilantes featured prominently in the early targets
because they were standing on street corners in Catholic areas and
could be fired at from a fast moving car. UDA colonel 'John', who
warned his fellow vigilantes that unless they were armed they
would be sitting ducks for republican murder squads, knew what
he was talking about: he was a 'duck shooter'. People who drank
late outside their own area and then walked home towards an
obviously Catholic part of town were also easily identifiable and
made easy targets. Other victims were Catholics who stumbled
into a loyalist vigilante patrol.

Sometimes there was a 'reason' why a particular person was
killed. Phillip Fay was shot dead by Albert 'Ginger' Baker, a
member of the east Belfast UFF team, because he was a Catholic
who worked as a barman in the Girton Lodge hotel in east Belfast.
The Inner Council of the UDA met in the Girton Lodge and
someone was concerned that Fay might have overheard something. That was reason enough to order Baker to shoot him, which
he did with efficiency and no qualms.

The Politics of Vocabulary

Although most serious journalists and analysts scorn the IRA's
claim that the people it kills are 'legitimate' targets, there is no
doubt that the IRA has been more successful than its loyalist
counterparts in the war of propaganda over the legitimacy of
murder. The republican advantage lies more often in avoiding the
'sectarian' label.

There is no doubt that most loyalist killings in this period were
'sectarian' in the sense that people were killed because they were
Catholics. Only rarely did the victim have some other
characteristic that identified him as an 'IRA man' or a 'republican'

or a member of some other group which the UDA views as providing legitimate targets. Awareness that killing Catholics at random is not something which can be defended in terms of the role which the loyalist paramilitaries claim for themselves leads them often to deny responsibility for their murders.

What is often overlooked or outrightly denied is the degree to which the IRA are also 'sectarian'. Kelley wrote: 'despite the climbing death toll and the increasingly casual and sadistic violence, the Provos had not become completely battle-hardened by the spring of 1972. They were still reluctant to shoot someone simply because he or she was a Protestant.'[18] This is romantic nonsense; PIRA was one of the main causes of the climbing death toll! A much more honest assessment was given by Bishop and Mallie in *The Provisional IRA*:

The non-sectarian principle meant little to many of the new recruits. Indeed some of Donnelly's intake 'joined because they hated Protestants', although he says that 'this feeling later wore off'. The actions of the Protestant murder gangs in the following years ensured that sectarian assassinations became part of the Provisional's routine activities.[19]

As an example, one might note the August 1973 case of a Protestant who was stopped walking home on the Cliftonville Road by three men. He was asked his religion and, when he gave it, he was shot in the mouth. He survived.

There could only be any truth in Kelley's view if he confined his remarks to 'shooting'. IRA men might have been extremely fussy about who they shot (actually they weren't); they were certainly casual about who they blew up. In 1971, well before the UFF teams started their 'sectarian' murders, the IRA was bombing public houses in Protestant areas, and such bombs were only as selective as the pub was select. They were not police clubs or army base NAAFIs; they were ordinary pubs in working-class Protestant areas. The bombs were designed to kill 'Protestants' and they succeeded. Nor were such attacks the work of an ultra-militant and deviant fringe (as Lebow suggests of the Kingsmill massacre of Protestant workmen).[20] In August 1975 a bomb was thrown

---

[18] K. J. Kelley, *The Longest War: Northern Ireland and the IRA* (London, 1988), 170.

[19] Bishop and Mallie, *The Provisional IRA*, 181.

[20] N. Lebow, 'The Origins of Sectarian Assassination: The case of Belfast', in

into the Bayardo Bar on the Shankill, and two men standing outside were gunned down. A youth and a woman died in the attack. As the attackers drove off, one man machine-gunned a bus queue. The leader of the attack was a senior figure in the Belfast IRA leadership who was later prominent in the prison protests.

What seems very obvious to anyone who reads through the details of the dead of Ulster's Troubles is that, of those who are prepared to kill at all, many are quite happy to kill *anyone* of the other side. Loyalists and republicans are equally sectarian. However, the IRA has an easier time of it in the propaganda stakes for two reasons. First, its legitimate targets (narrowly defined) are more numerous than those of the loyalists. If one adds the total personnel of the security forces, their families, and those who work with or supply the security forces, one has a target population of over 100,000. A guess at the number of active republicans and their families might give a total of 20,000. The bigger the target, the more likely you are to hit it. Secondly, the population to which loyalists have to present their work as legitimate is more responsive to government and security-force arguments than is the population to which the IRA has to answer; east Belfast Protestants are more likely to believe RUC assertions about the innocence of a victim than are Ballymurphy Catholics, who tend not to believe anything the RUC says. Loyalist paramilitaries are concerned with maintaining the status quo, with defending the province against 'murdering cowardly rebel scum'. When one's justification comes from the future utopian goal of a united Ireland, 'mistakes' in the present are much easier to justify than they are when one is claiming only to represent and preserve the virtues of the present.

London Guns

Although loyalists possessed military skills acquired in the services, they were as short of serious armaments as was the IRA. Although the WDA had collected money for arms, it had acquired very little. Having pushed the first chairman aside, Charles Harding Smith

---

A. D. Buckley and D. D. Olson (eds.), *International Terrorism* (Wayne, NJ, 1980), 41–53.

had emerged as the dominant figure in the WDA and, with McKeague out of the way, as one of the leaders of the UDA in the city. In February 1972 John Campbell, a Belfast arms dealer and friend of Harding (as he was known), contacted a Mr 'A' and said he had £50,000 to spend on guns. Mr 'A' put him in touch with a Scottish arms dealer 'B', and Campbell arranged to meet 'B' in a London West End pub. He took with him Harding Smith and RUC officer Robert Lusty. Unfortunately, 'B' was a Lanarkshire special constable and his principal was a Special Branch officer. Police watched as Campbell, accompanied by John White and Bobby Dalzell, two of Harding Smith's closest associates, and Lusty, met 'B' and his principal in a room at the Hilton on 29 April. The four men were arrested. Later that evening Harding called at Scotland Yard and said he knew the four men but refused to give any further information. He was also arrested.[19]

Early on in the trial, the case against Lusty was dropped. White and Dalzell claimed they were just at the Hilton having a drink and knew nothing. Harding Smith and Campbell did not deny the details of what had transpired but offered an interestingly different motive for their behaviour. They argued that they were trying to trap IRA gun-runners. Campbell claimed that he believed 'B' was supplying the IRA and was trying to trace the source of the weapons. Both men were discharged and, on 20 December, Smith returned to Belfast and the west Belfast UDA.[21]

In the view of the verdict, one cannot argue with Smith's account of his actions, but his erstwhile colleagues point out that, had he actually purchased the £350,000 worth of guns that was sometimes talked about, he would have acquired a position of unchallenged authority in the UDA and of immense power in Northern Ireland.

During Harding's absence the UDA grew enormously; a reasonable guess for the end of 1972 would be about 26,000 due-paying members. It also changed its structure to take on a deliberately military shape. Areas became 'battalions'. West Belfast was a battalion with three areas within it—Springfield, Highfield, and Glencairn (the Protestant west Belfast estates) became A company, Woodvale became B company, and the Shankill Road became C company.

[21] See *Guardian*, 12 July 1972 and *Irish Times*, 20 Dec. 1972.

The Ainsworth Avenue Stand-Off

Prods were still not used to being treated like Taigs. Harding Smith's arrest triggered one of the UDA's most dramatic and frightening displays of its potential: some twenty thousand men marched twelve abreast through the busy centre of Belfast to protest at his imprisonment.

Loyalists responded to any security-force action against them by contrasting that action with an apparent unwillingness to confront the IRA. In particular, the UDA's leaders were unhappy about the government's tolerance of Catholic 'no-go' areas. For long periods since 1969 the western Belfast estates or 'Free Derry' had been outside the effective control of the state. The security forces rarely entered and the IRA was free to organize, train, stockpile weapons, and weave itself into the fabric of the community. Apart from the practical advantages 'no-go' areas gave to the IRA, their existence was a powerful symbolic affront to Protestants. The rebels were able to live outside the law. Unionists had always criticized nationalists for being willing to take such benefits of British citizenship as social security, while refusing to support the state: 'they reject the Crown but they're loyal to the half-crown'. The 'no go's were the final extension of that.

At two periods of intense communal violence—August 1969 and July 1970—loyalists had also erected barricades for protection and created their own 'no-go' zones. In 1972 UDA set up what it promised to be the first of a series of 'no-go' areas that were different in purpose. They were not primarily practical measures of defence but symbols, political bargaining counters, directed at the British army and government. They would be removed when the British army moved into Catholic west Belfast and the Bogside in Derry. In a co-ordinated action, McKeague's Red Hand Commando (RHC) barricaded an area of the seaside town of Bangor.

As an aside, it is worth noting the part-time nature of UDA involvement. Like the Inner Council meetings and the mass demonstrations, barricading loyalist areas was something that was done primarily at weekends, so that it did not interfere too greatly with the working lives of the many UDA men who had jobs. In Monkstown the rather ritualistic nature of the barricades was given away by the local UDA commander promising to return to their owners on Monday morning the vehicles that had been commandeered to block roads.

On 21 May the second weekend of barricades saw serious confrontation with the army. In east Belfast, paratroopers stormed newly erected barricades and a night of rioting followed. On the evening of 3 July, the commander of a west Belfast UDA company and a small number of men faced up to the Paras. The UDA wanted to create a 'no-go' area in streets just north of March Street, between the Springfield Road and the Woodvale Road. This was a borderline area between the Protestant Woodvale and the Catholic Falls. The small pocket had been mixed, but the flight of 1971 had seen a major reorganization around Ainsworth Avenue, and it was now overwhelmingly Protestant. About fifty Catholic families still lived there, and the army had decided that barricades would not be tolerated.

On the afternoon of Monday 3 July the battalion commander in the area was told by the UDA that 2,000 families were insisting on living inside barricades, and soldiers moved in to stop another convoy of Protestants arriving with road drills and other such equipment.[22]

After some bargaining, the local UDA thought they had won an agreement from the colonel commanding the First King's that the army would build barricades and allow three army and three UDA patrols inside the area every day. Cases of intimidation of the fifty Catholic families isolated within the barricaded area would be referred by the army to the local UDA chief, who promised to deal with them! But shortly after agreement was reached the colonel was summoned back to base and told that it was unacceptable. 'No-go' areas were not to be permitted. As word spread that 'something was on', large numbers of uniformed UDA men from all over Belfast came to the Woodvale Road and down it into the seven disputed streets. According to the Radio Ulster news report: 'Ranks of the UDA stretched from the confrontation point at March Street to the Woodvale Road and beyond, the front line carrying army style riot shields and sticks faced soldiers carrying similar equipment.'

Leaders of the two sides, who had been talking inside a 'Pig' (as the armoured personnel carriers were affectionately known), parted and the UDA men, swollen now from their early numbers, took up their positions, ready to take on the troops. General Ford, GOC Land Forces, arrived around nine o'clock and started talks with Herron, Jim Anderson, Sammy Doyle, and Davy Fogel. At ten he left, no agreement having been reached. Finally he returned an hour later, having apparently consulted William Whitelaw, the Secretary of State for Northern Ireland, and conceded the UDA's demand. Although the UDA would not be permitted to seal off the area, small barriers were allowed and the UDA was allowed to maintain groups of men who 'patrolled' alongside the army. 'That was our best fuckin night. Brilliant! Thousands of them just turned up. I don't know how they got there that quick. And the army backed off. We fuckin won. All bluff but we did it.'

The Ainsworth Avenue confrontation was a major victory for the UDA. If any Catholic was still in doubt, it demonstrated the might of the working-class Protestant people and their potential for violence. By showing the army and the UDA apparently 'working together', it bolstered loyalist paramilitary morale. Thirdly, and most importantly, it was invaluable recruiting publicity for the UDA. How could young loyalists not be attracted to an organization that could face down the army?

The IRA Truce and Lenadoon

The UDA followed the success of Ainsworth Avenue by breaking the IRA truce. Even with hindsight it is difficult to disentangle the various army, Stormont, and Westminster interests that caused security policy to waver between such acts of oppression as the lower Falls curfew and the tolerance that was shown towards Free Derry in the Bogside. However, we can identify one clear strand of British thinking in 1971 and early 1972 and that was to negotiate with the IRA. Towards the end of May the Official IRA (OIRA) declared a cease-fire. On 29 May PIRA said it would not be following suit. Two weeks later Sean MacStiofain said the PIRA was willing to discuss its peace plan with the Secretary of State, but Whitelaw rejected the advance. On 22 June PIRA announced that, with effect from the 26th, it was suspending operations. Whitelaw said that the government would 'reciprocate'.

Leading Provisionals Sean MacStiofain, David O'Connell,

Gerry Adams, Martin McGuinness, Ivor Bell, and Seamus
Twomey were flown to London (some of them from prison) to
meet Whitelaw. Unionists were appalled by this apparent act of
betrayal; their government was negotiating with the murderers of
soldiers.[23] Loyalist paramilitary leaders were determined to force
an end to the truce and they managed it with an incident at
Lenadoon in the south-west of the city.

The dispute concerned territory and houses that were empty
because persistent IRA sniper fire had driven out the Protestant
occupants. The vacant houses were allocated to Catholic families
who had been intimidated out of Rathcoole, the solidly Protestant
estate on the northern outskirts of the city. In a classic insistence
of not giving an inch of territory to the enemy, the south Belfast
UDA, led by Sammy Murphy, refused to allow the Catholics to
occupy the houses. The local IRA insisted that the army hold back
the UDA while the families were installed. From Friday afternoon
through Saturday the army tried to mediate between the two sides,
but the UDA was intransigent. On Sunday a large crowd of
Catholics gathered and began to stone the army. The army retaliated with CS gas and rubber bullets. IRA snipers again took up
positions and began firing. The two-week-old truce was at an end.

There is interesting confusion about who first fired metal
ammunition. The Provisionals believe that the British army fired
first, while forcing the mob back up the hill.[24] Hamill, who had
access to good military sources, is not sure and notes 'some
reports suggesting that the Officials [IRA] opened fire first to
make sure that the Provisionals really did become involved in
breaking the cease-fire'.[25] Well-informed UDA sources told me
that they engineered the breakdown by sending a carload of armed
men on a dangerous run into Lenadoon, behind Catholic 'lines',
where they fired in the air and precipitated general shooting. In all
likelihood the cease-fire would have broken down soon, even
without the Lenadoon incident. The IRA leaders' talks with
Whitelaw had made it clear to them that the British government
was not going to give them what they wanted and they were keen to

[23] Lord Carrington was present at the talks as Defence Secretary. It is a mark of
the Northern Ireland Office's insensitivity that he could be suggested as the
'neutral' chairman for the 1991 cross-party talks.

[24] *Republican News*, 14 July 1973.

[25] Hamill, *Pig in the Middle*, 111.

return to the offensive. None the less, the UDA had again confronted the army and won itself a major piece of publicity.

East versus West in the UDA

The Ainsworth Avenue and Lenadoon victories, and the major boost to recruitment which they brought, had been won without the participation of Harding Smith, who had spent the summer in a London jail. On his return Harding resumed control of the west Belfast UDA and was appointed 'joint chairman' with Jim Anderson of Woodvale. Tommy Herron, who was the first full-time paid UDA officer, was the brigadier of east Belfast and vice-chairman.

Apparently encouraged by Smith, a campaign to smear Herron began. On 17 January 1973 *Ulster Militant*, a UDA magazine edited by Sammy Smyth, reported that two hundred members of various battalions had met and agreed in a burst of self-criticism that the UDA was using intimidation to extract money, was badly organized, and was using its members to act as bouncers in unlicensed clubs.[26] Rumours circulated that Herron, whose mother was a Catholic, had relatives in the Official IRA.[27]

In the introduction I stressed the difficulty of ever being sure of what was really going on in the UDA and UVF; much of what the UDA did was illegal and the UVF was a proscribed organization. We can be confident that Herron was a committed UDA activist who had little or no time for Catholics and less time for organized republicanism. However, the assassination of a close relative of Herron suggests a gleam of plausibility in the accusation of links with the OIRA. Michael Wilson, Herron's 18-year-old brother-in-law, was shot dead in June by two masked men who entered Herron's house while he was away. At the time, it was reported as a botched IRA attempt on Herron, but the widely believed gossip was that Wilson had been killed by UDA men on Herron's orders because he had been passing information to republicans in the Markets area of Belfast (an Official, rather than Provisional, IRA stronghold). That link may explain the rumour that Herron had republican contacts.

[26] *Ulster Militant*, 17 Jan. 1973.
[27] *Irish Times*, 18 Jan. 1973.

Despite the rumblings, Herron was not displaced from his power base in east Belfast. Two days after the critical comments appeared in *Ulster Militant*, a meeting of local UDA commanders reaffirmed support for Herron and denounced the campaign against him. Herron stayed in charge of east Belfast until his assassination in September 1973.

While the campaign against his rival was rumbling, Harding consolidated his own position in west Belfast. Despite returning empty-handed from London, he was sufficiently popular in west Belfast and sufficiently ruthless to remove threats to his position. By all accounts a not particularly bright man (a man who worked closely with him said he was 'near illiterate'), Harding frightened a lot of people and was able to get his way by using one of his three companies against the other two. The first of his rivals to go was Davy Fogel, who had taken over Woodvale in his absence. Fogel was 'arrested' by Harding Smith and held for three hours while it was explained to him that Harding was back and that Fogel could stay only if he accepted that fact. He took the hint, left the country, and gave his story to the British papers.[28] In a press conference held to counter some of Fogel's claims, Herron said that it was at his command, not Harding Smith's, that Fogel was taken to east Belfast for questioning, and that Fogel had been under a cloud of suspicion for some time. Apparently six months earlier the Association had been tipped the word by a high-ranking member of the security forces that Fogel was a 'danger to the UDA'. For the obvious reason that it may have damaged the organization's reputation, Herron did not make public the reason whispered among UDA men: Fogel was reputed to have pocketed large sums of money that were meant for the organization.[29]

There were two interesting subtexts to that press conference. First, Herron was keen to stress his own position of authority in the UDA. Secondly, Harding was not a man for the limelight. He lacked the confidence for public prominence and, although he wanted to be in charge of the UDA, he did not seek or welcome the responsibility for public presentation of the organization's aims and intentions.

[28] See *Sunday Times*, 28 Jan. 1973, for Fogel's story.
[29] As we shall see (Ch. 7 on racketeering), this accusation was standard.

Over-Explanation

The casual reader may prefer me to tell the story of the UDA without frequent references to sources and other studies, but there are some mistakes in the literature on the early UDA which cannot go uncorrected. An error that has misled many subsequent analysts is Dillon's and Lehane's 'left–right' explanation of rivalry between UDA bosses. They believe that Ernie 'Duke' Elliott, Davy Fogel, and Tommy Herron were socialists and were for that reason opposed by Harding. They also believe that the first and third were gangsters and that Harding wanted to stop racketeering.[30] Unfortunately this has become the orthodoxy, and the same line is taken by Paul Foot.[31] It is entirely mistaken. Not one of the UDA men I have interviewed, irrespective of his relationship with Harding, has offered a similar analysis or anything that would support it.

Politics in the conventional sense had little or nothing to do with the conflict between the UDA leaders. Personal animosity was a major consideration, but equally important was the competition for status, both personal and group. Put simply, many UDA men wanted to be top dog in the top team. Such competition can be healthy for an organization if it is controlled and channelled so that teams compete in pursuit of the *organization*'s goals. The UDA managed that too rarely. Internal rivalry was a major problem for the UDA, and I want to spend some time looking closely at the Dillon and Lehane explanation. The first part of the record that needs to be set straight concerns the murder of 'Duke' Elliott.

Elliott was a 'Lieutenant-Colonel' in the UDA and second-in-command to Fogel in Woodvale. On 6 December he was reported to have been kidnapped. His body was found the next day in a cardboard box in the back of the official car of the WDA. He had been killed by a single-ball shotgun blast in the face at close range. A second man was found badly beaten and wandering in the Ainsworth Avenue area. He told the police that he and Elliott had been stopped by three IRA men the previous evening when they were crossing the lower Falls to go for a drink in Sandy Row.

---

[30] Dillon and Lehane, *Political Murder*, 144–50, 165–74.
[31] P. Foot, *Who Framed Colin Wallace?* (London, 1990).

Dillon and Lehane report: 'There is little doubt that Elliott was killed by his own side in the midst of a very serious upheaval in the Protestant camp.'[32] They argue that Elliott was killed because of Harding's return and his supposed campaign to clean up the UDA. However, there is a minor problem with dates. When Elliott was shot, Harding Smith was still on trial in what looked like a very strong prosecution case. Nobody in the UDA expected to see Harding back in Belfast for a very long time. Hence nobody would have been doing Harding's dirty work, even if it had been his wish to get rid of Elliott. In those circumstances, reasons why Harding might have wanted rid of Elliott are irrelevant, but those offered by Dillon and Lehane are spurious. Elliott's criminal record was not held against him (I will return to that in a moment), and he did not have 'a sharp left-wing philosophy'.[33]

Elliott was killed because of team rivalry. The WDA had left some guns with the Sandy Row UDA for safe-keeping and wanted them back. According to a south Belfast UDA man who was involved in the killing, Elliott and three companions went to a UDA drinking club that went under the name of the 'St George's Recreation Club' to demand their return. Elliott put a gun to the head of the barman and his companions took three hostages at random from the bar and led them out to the van, saying they would be released when the guns were returned. Someone alerted a local UDA man who had a shotgun.

Elliott was shot in the legs. Two of the team got away with one hostage. Elliott and one companion were (in the words of one witness) 'mercilessly beaten' and taken back into the club. Somewhere in the fracas, Elliott was killed by the shotgun. His companion was exchanged for the Sandy Row hostage.[34]

The murder of Elliott tells us a lot about the UDA. It reminds us of the intense rivalries which existed between different areas. It alerts us to the almost casual use of serious violence. It also points to the role which alcohol played; as in many UDA actions, 'drink had been taken'. But it had nothing at all to do with left-wing politics.

The notion that Harding was concerned to clean up the

[32] Dillon and Lehane, *Political Murder*, 146.
[33] Ibid. 148.
[34] *Sunday World*, 14 Oct. 1984.

organization's rapidly tarnishing image is also misleading. Smith periodically tried to control racketeering in his area, but none of those I have interviewed believes he had anything against it in principle. It is true that, in April 1973, posters signed by the UDA, Orange Volunteers (OVs), RHC, and UVF appeared in west Belfast threatening severe punishment for law-breakers, especially those purporting to be loyalist militants,[35] and that Tommy Herron did not mount a similar poster campaign in east Belfast. But to suppose that this represented any serious conflict of principle between the two men is naïve and supposes that Harding was serious about ending rackets. Such clean-up campaigns were, and still are, part of the stock-in-trade of paramilitary organizations and are regularly deployed in an attempt to win some support from the community; the rackets themselves are privately condoned because they are a necessary part of such organizations' fund-raising.

A west Belfast UFF team was accused of hijacking a lorry of alcohol and cigarettes from the Shankill. Harding, in a classic example of his technique of using one 'company' against another, had another team round it up and take the members to the Bricklayer's Arms in Wilton Street, where they were beaten up and then 'put off the Road'. An observer added that some people wanted them killed, but Harding regarded the pistol-whipping as sufficient punishment. This story may have been the basis for supposing that Harding wanted to clean up the organization, but the UFF team was punished for crossing Harding, not for the act of stealing itself. Given his power, it is hard to reconcile the idea of Harding as a 'white knight' with the very large number of robberies and extortions which took place on his patch.

Dillon and Lehane may have got the reasons for internal UDA feuding wrong because they confused two west Belfast 'Smiths'. When Herron issued a press statement replying to the rumours accusing him of collusion with Catholics and claiming that they were being spread by a man, not even a UDA member, who was 'seeking to break up the organization and take power for himself',[36] he had in mind not Harding Smith, but Sammy Smyth, sometime editor of Ulster Militant and a loose cannon who

---

[35] Guardian, 11 Apr. 1973.
[36] Dillon and Lehane, Political Murder, 167.

enjoyed an exciting and erratic relationship with the UDA. It was Sammy, not Harding, who was making a fuss about Herron's rackets.

It would also be a mistake to suppose that Harding and Herron disagreed in some fundamental or systematic way about the sectarian murder campaign. Again one need do no more than note that both east and west Belfast had very active UFF teams of 'operators'.

Black Propaganda and the Ulster Citizens' Army

Although it is only a very minor part of the big picture, black propaganda has played a small part in muddling this period of the UDA's history. In October 1972 a circular was distributed to Belfast papers claiming that a new force, 'Composed of the more socialist-orientated and class-conscious members of the UDA', had been established because of 'growing dissatisfaction, frustration and anger within UDA ranks' over a lack of firm response to security-force actions against loyalists. The new group called itself the Ulster Citizens' Army (UCA). In later press statements the UCA presented itself as a left-wing and incorruptible defender of the loyalist working class and used that persona to attack the UDA and UVF for corruption and sectarian murder. As one of the UCA's press releases of 1974 put it:

[The UCA re-affirmed that] they would continue to struggle against the fascist sectarian regimes of the UDA, UVF and their front organizations to bring about their ultimate destruction. Although the UCA was formed in 1972 to protect the Protestant working class and working class homes we feel that we cannot stand idly by while members of the Catholic working class community are slaughtered without cause.

The document went on to list the names and addresses of thirteen leading UDA and UVF men who, it was claimed, were responsible for the sectarian murder campaign. It also specifically accused Andy Tyrie, by then leader of the UDA, of having murdered a Shankill Road Protestant at his home in Wilton Street in 1970.

On the grounds that dead men could not argue, the UCA claimed Tommy Herron and Duke Elliott as 'Lieutenant-Colonels' by placing *in memoriam* notices in the *Belfast Telegraph*. Their membership of the UCA took on such solidity that as recently as 1990 a newspaper feature on Tommy Herron repeated the claim.[37] The UCA claims for Herron and Elliott seem to have been the main reasons why they have been retrospectively characterized as 'left-wing' critics of Harding Smith.

The question of the UCA has become hopelessly intertwined with the general tangle around the person of Colin Wallace. Wallace was the civilian who was the army's chief information officer at Lisburn headquarters in the early 1970s. As a well-informed local, he quickly became more than just an issuer of press statements and he seems to have worked on intelligence matters and 'black propaganda' at a high level. He was suddenly removed from his post in Ulster in 1975, after he was found to have passed a classified document to *Times* correspondent Robert Fisk. He went to work for a local authority in England. In 1980 he was charged with killing the husband of a woman with whom he worked and with whom he had become involved. He was sentenced to ten years' imprisonment for manslaughter. He maintains that he is innocent of that crime and had been framed because of his involvement in MI5 and MI6 clandestine operations.[38]

When the UCA press statements appeared again in 1974, two reporters from the *Daily Telegraph* were tipped off to visit a 'George' or 'Ron' Horn, an ex-serviceman and music teacher living in Antrim. According to a later UDA version, Horn apparently admitted his part in the fabrications.[39] At the time, the UDA was given the same hint, but, fortunately for Mr Horn, the men sent to pick him up became suspicious about the ease of the operation and wondered if they were being used. They were. Ron Horn had recently married a woman who had previously been the girlfriend of Colin Wallace. As Wallace admits that the UCA documents were produced at Lisburn, one possible interpretation of the tip-off is that Wallace was trying to have his rival killed. An alternative, which Wallace prefers, is that Horn was fingered by someone else in the Lisburn unit so that investigations would bring the story back to Wallace and cast doubt on anything else he

[37] *Sunday Life*, 4 Feb. 1990. See also W. D. Flackes and S. Elliott, *Northern Ireland: A Political Directory, 1968–88* (Belfast, 1989), and Foot, *Colin Wallace*.

[38] The Wallace version is given at length in Foot, *Colin Wallace*, and challenged by McKittrick in the *Independent*, 2 Sept. 1987, which should be read with the qualifications made in the *Independent*, 9 Mar. 1990.

[39] *Ulster Loyalist*, Christmas 1974.

might have to say. As Foot plausibly puts it: 'The information could well have been planted on the UDA in the first place precisely because it would, in the end, publicly rebound on Colin Wallace, as it did.'[40]

Fortunately my interest is in the UCA and not in the possibility of Colin Wallace twice in six years doing harm to the husbands of his women friends. Wallace believes that the UCA existed before Lisburn picked it up and exploited it. Foot reports that 'no one, least of all Lieutenant Colonel Jeremy Railton, Head of Information Policy . . . doubted that the Ulster Citizens' Army had genuinely existed and had certainly not been formed by the British Army'.[41] The British army may not have been the inventor of the UCA. It is just possible that the very first press statement was the work of Sammy Smyth—the attack on those elements of the UDA which were supporting Bill Craig and his Ulster Vanguard was certainly a favourite theme of his—but the name is wrong for anything Smyth would dream up. Both sides in the Irish conflict are very traditional about names, and 'Citizens' Army' smacks of nationalist and republican ambitions. But, whoever wrote the very first broadsheet, the posthumous claims that Herron and Elliott were UCA leaders have all the hallmarks of black propaganda, and we can be sure that the UCA had no material existence. There were no UCA murals or enduring graffiti. The significance of this omission should be stressed. Paramilitary organizations, especially those that grew from vigilante groups, are primarily territorial, and the murals that decorate gable end walls and the 'rolls of honour' in drinking clubs are important signs of identity. The second reason to doubt the existence of the UCA is that no one has ever claimed membership of it. The third is that none of the very many well-connected loyalist paramilitaries I have interviewed were in it, or ever knew anyone who was in it.

Community Leadership

The UVF was from the first a 'military' organization, and new members expected to be involved in violence. The UDA's development from vigilante groups (and its legality) meant that it drew

---

[40] Foot, *Colin Wallace*, 158.
[41] Ibid. 150.

in a different sort of figure, the trade-union activist with a broader vision of what the loyalist working class could be doing.

The mass flight of population had caused chaos in the institutional arrangements for housing allocation. The fighting in Lenadoon over vacant houses has already been mentioned. The breakdown of law and order meant that councils were in no position to allocate vacant properties rationally. Squatting became common. In March 1973 over five thousand families in the greater Belfast area were squatting illegally. The job of housing allocation fell to individuals who had some sort of informal position of community leadership. More generally, the fact that security-force attention was given over almost completely to policing civil disorder meant that local social control was left in the hands of those people who were willing to give any sort of lead. A number of men were pushed by their own communities into the role of local representatives and became prominent in the 'social' or 'political' (as distinct from the military) side of the UDA.

The number of internments and arrests of loyalists created a need for information on legal rights, and Sammy Smyth and Harry Chicken responded by forming Ulster Citizens' Civil Liberties (UCCL) as a loyalist alternative to the National Council of Civil Liberties (NCCL). After a number of weekends of instruction from Queen's University law lecturers, Smyth and Chicken prepared a series of documents on the rights of people taken into custody, and developed reputations as counsellors. With others who later held senior but 'non-military' positions in the UDA, both were also active in encouraging community-action and tenant groups.

Restructuring and the Rise of Andy Tyrie

In early 1973 Jim Anderson, who was joint chairman with Harding, announced that he wanted to stand down. A mass meeting of UDA commanders was held in the Park Avenue Hotel in late March. Apparently more by accident than design, Andy Tyrie— Company Commander for A company, the west Belfast estates— was appointed to chair the conference.

Tyrie came from a lower Shankill Road family. Born in 1940, he was 11 when his family moved to Ballymurphy, which was then a mixed estate. He worked for a short time as a gardener with the city corporation before becoming a machinist, first in a feed mill in York Street and then with Rolls Royce in east Belfast. At the age of 18 he joined the Territorial Army (TA) and remained in it for seven years. In 1967 he was invited to a meeting in an Orange Hall where he was sworn in to the UVF. When the communal violence erupted in 1969, Tyrie was living in New Barnsley, an estate on the western fringe of the city, and he became one of the organizers of the evacuation of Protestant families. He moved to the entirely Protestant estate of Glencairn, where he became commander of A company of the UDA.

Pressure to streamline the UDA led to a decision that the organization should have just one chairman and one of Tyrie's first jobs was to preside over the election. Whether Harding saw this as a chance to achieve what he saw as his rightful position is not clear. Although the story is sometimes told as a contest between Harding in the east and Herron in the west, I suspect that Harding had little interest in active control of the whole organization. Supremacy and autonomy in his own patch seems to have been more his goal.

Contrary to Dillon's and Lehane's assertion that Anderson disliked Herron, the two men were, in the words of a man who worked closely with them, 'buddy, buddy', and shared a dislike of Harding, whom they were committed to excluding from the chair.[42] The contest would have been deadlocked between Herron and Harding Smith; to give the job to either would have run the risk of the other walking out. The outcome was the election of Andy Tyrie as UDA chairman. As McKittrick put it: 'He had handled the conference smoothly and well; he was a likeable sort; and with no real power of his own he provided no threat to the brigadiers. He was the ideal compromise candidate.'[43] More than that, he was a west Belfast man; he would be supported by cast Belfast for not being Harding and by west Belfast for being local.

Harding Smith and Herron left the meeting expecting that Tyrie would be a figurehead and they could continue to run their own empires as previously. Initially they were right. For some time after his election Tyrie continued to work full time at Rolls-Royce,

[42] Dillon and Lehane, *Political Murder*, 227.
[43] *Irish Times*, 12 June 1973.

but gradually his control of the organization was consolidated and he remained in charge for sixteen years.

The Murder of Tommy Herron

The evolution of Tyrie from chairman to 'Supreme Commander' was helped markedly by the murder of Tommy Herron.

At about 12.30 on the afternoon of Friday, 14 September 1973, Herron gave the keys of his car to one of his bodyguards, saying he would be away only for a short time and asking the man to move the car, which was parked in a restricted zone, should the police come along. He left UDA headquarters on the Newtownards Road, as if just going for a brief walk, but he did not return. According to one account, Herron joined a woman and they got into a minibus with darkened windows.[44] According to another, Herron joined three well-dressed men in a red Ford Cortina.[45]

Two days later his body was found by the side of a road near Drumbo, to the south of Belfast. He had been killed with one neat bullet through the head, after his jacket had been pulled over his head. His arms were folded neatly on his chest and his legally held gun was still in its shoulder holster. There were no signs of any struggle.

Who killed Herron remains a mystery. What was quickly agreed by all parties was that it was not a republican murder. The IRA would not have left Herron's gun on his body. A good sidearm was valuable to any paramilitary organization and, even if the IRA had had enough weapons, the use of a UDA gun in a number of murders would have nicely confused ballistics data and made the police job more difficult. Secondly, it is unlikely that the IRA could have sent men into the heart of Protestant east Belfast and, without a fuss, persuaded Herron to get into a car of strangers.

The rumour mill began to grind, and a number of explanations were elaborated. A problem concerns motive; there was both too much and too little. Herron was not universally liked. He had fallen out with the RHC by trying to commandeer the income from McKeague's *Loyalist News*. An RHC team beat him up and

[44] *Sunday Life*, 4 Mar. 1990.
[45] *Hibernia*, 21 Sept. 1973.

there was no retaliation.[46] There was also persistent rivalry with most of the other senior UDA figures, which was so intense at times that one leading man could say of the Inner Council that 'they always had their minders with them. They were all scared of each other.' That Herron went off without his minder suggests either that he was going to meet someone he knew and trusted or that his abductors were very lucky in their timing.

In one type of story, the crime was the work of other senior UDA men. In one version, Herron was shot by the east Belfast UFF because of a dispute about takings from a bank robbery. In another, he was killed by a south Belfast UDA man for sleeping with his wife. Both are plausible, but an internal UDA investigation could find no compelling evidence for either of these or similar accounts.

Another school of thought blamed British security forces. There is no doubt that service personnel were involved in sectarian murders in this period, and Herron's much-publicized 'declaring war on the Army' would have made him a marked man. There is the (admittedly tainted) evidence of Colin Wallace that Charles Harding Smith, the other most significant UDA figure, was also the target of an attempted murder.[47]

The third strand of thought involves a 'bent' policeman who in 1973 was stationed in east Belfast and working for CID. Herron is reported to have received guns and information from the officer and may have been pressing him for further assistance. Feeling he was being pushed too far, the officer recruited an odd assortment of individuals to assist him. Although the story does not settle anything, it is worth recounting for the idea it gives of the murkiness of the war in Northern Ireland. Two young Andersonstown Catholics, Vincent Heatherington and Myles McGrogan, were charged with taking part in the shooting of two RUC men at Finaghy Road in Andersonstown in May 1974 and remanded to Crumlin Road prison. There they joined the Provisional wing of the prison. After lengthy interrogation by the IRA, Heatherington 'broke down' and confessed to being part of an army-sponsored

[46] Ibid. 2 Feb. 1973.
[47] K. Lindsay, *Ambush at Tully-West: The British Intelligence Services in Action* (Dundalk, 1979), gives in detail the story of the security-forces attack on William Black. Wallace (in the *Sunday World*, 18 Feb. 1990) suggests that the intended victim was Harding Smith.

gang which included an English woman and an east Belfast Protestant Gregory Brown.

In Belfast they had their own weapons supply and were permitted to carry
out their own robberies so that these would create disruption and confusion and cause the IRA to suspect that some of its own members were
lining 'personal pockets'. They also had explosives to carry out no-warning
bomb attacks to discredit the IRA.[48]

Heatherington gave his interrogators names of other IRA men
whom he believed to be informers and said that he and McGrogan
had been sent into the prison to win the confidence of and then
poison three leading Provisionals. Credence was given to his story
when a search of the prison turned up a stash of poison. Later
still, Heatherington is supposed to have told his questioners that
his previous information (which had caused considerable internal
tension and reorganization in the IRA) had been false and that
he had been instructed by his army handlers to divulge the
information.

McGrogan and Heatherington were moved to a protective
custody wing of the prison. In March 1975 they were acquitted of
involvement in the Finaghy Road killings. According to *Hibernia*,
Heatherington then worked for the south Belfast UDA and was
involved in the bombing of two Catholic pubs in west Belfast.[49]
Apparently in revenge for the trouble caused by their disinformation, the IRA murdered Heatherington in 1976 and McGrogan
a year later.

The connection between this curious episode and the Herron
murder is that Heatherington told his Provisional interrogators
that his gang had murdered Herron. The information was passed
on to the UDA. No action was taken immediately, but on 14 May
1976 a UFF team murdered Gregory Brown as he walked along
the Cregagh Road in east Belfast with a group of friends. The
statement claiming responsibility said that he had been shot for his
part in the Herron killing.

I have already made the point a number of times, but it must be
stressed that this is only one story and a not very plausible one.
The source for it was Heatherington himself and he was clearly
involved in systematic deception. Why should the IRA pass on

[48] Dillon, *The Dirty War* (London, 1990), 80.
[49] *Hibernia*, 30 July 1976.

such information to the UDA? The UFF repeated it when they killed Brown, but that does not mean that they believed it, given the many other reasons why they might have wanted Brown, a hard man and a hoodlum, dead. Perhaps the final word should be left to one of the UDA men involved in the internal investigation:

We really never knew. Nothing reliable has come out yet and that means either a very very professional job or something one-off, a personal thing that no one else was involved in. It might have been woman trouble. He had a lot of that! Lots of people might have wanted Tommy out of the way but we couldn't find any one person who had enough of a motive and the opportunity.

Whatever the motive and whoever the agent, the killing of Herron did not seriously damage the UDA, which in the three years since 1971 had grown and evolved. Indeed, given Herron's erratic behaviour and quick temper, his departure may have been to the organization's advantage. It had a mass membership and an increasingly articulate and influential central organization. It had brought in a number of more politically minded community activists. It could turn out very large numbers for mass demonstrations. It could mount a major pub-bombing campaign in retaliation for the IRA's attacks on pubs in Protestant areas, and the assassination campaign continued. There were still major tensions between the military and political sides—between those who saw their role as counter-terror and those who saw their job as providing social and political leadership to the loyalist working class. There was still considerable rivalry between teams from different areas, but by the end of 1973 the UDA could reasonably see itself not as a rag-bag of gangs and vigilante groups but as a major player in the confusion that was Ulster politics.

4

Paramilitaries and Politicians: The 1974 Strike

THE Troubles had broken the Unionist Party. The militant right of unionism was outside it altogether, as it always had been, but until the instability of the early 1970s few people supported Ian Paisley's Protestant Unionist Party (PUP) and not many more were impressed by it.[1] Instances of disputes within the Unionist Party have already been mentioned. At various points during 1971 a number of senior right-wing Unionists talked to Paisley about forming a new party, but when the time came they pulled back. Their caution came both from their suspicions of Paisley's ambition and from their belief that all was not necessarily lost with their old party. Although each of the three Prime Ministers—O'Neill, Chichester-Clark, and Faulkner—controlled the top levels of the party machinery and the government (in so far as anyone other than the army GOC was in charge of that), many of the local constituencies were right wing. The possibility of regaining control of the party was enough to dissuade many of the more senior right-wingers from joining Paisley when in September 1971 he formed the Democratic Unionist Party (DUP).

The slightly less militant right wing of unionism—represented by such politicians as the Revd Robert Bradford, the Revd Martin Smyth (Grand Master of the Orange Order), Captain Austin Ardill, and John Taylor—remained in the party but critical of its direction. Chief amongst the thorns in the side of Brian Faulkner was William Craig, the Minister for Home Affairs fired by Terence O'Neill and easily beaten by Faulkner in the election to succeed Chichester-Clark. In October 1971, shortly after the DUP had been formed, Craig's decision to stay with the Unionist Party was rewarded when he was elected chairman of a steering committee representing forty-three of the fifty-two constituency associations. That meeting pledged to

[1] For a history of the PUP and details of its election results see S. Bruce, *God Save Ulster!: The Religion and Politics of Paisleyism* (Oxford, 1986).

formulate policies which will be acceptable to official Unionist constituencies throughout the country [and from which] a lead would be given in uniting the loyal people of Ulster so that their concerted voice will be listened to at Westminster, Stormont and above all at the Ulster Unionist Council.[2]

Brian Faulkner became Prime Minister in March 1971, but, like an arthritic hand, his grasp on the situation and the office steadily weakened until the British government shut down Stormont a year later. In a manner more imaginative than that of previous Stormont premiers, Faulkner did everything he could to discover political changes which would satisfy the Catholic minority without further alienating the Protestant majority. He also did everything he could to satisfy the demands of Protestants for an improvement in the security situation, but such measures as internment simply increased Catholic hostility and provided more support for the IRA and thus more violence. Reform alternated with repression and all against a steadily mounting death toll.

Some figures will give an idea of just how violent the province had become. In 1970 the security forces recorded 213 shooting incidents and 153 explosions and defused 17 bombs. In 1971 there were over a thousand explosions and nearly two thousand shootings; 493 bombs were defused and there were almost five hundred major robberies. The following year there were over ten thousand shootings, 1,382 explosions, 471 defused bombs, and 1,931 robberies. In 1971 the Troubles caused 174 deaths; the next year the total was 467; and that in a country with a population of around 1.5 million.[3]

The high death rate was an expression of political instability. The IRA killed because it saw a real chance of destroying the Stormont state; the Protestants killed because they saw a real threat of a united Ireland. An essential element of instability, a random wobble, was the London rumour factory. The only thing everyone knew was that the present could not continue, and so the talk was always of 'initiatives'. It would not be too cynical to say that the Westminster government was deliberately porous. Ideas were 'market tested' by being leaked to the press so that

---

[2] H. Kelly, *How Stormont Fell* (Dublin, 1972), 122.

[3] Further details of indices of political violence are given in the Statistical Appendix.

the strength and direction of the response could be gauged. The unfortunate consequence was an almost permanent state of trepidation.

It is against the background of a murder rate of almost ten per week and frequent political initiatives—wars and rumours of wars—that the loyalist paramilitaries became involved in politics. The politics of the UVF will be the subject of the next chapter. Here I want to consider relations between the UDA and unionist politicians, and the 1974 Ulster Workers' Council (UWC) strike.

The Loyalist Association of Workers

The trade-union organizations of the Protestant working class were an important colour in the mosaic of loyalism. As early as 1969 a small group of shipyard workers had formed the Workers' Committee for the Defence of the Constitution. Like Gusty Spence, Billy Hull was from the Shankill Road and worked as a stager in the Harland and Wolff yard. He was also convenor of the engineering shop stewards in the yard. Hugh Petrie was active in the Amalgamated Engineering Union and a precision engineer with Short Brothers. With two others, they set up their committee to oppose the republican threat behind the civil-rights movement.

In early 1970 a room was rented and posters put up in most of the major industrial operations. About thirty-five men, including 'representatives of workers in most of Belfast's largest industries', turned up for a meeting that was something of an anti-climax.[4] At least one man came under the impression that he and his friends were to be given guns. They were not, but the foundations for a province-wide organization were being laid.

The Workers' Committee became the Association of Loyalist Workers before Hull had the bright idea of making a pun of the acronym by swapping the first two words round. Posters were pasted up saying only 'LAW is coming'. But it was increasing instability rather than clever slogans that ensured that Hull and Petrie found themselves getting a good hearing at factories in towns around the province. Initially the movement was focused on the demand to end the 'political levy' which all union members

---

[4] R. Fisk, *The Point of No Return: The Strike which Broke the British in Ulster* (London, 1975), 26.

inadvertently contributed to the funds of the Labour Party. Quite reasonably, loyalist trade unionists did not see why they should be financing the anti-unionist policies of Labour. But gradually its role broadened. When the three young Scots soldiers were murdered, Petrie suggested and Hull announced a protest march to the City Hall and almost the entire Harland and Wolff work-force of nine thousand marched behind him.

Although the Workers' Committee had been sufficiently aware of the dangers of being co-opted by politicians to agree at the first meeting not to affiliate to any political party, LAW was soon to be found lining up behind Bill Craig, who had launched his 'Vanguard Movement' on 9 February 1972. Four days later Craig was the main speaker, with Billy Hull and Martin Smyth, at a rally in Lisburn, organized by LAW and stage-managed by the UDA. Riding in an ancient 'limousine', Craig was accompanied by motor-cycle outriders on his entry to the field. He walked slowly along the ranks of uniformed UDA men, shaking hands here and there.

His speech, as always, consisted of complaints about IRA violence and the security situation, constructed around a critique of the political reforms that had been introduced since 1969. But there were two noteworthy novelties. The first was his apparent willingness to encourage violence. At one point he said: 'We are determined, ladies and gentlemen, to preserve our British traditions and way of life. And God help those who get in our way for we mean business.'[5] The second was his encouragement of mass mobilization. In the final part of his speech he read out a long and plodding 'Ulster Covenant', modelled on the 1912 version, which pledged the loyal Ulster people to resist almost anything the traitorous British government might suggest. When he had finished, Craig asked all who agreed with the declaration 'to raise your hands three times and say each time "I do"'.

Similar rallies were held in Bangor and Rathfriland on 19 February. At each the martial rhetoric was more pointed and the numbers greater. At Bangor he introduced a new variant on an old theme. All unionists were in favour of the return of the B Specials, but Craig went one better and advocated the reformation of the old Ulster C Special Constabulary.

[5] Kelly, *How Stormont Fell*, 124.

On the 25th ex-Stormont junior minister John Taylor was shot and seriously wounded in Armagh; the next day a bigger Vanguard rally was held in Omagh, and Martin Smyth, Grand Master of the Orange Order, 'inspected' the UDA men.

In the Vanguard rallies we have the coming together of all three strands of loyalism: dissident politicians, Protestant trade unionists, and the vigilantes in the UDA. The important novelty was that the second and third groups were not just on the field listening and applauding; they were on the platforms with their 'social betters', making the speeches.

A crowded restaurant in the centre of Belfast, the Abercorn, was bombed by the IRA on 4 March. Two women were killed and 130 people were injured, many of them very seriously. Two sisters who had been shopping for a wedding dress were having a coffee. The one who was getting married lost a leg, an arm, and an eye. Her sister had a leg blown off. The leaders of LAW met and decided to call a one-day strike to protest at the security situation. Brian Faulkner tried to persuade them that 'any disruption in industrial production could only play into the hands of the IRA as it would be damaging to Northern Ireland both economically and constitutionally'.[6] More surprisingly, Ian Paisley was not enthusiastic about the stoppage and announced that, while he disagreed with the principle, in the interests of loyalist working-class unity 'all loyalists should abide by the decision of the majority in their place of employment'.[7]

The strike was a success. Although there was little impact outside Belfast, stoppages at the power-stations so reduced power that electricity supplies were disrupted in the middle of the day and the big Belfast firms—Harland and Wolff, Shorts, Mackies, ICL, and Sirocco—shut at lunch, as did AEI in Larne. Two-thirds of the work-force of the ICI plant at Kilroot walked out.

On 18 March LAW and Vanguard held a rally in the Ormeau park in south-east Belfast at which over sixty thousand people, many of them in paramilitary uniform, heard Craig, Martin Smyth, Billy Hull, and Sir Knox Cunningham (the Unionist MP for South Antrim). Three days later, Faulkner, deputy Prime Minister Andrews, and two senior civil servants flew to London for a

[6] Northern Ireland Information Service press release, 5 Mar. 1972.
[7] Press statement, 8 Mar. 1972.

meeting with the Prime Minister Edward Heath, the Home Secretary Reginald Maudling, Lord Carrington, and William Whitelaw, the leader of the House of Commons. The GOC NI General Sir Harry Tuzo was also present. After an apparently routine report by Faulkner, in which he presented his usually misinformed assessment of the security situation, Edward Heath surprised the Northern Ireland delegation by announcing that:

The British had not only decided to take over complete control of security matters, including the Royal Ulster Constabulary, the RUC Reserve and all executive responsibility for law and order, but they had also decided to take control of the courts, responsibility for the administration of law and justice including the organization of and appointments to the bench, all matters of public order, prisons and penal establishment, all special powers, public prosecuting and power to create new laws and penal offences. In other words, they had decided to take every single worthwhile power in the security and legal fields away from Stormont.[8]

Stormont could continue with fewer powers than a good-sized borough council, but nothing that mattered would be trusted to a Unionist government. At the end of a meeting which lasted nine hours, the Stormont delegation returned to Belfast fully aware that the cabinet would have no choice but to resign. That decision was made at a full cabinet meeting on Wednesday and on the next day Faulkner and Andrews flew back to London to discuss the details of the transfer of power to London. As dramatic counter-point, a huge bomb destroyed the Great Victoria Street railway station in Belfast. Only prompt evacuation had saved many lives.

(On Friday, 24 March, Heath rose in the House of Commons to announce that Stormont was being prorogued and that the province would be ruled directly from London, with William Whitelaw as Secretary of State for Northern Ireland.)

The loyalist response was immediate. Vanguard and LAW announced a two-day strike from Monday. Many workers supported the strike voluntarily; many of those who did not were 'persuaded' to stay away from work by large numbers of UDA men. And those who made it to work found that they had wasted their time. Despite having only the weekend in which to send instructions to the power-station work-forces, Billy Kelly, the unofficial leader of the electricity workers, so reduced the power

---

[8] Kelly, *How Stormont Fell*, 136.

within a few hours that supply had to be stopped to the major factories in the Belfast area.

That was Monday. On the second day of the protest, some ten thousand loyalists led by paramilitary units from all the Protestant areas of Belfast, converged on Stormont. Bill Craig came out on the balcony to address the crowd. For a moment it looked as if he was crowing over the Prime Minister's defeat, but Faulkner, showing a political sense that had been previously missing, brought his resigning cabinet out on to the balcony, to show that they were on the same side as the protesters. Craig and Faulkner shook hands and for a moment the Protestant people were united in their humiliation and anger at Westminster's capitulation to 'rebel demands'.

There was one major figure missing. Paisley's response to direct rule (of which he had received good warning) was quite different from Craig's. Instead of demanding a return to Stormont government, Paisley argued for full integration with Great Britain. Partly because of this policy disagreement and partly because they were rivals, Paisley very deliberately absented himself from Craig's rallies.

LAW and UDA

Relations between LAW and the paramilitaries were close. This should be no surprise, given that they recruited from the same constituencies. Billy Hull and Gusty Spence were working-class Protestants from the Shankill Road. In Londonderry the UDA was formed by the same people who organized Protestant shop stewards into a group that affiliated with LAW. The secretive and illegal nature of the UVF kept it small, but thousands of people were involved in the various vigilante groups that became the UDA. As one LAW official put it:

A lot of LAW people, ordinary workers, were going home for their tea and putting on their uniforms and going out on patrol with their street defence groups. When the UDA was formed we had a lot in common. It was suggested by some people that we become the political side of loyalism and the UDA become the military side.

To an extent this was the division of labour which evolved, but there was a lot of overlap. Billy Hull was vice-chairman of one of the very first UDA meetings called by Alan Moon. He and Hugh Petrie had been in London with Charles Harding Smith, addressing a loyalist rally, when Harding was arrested in the Hilton Hotel arms case. They told Fisk that they had been planning to go with him to the Hotel but were warned off.[9] However, they could not contact him in time.

LAW was a work-place-based movement and drew its leadership from people who were active in the trade-union movement. Glen Barr, Billy Hull, Hugh Petrie, and Bill Snoddy were all experienced shop stewards, convenors, or union officers. They were all immensely more articulate than Charles Harding Smith or Tommy Herron. This suggests an imbalance in the roles which could be played by the two groups. The LAW activists could, if they had wanted to, lead paramilitary units and at least two did. Hugh Petrie was a senior figure in the Vanguard Service Corps (VSC) (the paramilitary wing of the Vanguard movement) and Bob Marno led the OVs. But, as we will see, paramilitary leaders could not easily move the other way.

Politicians and the UDA

Ties with right-wing unionist politicians were slightly less straightforward than those with trade unionists. In March 1972 the Woodvale company of the UDA came out strongly in support for Craig:

It cannot be stressed often enough how essential it is to have COMPLETE UNITY of Ulster's loyalists . . . For almost three years our cry has been, 'Who will lead us?', 'Who will unite us?', and 'Who will speak on our behalf?' Now—these questions have been answered—Leadership—Unity—and Voice—through the Organisation of 'ULSTER VANGUARD'. . . . We, the members of the Defence Volunteers, who have committees in all areas of Belfast, and most areas of the province, have pledged our full support to this vast, and ever-growing organisation.

Although this sounds like ringing endorsement, it was a qualified message of support, for it went on: '[VANGUARD] is open to all Loyalists no matter what political line they follow, for this is NOT a political party, but an Organisation that is determined there will be

---

[9] Fisk, *The Point of No Return*, 36.

no tampering with the Constitution.[10] That is, the vigilantes supported Craig so long as he did not behave like a politician. As with Paisley, support for the right-wing mavericks of unionism was greatest when they succeeded in presenting themselves as being other than politicians, as men interested in saving their country by uniting the loyalist people. As soon as they seemed to be acting like politicians, support shrank.

The previous month, John McKeague's *Loyalist News* also endorsed Craig:

What Ulster needs to-day is a leader, one that every Loyalist looks up to and supports. . . . The man we believe can do it is William Craig. We have said before the task will be great but William Craig is a very capable man. . . . Like Winston Churchill he must now be called upon to lead Ulster in her time of crisis.[11]

After the Bangor rally of February, the editor of the *Dundonald UDA News* reflected on his impressions:

One could actually feel the sincerity of the speakers and as the rally progressed one got the feeling that for once here were men to look up to. . . . We, of this news-sheet, made our minds up to advise all shades of loyalists, irrespective of their principles, to shelter under the banner of Ulster Vanguard and go forward to victory over all enemies of our beloved Ulster.[12]

Sections of the UDA disagreed with this line. Sammy Smyth, the editor of *Ulster Militant*, was given 'a severe doing' for publishing a strongly anti-Vanguard editorial in which he wrote:

The Ulster Defence Association owes its birth and strength to the promise given that there would be no political involvement of any kind. While it adheres to that promise, it will remain strong and viable; once it enters the political arena then it will start to disintegrate.[13]

The already-mentioned UCA press release (see above, p. 69) is significant, either because its anti-Vanguard sentiments were those of Smyth and his circle or because its military intelligence authors expected its sentiments to find a receptive audience. In addition to those sections of the UDA who were universally sceptical of all

[10] *WDA News*, 8 Mar. 1972.
[11] *Loyalist News*, 12 Feb. 1972.
[12] *Dundonald District UDA*, 26 Feb. 1972.
[13] *Ulster Militant*, Feb. 1972.

politicians, some UDA men preferred Ian Paisley, who had been consistently critical of Unionist Party politicians.

For their part, the politicians were concerned about the rogue elephant nature of loyalist paramilitarism and the possible costs of being too closely associated with murderers and bombers, but LAW men consistently supported UDA actions. In a response to a call from Catholic politician John Hume for loyalist killers to be pursued as vigorously as their republican counterparts, the LAW leadership said:

The membership of LAW will not stand idly by if their leaders or the leaders of any loyalist organization are arrested at the say-so of Mr John Hume. We would point out that over the past 4 to 5 years of IRA violence and atrocities, Mr Hume has not been heard to call for the arrest of IRA leaders. On the contrary, certain of his colleagues in SDLP [Social Democratic and Labour Party] have publicly shared platforms with admitted IRA members and leaders. We did not see Mr Hume hot-footing to Westminster to demand the arrest of IRA leaders following the Aldershot bombing for which the IRA so proudly proclaimed responsibility. Not to mention the Abercorn and Donegall St tragedies, Oxford Street and Bloody Friday, nor have we forgotten Mr Hume's 'United Ireland or Nothing'. We would remind Mr Hume that people who live in glass houses should not throw stones.[14]

On Monday, 5 February 1973, two members of the east Belfast UFF squad were 'interned without trial' under the Special Powers Act for a grenade attack on a Catholic working-men's bus which killed one man and wounded a number of others.[15] Although large numbers of Catholics had been interned since August 1971, these were the first Protestants, and the response was vigorous. Craig tried to persuade Whitelaw to change his mind and, when he failed, was forced by LAW and the UDA into backing a call for a two-day strike. The electricity workers again managed to reduce the supply, but the most memorable part of the action was the rioting that broke out in south and east Belfast, as 'Tartan gangs' fired shops and houses.[16]

[14] LAW press release, 31 Jan. 1973.
[15] For a detailed account of the attack see Dillon, *The Dirty War* (London, 1990), 260–1, and M. Dillon and D. Lehane, *Political Murder in Northern Ireland* (Harmondsworth, Middlesex, 1973), 182–3.
[16] The Tartans were youth gangs whose members wore tartan scarves and patches, supposedly using a type of tartan to identify their particular gang. Some

Brian Douglas, a 23-year-old fireman who lived with his blind widower father, was shot dead by a loyalist sniper while trying to put out a fire in Bradbury Place, just south of the city centre.[17] In the Willowfield area of east Belfast, a Catholic church was ransacked.

Rioting and shooting dead a fireman worried unionist politicians. They were also concerned about the ambitions of the working-class leadership of LAW. Although many members wanted to confine the movement to trade-union issues and tactics, others wanted a straightforward political party. In August 1972 some people in LAW and the UDA flirted with the idea of a party. As the *WDA News* announced:

For too long the Unionist Party has been maintained by massive working class support, yet its policies seldom reflected the problems of the working man. The working class have been represented too long by landlords such as O'Neill and factory owners such as Brian Faulkner. For mild socialist policies we had to turn to the Labour Party and the nationalist minded parties . . . Now the Unionist people have a working class orientated party, one that is uncompromising on the issue of Northern Ireland's freedom and her constitution.[18]

Nothing came of that initiative, but the potential threat to the position of established political leaders and activists was clear.

The two sides could also compete over military matters. The more astute paramilitary leaders were concerned that the politicians might start their own paramilitary organizations. Craig formed his VSC, but it failed to attract many UDA men. The second concern was that the UDA might be reduced to the role of political 'bouncers'. Robert Fisk, then the *Times* correspondent, has the marvellous story of Herron phoning him up late at night to complain that Craig was just using the UDA as a vehicle to power: 'he suggested that the UDA was being asked to "march on Rome" while Mussolini "took the train"'.[19]

---

commentators thought the tartan honoured the three young Scots soldiers murdered by the IRA; others that it was just a fashion started by Edinburgh pop group the Bay City Rollers. No ex-Tartan I talked to could remember the origins.

[17] The sniper is reliably reported to have been killed by the UDA for his error.
[18] *WDA News*, 14 Aug. 1972.
[19] Fisk, *The Point of No Return*, 41.

The Power-Sharing Assembly

Direct rule was always seen as a temporary expedient and Whitelaw quickly formulated plans for a new devolved government. The main elements of this initiative were a devolved assembly elected on the basis of proportional representation (so that the minority would have a greater representation) and a conference of elected representatives and the British and Irish governments to consider future political directions. Although the idea of a 'power-sharing executive' was not clearly formulated until after the elections to the assembly, it was a popular topic of rumour and debate, and the elections in June were effectively a referendum on that possibility. The Catholic vote went overwhelmingly to the SDLP, while the unionist vote was split.

Some Protestants were members of the small newly formed and non-sectarian Alliance Party. Most were still members of the Unionist Party, but it was one party with two policies. Party leader and former Prime Minister Brian Faulkner had made it clear that he was willing to consider power-sharing, and a number of candidates supported him. Other constituency associations had proposed candidates who campaigned against the white paper. Paisley's DUP was anti-power-sharing and Craig's Vanguard Movement had constituted itself the Vanguard Unionist Progressive Party (VUPP) in time for the May local government elections, which provided useful practice for the assembly elections.

Apart from what the final outcome presaged for the fate of the assembly, the election was interesting because it provided the first public test of the political popularity of paramilitary leaders or people openly identified with paramilitary organizations. Although Dillon and Lehane are badly wrong to portray Herron as a socialist, it is certainly true that he had more interest in politics than most UDA leaders. From almost the start of his involvement, Herron argued that working-class loyalists should be able to vote for working-class loyalists. When they did get the chance, the results were not reassuring.

In north Belfast, Billy Hull of LAW and Tommy Lyttle, Harding Smith's right-hand man in the west Belfast UDA, stood as Vanguard candidates and polled badly. While Fred Proctor and Frank Millar, two working-class loyalists with strong grass-roots support, got 2,112 and 4,187 first preference votes respectively,

Hull got 852 and Lyttle 560.[20] Standing as an independent in West Belfast, Hugh Smyth—who was close to some UVF men— was elected. In East Belfast, Tommy Herron got only 2,480 first preference votes, while Mrs Eileen Paisley for the DUP got 5,518, and in total four unionists got more first preferences. Compared to Hull and Lyttle, this was a good vote, but it fell far short of what he had expected. Herron claimed that the British government had been so worried about his power that they had stolen his votes from the boxes. Glen Barr (the UDA's political spokesman), who must have known better, repeated the claim and even suggested, when Herron was lifted by the army with over £2,000 in cash on him, that he was being harassed because he was getting near to the truth of the missing votes.[21]

The votes were missing because his own people did not vote for him. His impression of what he should have got was based on people in the street saying 'Sure Tommy, I'll be voting for you' and then using the privacy of the booth to vote for the more respectable spokesmen associated with the DUP. The rejection of Herron by the voters was in part a response to his personality. He had a fiery temper and was well known as a hard man who could flare up easily. His rash 'declaration of war' on the British army caused a lot of potential supporters to question his judgement. People who knew him well told me that many people respected him as a paramilitary commander but they wanted someone a bit quieter, a bit better educated, and a bit less aggressive as a political representative.

With so few candidates to consider, it is difficult to compare performances and draw general conclusions, but a number of observations can be made. Glen Barr was elected in Londonderry. Although he was a founder of the local UDA, he was better known for his trade-union and LAW work, and, unlike Herron's, his involvement in the UDA was clearly on the political wing. Hughie Smyth, who was close to some Shankill UVF men, was elected in west Belfast, but even those who thought he was 'UV' associated him only with the political and social wing of the organization. No one thought he was a hard man. It does seem that working-class

[20] W. D. Flackes, and S. Elliott, *Northern Ireland: A Political Directory, 1968–88* (Belfast, 1989), 315–19.
[21] *Belfast Telegraph*, 23 Aug. 1973.

loyalist community leaders could win elections (always with far fewer votes than mainstream unionist politicians) even if they were thought to have paramilitary ties, but people who were unambiguously paramilitary figures were not popular as political representatives.

The overall results of the election on 28 June 1973 gave those in favour of the power-sharing white paper a majority. Faulkner had 22 pro-assembly unionists, the SDLP had 19, and Alliance 8; a total of 49 in favour of the experiment. There were 8 anti-power-sharing Unionists, 8 DUP, 7 Vanguard, and 3 independent unionists. This gave Faulkner a healthy majority (if he could hold all his unionists to the line). In negotiations with the SDLP and Alliance he worked out a system which would make him Premier and Gerry Fitt, the leader of the SDLP, Deputy Prime Minister. The executive would consist of eleven voting ministers—six Unionists, four SDLP, and one Alliance—and three non-voting department heads, two of them SDLP and one Alliance. The big concession to the SDLP for their involvement in the government of the North was an inter-government Council of Ireland, which would allow issues of mutual interests to be discussed and, should the majority in the north desire it, provide a framework for the future unification of Ireland. This they could present to their supporters as an implicit recognition of the legitimacy of nationalist aspirations.

The Civil Service College at Sunningdale was the venue for discussions between the embryonic executive and the British and Irish governments. Francis Pym, who had succeeded William Whitelaw, made a serious political mistake in initially refusing to invite the loyalist leaders on the rather feeble grounds that they had already refused to take part in the executive. Later he changed his mind and invited them to part of the discussions—they refused—but British maladroitness had been such that they were able to present the whole scheme as undemocratic.

Faulkner's executive took office on New Year's Day 1974. It had hardly been in office two months when its legitimacy was seriously undermined by the results of a Westminster general election. In what would turn out to be a perverse parallel, Edward Heath had called an early election on the issue of trade-union militancy (he was against it) and lost to Labour. In Ulster, the elections were taken as a referendum on the Sunningdale agreement. Having only just taken office in the power-sharing experiment, the three parties that favoured it were offered the opportunity of Westminster elections to stand against each other. To maintain the momentum of the executive, liberal unionists and nationalists should have formed a pro-power-sharing coalition and fielded only one candidate in each seat, but to have done that would have laid each open to the charge of having gone over completely to the other side. While claiming to be committed participants in the new arrangements, Faulknerite Unionists, Alliance, and SDLP candidates competed against each other. In contrast, Paisley's DUP, Craig's Vanguard, and the anti-Sunningdale Unionists led by Harry West formed a 'United Ulster Unionist Council' to present a common front against the power-sharers, and won eleven of twelve seats. Those opposed to the executive took 51 per cent of the vote, while the parties which supported Faulkner gained only 41 per cent.[22]

More importantly for understanding the loyalist environment, one should note the proportions of the unionist vote. Faulkner's candidates took only 13.3 per cent of the vote; unionists who were opposed to power-sharing took 51 per cent. The majority of the population of Northern Ireland was unionist; now a large majority of unionists was opposed to the system of government which had just been introduced.

This was what the loyalist politicians needed. With this result they could present their campaign to get rid of the executive as the legitimate expression of the democratic will that had been denied a voice at Sunningdale.

Strike

In mid-1974 LAW was no more. It had been torn apart early the previous year over a proposed rent-and-rate strike. Hull had heavily backed the protest, which was unpopular because that was the sort of thing rebel Catholics did, and then backtracked after his colleagues had voted for the policy. LAW men had also been divided in their attitude to the violent protests against the first

[22] Flackes and Elliott, *Northern Ireland*, 319–22. Contemporary opinion polls showed a clear majority of Protestants in favour of the experiment, but this is probably a result of the well-known tendency of survey questionnaire respondents to present themselves in an incorrectly moderate light.

internment of loyalists. However, individuals were still organizing loyalist workers and a new structure—the UWC—was in place.

Among the paramilitaries, the main initiative was the formation of the Ulster Army Council (UAC) as a talking shop for the UDA, UVF, Ulster Special Constabulary Association (USCA), and RHC. Among the leaders of the skilled workers, the notion of a strike was again gaining ground. As early as July 1973 Craig had held talks with Petrie and power-workers from Ballylumford to talk about a general strike. Power-workers had also been talking to Glen Barr (the UDA's political spokesman, vice-chairman of Vanguard, chairman of the UWC, and a former shop steward at the Coolskeeragh power-station in Londonderry) and Andy Tyrie, the chairman of the UDA.

It only required the three elements—politicians, paramilitaries, and workers—to be mixed. A co-ordinating committee was formed, with Harry Murray, Billy Kelly, and Tom Beattie of the UWC, Paisley, West, Craig, Barr, Tyrie, and Ken Gibson of the UVF, Bob Marno of the OVs, Col. Peter Brush of the Down Orange Welfare (DOW), Hugh Petrie for the Volunteer Service Corps (as the Vanguard Service Corps now called itself), and George Greene of the USCA. In identifying the groups involved, Fisk alludes mysteriously to two other organizations: 'At least one of them, represented by a factory foreman from west Belfast, was believed by the army and police to have been responsible for many of the sectarian murders of the past twelve months.'[23] One of these was the RHC; the other may well have been the UFF.

Despite this degree of organization, the politicians, either because they did not realize how well prepared were the workers or because they did not believe in the enterprise, did their best to wriggle out of calling a strike. At the end of April leaders of the three political parties met in Portrush (without telling the UWC!) and talked themselves out of the strike, settling instead for the old stand-by of a boycott of Eire goods. Harry Murray had planned the strike to begin on 8 May, but Paisley blew the gaffe by announcing it in a press statement.

The UWC decided that the only solution to the timidity of the politicians was to present them with a *fait accompli*. Barr and Tyrie wanted to have a very obvious 'peg' on which to hang the stoppage

[23] Fisk, *The Point of No Return*, 45.

and a clear objective. On 13 May Paisley, Ernest Baird (Craig's deputy), Austin Ardill, and John Taylor met Kelly, Petrie, Jim Smyth, and Andy Tyrie at a hotel in Larne. According to some of the Unionists there, Kelly said simply: 'We've got the strike organized—it begins tomorrow at six when the vote is taken in the Assembly.'[24] Initially reluctant, the politicians were eventually talked round. On the evening of Tuesday, 14 May 1974, Brian Faulkner won an important vote in the Assembly, when a loyalist motion calling for the rejection of the Sunningdale agreement was defeated by 44 to 28 votes. Just after the vote was taken, Harry Murray and Bob Pagels arrived in the press room at Stormont and announced that the UWC was calling an indefinite strike in support of the demand for new elections to the Assembly.

Although the strike was initially dismissed by the British government and the Stormont executive, it took only fourteen days to bring the province to such a degree of collapse that the executive resigned. Of the press corps, only David McKittrick, then with the *Irish Times*, appreciated the potential of the UWC and its support in the power-stations. By the end of the first day, Ballylumford was down to half capacity and large areas of Northern Ireland were experiencing power cuts.

Even with no popular support, the combination of power cuts and intimidation on the streets would have brought the province grinding to a halt, but the strike was genuinely popular in places. In Larne, DUP politicians mediated between local businessmen and the paramilitaries to produce a compromise in which certain 'essential services' would be allowed to operate in limited fashion while everything else closed down.

On the afternoon of the 17th—the fourth day of the strike— massive car bombs exploded in Dublin and Monaghan town, killing twenty-eight people. The three cars had been hijacked in the north. Of the two stolen from Belfast, one was taken from the Shankill Road. The third car was hijacked in Portadown. The source of the vehicles make it clear that it was the work of loyalist paramilitaries, although the UDA and UVF both denied any in-

[24] Ibid. 48. A general comment on Fisk: while he is reliable on the chronology and the basic facts, he underestimates the role of the UDA and overestimates the part played in the strike by the UWC and the leaders of the smaller paramilitary organizations, probably because they provided his main sources.

volvement. As usual the IRA insisted that there was security-force involvement, but it was actually the unaided work of the UVF.

By the end of the week the strike leaders found themselves in the unusual position of being called upon to make major executive decisions. Animals needed feeding and food supplies could not just be halted. So one committee member became 'minister of agriculture' with the job of issuing passes for emergency supplies of feed, and the suppliers helped by giving him an office in Andrewes Flour Mills at the docks. Hugh Petrie issued passes to a small number of Shorts workers who were needed to service delicate machinery. Decisions had to be made as to what was an 'essential service'. As the strike organizers proved they could do that job quite well, they gained further credibility and legitimacy.

'At first we had a few complaints', the Vanguard man said, 'but they were not so much about the strike as about the times food could be bought. We had three people ring against the strike; but most have been asking for help.' The paramilitary groups have been supplying milk for children after buying it from the Co-op. . . . 'We have even had some inquiries which have nothing to do with the strike,' the woman who owns the house said. 'One girl came on the phone in tears because her husband had hit her. Then we found out she had no sink or proper lavatory in the house so we fixed her up with them.'[25]

The strike committee controlled petrol distribution. In an interesting gesture, the first tanker allowed to deliver went to the Catholic Falls area. UDA officers accompanied tankers to their destinations and checked the credentials of motorists who queued for supplies. In addition to electricity shortages, gas was in short supply and consumers had to turn off their taps to prevent explosions as pressure dropped. In the country nearly four thousand gallons of milk were being poured away every day by farmers. Livestock suffocated in air-conditioned units when the power supplies failed.

There was, of course, intimidation. The paramilitaries were not going to run the risk of the strike failing. Vehicles were hijacked and made into barricades. Before the shortage of fuel supplies would have stopped it anyway, public transport was halted by the simple expedient of burning the first few buses; the rest remained in their depots. People driving their own cars to work were stopped and turned back. Tucker Lyttle had the simple but apparently

[25] *The Times*, 22 Mar. 1974.

effective idea of giving the men on the barricades cameras with which they were to photograph people who tried to get through. As he said: 'You may have called it intimidation but intimidation without violence is something very important.'[26] Men in camouflage jackets went from shop to shop, politely suggesting that it might be in the shopkeeper's interests to close. At Harland and Wolff's shipyard, eight thousand manual workers were called to a lunch-time meeting where they expected to hear rousing loyalist speeches. Instead an unnamed voice announced that any cars still in the car park at 2 o'clock would be burnt!

The only major incident involving Catholics came on the second Friday of the strike. Many of the pubs in north and east Antrim, predominantly Protestant areas, are owned by Catholics and, despite instructions from the UWC, these had remained open. Loyalists decided to 'persuade' them to close. Instructions were that no violence should be used, but the mixed UDA and UVF team which set off in two minibuses and a taxi had been drinking. They wrecked three pubs in Ballymena. At a fourth, the Wayside Halt, the two middle-aged brothers who owned the pub resisted and were shot dead by Belfast man Thomas McClure. The gang were so drunk that they did not have the sense to scatter. Instead they drove off to Doagh, where they were stopped by a police road block and arrested.

While the strike committee did their jobs extremely well, the success of the stoppage owed much to a number of other factors. First there was the unpopularity of the SDLP ministers in the executive. Many unionists not committed to the strike had little sympathy for Fitt, Hume, and Devlin, and many working-class Catholics had no great interest in seeing these 'uncle Toms' succeeding. Extremely important was the army's refusal to get involved. One suspects that it was unwilling to face two enemies, but the army command insisted against all evidence in seeing the strike as an industrial dispute and took no action to break block-ades or keep roads open. The RUC also refused to become involved. Again, the force might have been right to suppose that it could not take on the loyalists and win, but it did not try. Every reporter could find any number of examples of policemen stand-ing by while gangs of loyalists blocked roads and intimidated

[26] Fisk, *The Point of No Return*, 58.

motorists into turning back from their journeys to work. However, this should not be seen solely as a lack of will on the part of the security force. UDA squads were under very clear instructions not to confront the police head-on but, if challenged, to withdraw, wait a bit, and then set up another barricade round the corner.

The one security-force action against the strike committee was the arrest of the leaders in east Antrim. On the last Saturday of the strike the organizers received word that they were to be arrested, and a number took flight. Much to the derision of other paramilitaries, the leader of one of the smallest groups headed straight for the Stranraer ferry. That evening Harold Wilson spoke to the nation and, against the advice of Brian Faulkner and Merlyn Rees, referred to Ulster Protestants as 'spongers' and described the strike as a 'rebellion'. If it was the intention to arrest the leaders of the strike, the orders must have been countermanded. That night only one army section from the Palace Barracks in Holywood went out to arrest. One east Antrim UDA man described that day:

I was on my way to Hawthornden Road [the strike headquarters] when I was stopped and told to get offside because they were coming to break up the UWC. I went straight back to Rathcoole. Usually if there were any changes in orders about releasing goods or embargoes during my shift [at strike headquarters], I would come back down in the evening to Cloughfern Protestant Hall and tell all the OV, UVF and UDA commanders. That night I went down to Tiger's Bay to see if I could find Bert but couldn't. I came back, went to bed and at about a quarter to three the army came and put my doors in.

With twelve others from Rathcoole, he was taken first to Castlereagh, the main interrogation centre in Belfast, and then to Long Kesh internment camp.

Explanations for this departure from the army's previous policy of not getting involved in the strike vary. It might have been a mistake. Perhaps orders had been given for similar arrests in every area of the province and had been withdrawn, but the Holywood squads had already left their barracks.[27] This is possible, but,

[27] This view was taken by E. W. H. Christie of Lincoln's Inn, a well-connected lawyer who gave evidence for one of the interned at his hearing; see K. Lindsay, *Ambush at Tully-West: The British Intelligence Services in Action* (Dundalk, 1979), 122–36.

given that they could have been recalled by radio or even been instructed to release the men, it is more likely that arrests were made in this area because it was the base of the overall military commander of the UDA—the man in principle responsible for the pub-smashing fiasco which ended in two murders—and of the UDA men who were thought to have been responsible for a number of recent high-profile murders.[28]

Whatever the reasons for it, the east Antrim scoop was the exception. Through most of the strike the army joined the RUC in doing very little to prevent the UDA and UVF adding the necessary element of coercion that ensured the workers' industrial efforts would be successful. However, it would be misleading to observe that without adding that forceful intervention by the police and army would almost certainly have been counter-productive. The consequences of a complete shut-down of power would have been disastrous and the electricity workers always had that option as a 'trump'. Similarly, the strike organizers could have prevented essential feed stuffs reaching farmers and crippled the agricultural economy. The major port of Larne was a loyalist stronghold and any military intervention could have been followed by a complete close-down. Although it was galling for the government, the strike was sufficiently popular that to try and break it by using the army and police would have simply made it more effective.

Although, for some of the east Antrim activists, the strike was to end with them in Long Kesh, for the UDA and UVF as a whole it was an extraordinary success. With little or no help from unionist politicians, the military and the political wings of working-class loyalism had strangled the economy of the province and defeated a government initiative.[29] They had not only shown their muscle; they had also won a great deal of credibility with ordinary working-class people by showing they could actually manage the production

[28] However, this is not to say that the charges laid against the UDA men at their internment hearings were valid. As was often the case, gossip played a major part in the framing of charges, and they were often the wrong charges for the right men, and vice versa. For example, the 'political' leader of the south-east Antrim UDA was charged with crimes that could more plausibly have been laid against the 'military commander'.

[29] In order to understand the failure of the 1977 strike, it is important to note that it was not the British government that was defeated in 1974 but the government's specific policy initiative. By exaggerating their victory, some of those involved were led to quite false conclusions about their power.

and distribution of goods and services. In two years they had gone from organizing 'wee vigilante groups of ten men to patrol a street' to running the province. However, an important part of their work—the sectarian murder campaign—could not be admitted and the organizations continued to need 'fronts' such as the UWC.

The Defeat of the Paramilitaries

In an issue of *Combat*, the UVF magazine, Hugh Smyth said the UWC victory 'belonged to the workers and not to the politicians who did not declare their hand until it became clear that the workers were going to win'.[30] The strike showed both the strength and the weakness of the working-class loyalists. By combining paramilitary muscle and trade-union skills, they had vetoed a government initiative, but they failed to capitalize on the success and within a year the UWC organization had collapsed. As a senior organizer of the strike put it:

We were deeply disappointed. We went as far as we felt we could go. We had a goal which was to bring down the executive. That was achieved. But then the only political forum was Westminster and we had no one there. In the absence of representatives of working-class people like myself, Tommy Herron, Glen Barr, we had to leave it to the politicians and they muffed it. They done nothing.

Nothing, that is, except re-establish themselves. Harry West, who had been reluctant to support the strike and had barely been involved in it, was now to be found attending planning meetings and insinuating himself into initiatives. The above speaker so strongly objected to West's opportunism that, whenever West arrived at a meeting, he walked out, which was fine for his principles but did nothing to strengthen the working-class alternative to the old political parties. Paisley had arranged to be out of the country for a good part of the strike and was so little regarded by the strike organizers that when he once sat at the head of the meeting-room table he was told to 'get the fuck out of Glennie's chair'. Now he was back in full stride. In contrast to the politicians, who seemed confident and sure of their direction, the loyalists were divided.

[30] *Combat*, vol. 1 (4), p. 2.

The more radical ones were disappointed that Craig had not delivered on a 1972 promise to form a provisional government. They believed that the strike should have been continued until a positive political settlement had been achieved. The more moderate ones were pleased that they had achieved their goal.

A month after the return to work, the paramilitaries met for three days in the Vanguard headquarters at Hawthornden Road in east Belfast under the chairmanship of Glen Barr to formulate an agreed political direction. A variety of proposals were tabled. Curiously one of the more interesting ones came from Harding Smith. Harding had been quiet during the strike, happy to lend his weight to the business of making it stick but taking no leading part. Now the west Belfast men floated a package which included the idea of a three-month cease-fire, the exclusion of all politicians from deliberations, and discussions with both wings of the IRA. Quite how well thought out these proposals were is not clear. 'I'll bet that "no talks with Craig and West" business was Buckie's idea. He was a thick wee shite. You can just imagine him taking the huff, like, and saying "We're not fuckin talkin to youse!"'

If it was better conceived, the idea of talks with PIRA was not popular. Indeed, it was rejected by almost everyone, but, as is often the case, it was most vehemently opposed by those who were *least* active in the military side of any of the organizations.

Although he was excluded from the talks, Craig had his supporters at the meetings in the persons of the leaders of the DOW, OVs, USCA and the Volunteer Service Corps (VSC), and the proposal that loyalist politicians be shunned was rejected. Tyrie, Lyttle, and Bill Snoddy were unhappy about the west Belfast UDA notion (which had support from some sections of the UVF), because they saw it as the foundation for a new working-class loyalist party.

When the report on the conference was published, it represented something of a compromise. Although Barr's interpretation of the meeting was that there was general agreement on the need for negotiated independence (his own long-term goal), this was not highlighted. Talks with loyalist politicians were shelved until new elections made them representative, and it was proposed that there be an increase in the number of Westminster seats to twenty-two; a representative government in Northern Ireland in which majority rule was tempered with a proportional representation system for choosing chairmen for important committees; an end to Eire's claims to sovereignty; an end to internment; two-thirds remission for all political prisoners; no all-Ireland courts; and a return of the control of security policy to Northern Ireland.

However, all this fine-sounding policy meant very little, because the paramilitaries had no obvious venues or opportunities for pursuing such an agenda, unionist politicians were not going to give them any, and their own internal alliances were fragile. A number of the activists who were not members of the UDA or UVF appear to have been 'bought off' by hints from the political parties that they would be rewarded with council seats or other offices if they broke away from the Barr line (which was ironic given that Barr was himself the only one who held office in a political party!). Jim Smith and Harry Murray of the UWC attended an informal meeting of 'all sides' in Oxford despite the decision of the UUUC politicians not to go. Murray was criticized by the UWC both for going and for describing loyalist politicians as 'cowboys' who would 'argue to doomsday while people in the street go on suffering' (even though most loyalists believed exactly that).[31] The UDA and UVF backed Murray, but their own feuding brought an end to the umbrella UAC, and the UVF announced the formation of its own Volunteer Political Party (VPP). In September three leading LAW men—Harry Murray, Bob Pagels, and Harry Patterson—resigned from the UWC, and Pagels and Murray formed a Peace and Reconciliation Committee. The UWC predictably accused them of consorting with the enemies of Ulster, and Pagels resigned from the Peace Committee.

The political defeat of the paramilitaries was confirmed in October when the second Westminster general election of the year gave the loyalist politicians in the UUUC a chance to consolidate their position. Ken Gibson of the UVF stood in west Belfast. Glen Barr got into trouble with Vanguard for campaigning for Gibson against the UUUC-agreed candidate, but he need not have bothered. Gibson polled very badly. Gerry Fitt held his seat with 21,821 votes, while Johnny McQuade of the DUP came second with 16,265. Gibson got 2,690.

---

[31] M. Hall, *20 Years: A Concise Chronology of Events in Northern Ireland 1968–1988* (Newtownabbey, 1988), 53.

Dirty Tricks

There are many reasons why the paramilitary alliance that worked well during the strike fell apart and some of these will be discussed below, but here it is worth again mentioning the role of disinformation. As one leading UVF told me: 'Every time we started to get together, to work together, something would go wrong.' In some cases, they genuinely went wrong, but in others events or rumours were engineered to drive a wedge between the UDA and UVF.

One easy but important way of engineering confusion was to phone the BBC or one of the Belfast papers and deliver a spurious threat or claim for some action. It would not be too unkind to say that the local media did not have a reputation for investigative journalism. It is no accident that the journalists whose work I have found most useful worked for two Dublin publications: the *Irish Times* and *Hibernia*. The local media often published press releases and phoned in statements without thoroughly checking their origins. Frequently false claims were made by people purporting to be UDA or UVF spokesmen that their organization had been responsible for this or that action and such claims were published with little or no effort to evaluate them. When Jim Anderson and Billy Hull were shot and wounded by the IRA on 9 November 1974, there was a phone call to the BBC claiming the hit for the UDA Young Militants (YM). The YM certainly existed—they were really just a section of the UFF strong in west Belfast—but they had no reason to attack the ex-chairman of the UDA and an ex-LAW leader and plausibly denied all knowledge of what was actually the work of the Ardoyne Provisionals.

Such 'stirring' worked, because it was based on one big truth: there was endemic feuding within and between loyalist paramilitary organizations. Had the paramilitaries been driven by shared strongly held political beliefs, the machinations of British 'psyops' would have been less than deleterious but, when added to the tensions which already existed, they were an aggravation.

When the British government offered its next constitutional initiative—the Convention of May 1975—the three parties (UUP, DUP, and Vanguard) ensured that no loyalists were selected as candidates and distanced themselves from the paramilitary organizations. Herron's prediction about his men marching to Rome while Mussolini took the train turned out to be mistaken in one particular. His people were not even being invited to walk to Rome.

The Establishment of Andy Tyrie

Although the UDA had no more political influence at the end than at the start of the strike, the position of Andy Tyrie within the organization had been vastly enhanced. He had played a major part in promoting the plan and, with his closest supporters in the UDA, had effectively run the strike. The rise of Tyrie meant that Harding Smith was again under threat. Smith himself precipitated a crisis when he announced at an Inner Council meeting in Taughmonagh Club in south Belfast that west Belfast was seceding from the UDA.

The underlying cause of the dispute was Harding's view that west Belfast was the UDA and he was its leader. The occasion for the disagreement was the public response to the UDA trip to Libya. On 14 November 1974 Glen Barr, Tommy Lyttle, Andy Robinson from Derry, and Harry Chicken from Newtownabbey accepted an invitation from a Dublin-based 'Development of Irish Resources Society' (DIRS) to visit Libya and present the Protestant case to Colonel Gadaffi, who was a major backer of the IRA. DIRS was a group of Irish businessmen who were interested in the exploitation of oil off the Irish coast; they felt that the Irish government was not doing enough and were interested in involving the Libyans in some capacity. Walter Hegarty, the secretary, believed that the Libyans would be willing to lend £200 million to an enterprise development organization which could make low-interest loans to promising businesses. The Libyans wanted to import meat, and Ireland, north and south, wanted to export it. Hegarty seems to have been concerned that the civil unrest would put the Libyans off, and that the Libyans' support for the IRA would put the Irish off the Libyans. Inviting the UDA to Libya to explain its case seemed like a good way of promoting the business.

At that time, the success of the UWC had left the UDA thinking politically and there was rumour that the *Newsletter*, the unionist daily newspaper, was in financial trouble. Some of the more far-sighted Inner Council members were interested in the idea of buying the *Newsletter* and slightly shifting its political line so that it gave voice to the ideas that were later to emerge as *Beyond the Religious Divide*; for that they needed the sort of money one could not collect by robbing a few banks. They also had at the back of their minds the long-term goal of negotiated independence for Ulster, and that would require international support as well as vast amounts of money.

Led by Barr, the three senior UDA men went to Libya and spent a curious week alternately explaining Irish politics to bemused and ill-informed Libyans (Gadaffi apparently thought Dublin was occupied by British troops and that the 1974 strike was a popular revolution) and being followed by British agents.

When they returned they were astonished at the tone of the press reporting and in particular by the accusation from 'respectable' unionist quarters that they had negotiated with IRA men. There had been a delegation of Provisional Sinn Fein men in Tripoli at the same time. The two sides had not negotiated, but co-presence was enough for the politicians, who took every opportunity to depict the UDA and UVF as unprincipled gangsters in cahoots with the IRA.

It is symptomatic of Ulster politics and the UDA's place in them that everyone criticized the Libya trip. Paisley denounced 'such talks by the UDA or anyone else and those who engage in them have no mandate from the Ulster unionist people. The UDA leaders must be very naive if they think they can convert a terrorist chief like Gadaffi to Ulster's cause.'[32] The UVF made threatening noises, because the UDA had talked to the IRA's chief supplier. For the same reason the IRA was none too happy. Army headquarters dirty tricks department put in its tuppence-worth by circulating another UCA leaflet. This one was headed by a fetching logo which combined the Red Hand of Ulster with the republican socialist Starry Plough:

Glennie 'Wonder' Barr, UDA star of screen and radio, has been having tea parties with Colonel Gadaffi (Libya's Andy Tyrie) and members of the Provisional IRA in Libya. Like that other infamous Londonderry traitor, Governor Lundy, Glennie Barr was prepared to sell Ulster to those who supply arms and money to the IRA to kill loyalists. Ventriloquist's dummy Tucker Lyttle blurted out lie after lie when their treachery was discovered. . . . The blood of hundreds of murdered loyalists is witness to

[32] *Protestant Telegraph*, 30 Nov. 1974.

this UDA treachery and demands justice. We in the Ulster Citizens' Army promise all loyalists that justice will be done and will be seen to be done.[33]

On its return, a leading UDA man warned one of the Libya party: 'Be fuckin careful. The Brits is going to do youse. The Provies is going to do youse. Harding is going to do youse.'

The last one of these possible sources of fatal violence is the interesting one. Quite why Harding was irked is not clear. Although his views were not taken seriously by Tyrie, he had been informed of the plans in advance, and one of the team, Tommy Lyttle, was his spokesman and 'counsellor'. Perhaps, once he had seen the hostile reaction of the trip, he had decided that the Libya trip did not sound like the sort of thing a true blue loyalist should be doing, but probably he was simply feeling increasingly marginalized. In the post-strike UDA, he did not count for much.

In one argument he threatened to have Barr and Chicken killed. In another interesting reverse of the expected positions of the politicos and gunmen, a leading UFF man, whom Harding had 'put off the Road' but who none the less could frighten him, turned to him and quietly told him that, 'if anything happens to them two, even a Provie hit, you're dead'.

Shortly after, Harding announced that west Belfast was leaving the UDA and that in future all UDA men in his area would take orders only from him. Other Shankill men, including Tucker Lyttle, although they doubted the wisdom of the move, walked out with Smith. They were west Belfast men and, whatever they might later do behind the scenes, they had little option but publicly to support their undisputed commander. The UDA paper *Ulster* was edited from the Shankill office. The day that Harding declared independence from the UDA, he, Buckie McCullough, and John McClatchey walked into the paper's office and told the editor to get out. The editor thought they were joking and told them to 'fuck off and let me get on with this article I'm writing'. Then he realized someone had a gun to his head. He collected together his personal things and left for east Belfast. There he met Tyrie and Sammy McCormick, who had taken over from Herron as east Belfast brigadier. Tyrie had been placed under 'house arrest' in Glencairn by Harding's men, but they were unhappy about the

[33] UCA circular, Dec. 1974.

order and were none too rigorous in their surveillance. Tyrie had
been able to escape to the east. But his wife and children were still
there, so a convoy of three cars, two each containing four fully
armed men, drove up to Glencairn and collected Tyrie's family.

On 7 January six members of the Inner Council met and Tyrie
sought and received the backing of the other brigades. Smith
responded by calling a counter-meeting at the Shankill headquarters and inviting all the brigadiers and the chairman, but
Tyrie and Payne, who was now a loyal lieutenant of Tyrie, did
not go.

As one west Belfast activist, who was in prison at the time,
succinctly put it: 'Smith tried to take the organization and he
forgot that the organization is bigger than any one individual.'
Coercion drives out loyalty. In using one 'company' against another
Harding had to this point prevented successful challenges to his
position, but he had also ensured he had few friends and, in
putting Davey Payne 'off the Road',[34] he had made an awesome
enemy. Threatening Barr and Chicken had lost him the support of
the more political men. By threatening Tyrie's family, he had
forced the issue of overall control.

Harding's various chickens came home to roost on 14 January,
the day after a police escort accompanied Tyrie's possessions from
Glencairn to his new home in east Belfast. Three UDA men, one
a close associate of Tyrie, took over an optician's shop opposite
the Shankill headquarters and waited until Harding and Lyttle
appeared at the first-floor windows. The marksman paid no
attention to Lyttle but put two .300 bullets into Harding's chest.
In a wonderfully disingenuous press statement designed solely
for external consumption, the Inner Council said that it deeply
regretted the attack and was 'keeping an open mind as to who was
responsible'.

Astonishingly, Smith made a rapid recovery from his injuries
and tried to return to control of west Belfast. In his absence, Tyrie
had used his considerable diplomatic skills to restore harmony
between east and west. First he met Lyttle, Buckie McCullough,
and Tommy Boyd (the three most senior west Belfast men) in the

---

[34] On Payne, see Ch. 10. The loyalist view that 'putting someone off the
[Shankill] Road' was a serious sanction is interesting in showing the narrow
horizons of many loyalists and the inability of the command to pursue rational
punitive action against those who were held to have infringed.

Europa Hotel and talked them round. Then, in a tense meeting in a small club in Woodvale, Tyrie persuaded the rest of the major figures in the west that Smith had been self-interested and a liability to the organization and, in particular, that he had been planning to start a war with the UVF.

As usual I have to repeat the caution that all one has to rely on in trying to understand these events is rumour. I report these items of gossip, not because I know them to be accurate, but because they give some idea of relations within the UDA and between the UDA and UVF, and because the rumours themselves created and sustained ill-feeling.

As we will see in the next chapter, the UDA and UVF were engaged in serious feuding. It should be remembered that, especially in west Belfast, there had been considerable overlap between the UDA and UVF in the early days of the Troubles. A number of leading west Belfast UVF men had been with Harding in the WDA. But the two organizations were now in competition for members, resources, and prestige. In the lead-up to his attempt to take over the UDA, Harding had asked for a meeting with the UVF brigade staff and at a meeting in the west Belfast Orange Hall had suggested a merger. As one of them blithely put it: 'We told him to piss off,' and it is said he was shown off the premises at the muzzle of an Armalite. Rumour has it that Harding then tried to start a shooting war with the UVF by having the leader of the YCV, 'The Dog', shot. When that failed he is reported to have suggested that a popular west Belfast UDA man be killed in such a way as to implicate the UVF and justify a shooting war.

Kevin Myers offers a different and less plausible account for the fall of Harding Smith.[35] When three Shankill UDA men were interned, evidence was given at their internment hearings in Long Kesh which they believed could only have come from Harding. Myers's gloss on this is that Harding was fearful that too much killing would cause the security forces to arrest and intern him and was thus willing to shop some of his more militant members to save his own skin. Although I was told the same story, it was denied by a number of men who had no reason to like Harding.

Whatever the truth of whatever it was that Tyrie argued, it

[35] *Hibernia*, 18 Apr. 1975.

worked, and, in the brief period he was in hospital, Harding lost the support of his own brigade. When he returned to work, he was again attacked. A masked man entered his office, and shot and wounded him. Some reports said that the last three bullets were all defective; others that the gunman deliberately spared his life. Whatever the truth, Harding took the hint and left for England.

Conclusion

With the enforced retirement of Charles Harding Smith, the UDA completed its evolution and settled into a period of organizational stability under the leadership of Andy Tyrie. The man originally chosen as a powerless figurehead and a compromise between Herron and Harding had outstayed both of them and established himself as the unquestioned authority in the organization. But, although the UDA had demonstrated its power in the 1974 strike and continued through its UFF arm to pursue terror with a campaign of sectarian murder, it was not clear what its role would now be in the uncertain future of Northern Ireland.

5

The Men in Black

BETWEEN the proroguing of Stormont and the end of the UWC strike, the UDA attracted far more media attention than the older UVF; it was legal, it was big, and its leaders liked publicity. Away from press attention, the UVF had slowly been growing and re-organizing. In 1971 the *Sunday Times* Insight team described the UVF as having 'no organization and little potential leadership ... no more than half a dozen men have any leadership ability, one of them half-mad'.[1] In the previous two years it had done little more than rob a few banks, damage the Wolfe Tone memorial in Bodenstown, Co. Kildare, blow up a high-tension electricity pylon in Co. Dublin, and bomb the home of nationalist MP Austin Currie. Yet by early 1973 an *Observer* journalist could describe the UVF as 'the most respected and feared of all the Protestant organizations'.[2]

For some, the very lack of publicity was part of the mystique and appeal of the UVF. Everywhere there was the name 'Spence' and the famous cartoon-like image of a man with a prominent jaw, dark glasses, and black commando cap. Yet few people had UVF contacts. A man who joined the UDA in east Belfast said: 'I wanted to get involved. I couldn't join the UVF because they were just a myth. Everybody had heard of them, like, but they weren't around. Nobody knew anybody in the UVF.' Recruitment was slow, by word of mouth and personal recommendation, much as it had been in the pre-1969 period. One young man, whose father had been shot dead by an IRA sniper, wanted very much to join the UVF but had to press a friend in the organization a number of times before he was considered for membership. In so far as the UVF had a public rallying-point, it was the symbol of the 'men behind the wire'. As the masthead motto of the magazine *Orange Cross* (which was run by Gusty's nephew, Eddie Spence) put it: 'Their only crime is LOYALTY!'

---

[1] *Sunday Times*, 12 Sept. 1971.
[2] *Observer*, 18 Feb. 1973.

Despite the mythology that was developing around Spence as the symbol of working-class loyalist resistance, the prison authorities decided in 1972 to give him two days' parole to attend his daughter's wedding. That the parole was granted when the UDA was raising the political temperature in Belfast with its 'no-go' areas seems even more bizarre, but on 3 July 1972 Spence was freed from prison. He did not return for four months.

According to the account given to the police and the press, Spence was being driven back to the prison at the end of his leave by his nephew Frank Curry when their car was stopped by armed and masked men. Curry was rough-handled and Spence was kidnapped. The first speculation was that the IRA had pulled of a major coup, but the following day the UVF announced that it had Gusty and would only release him if he was given a fair retrial for the Malvern Street murder. For four months Spence moved freely around west and north Belfast. While the security forces were apparently having so much trouble finding him, an ITV camera crew had no difficulty arranging a meeting. Accompanied by a five-man guard, Spence denied that he was the leader of the UVF and insisted that he was being held against his will. He maintained that his trial had been a farce and that he was innocent of the shooting of Peter Ward. He condemned sectarian assassination: 'Random killing is to be deplored at any time and I would say to anyone engaged in sectarian murder "Cease it!" If they feel they must become involved in the fight, they should join an appropriate organization.'[3] Note the distinction between joining an organization and sectarian murdering, which nicely ignores the fact that most sectarian murder was being done by members and even senior officers of 'appropriate organizations'. He interestingly played down his heroic image:

What I'm saying is this. I didn't take the actions with which I was charged. I'm not saying I didn't take any actions. Gusty Spence the hero is a myth. The person who sits before you now is truly a humble and sincere man, some people would say misdirected, that is a matter for conjecture. I am sincere in anything I have ever done and I shall be sincere in anything I ever do. But as far as the hero bit's concerned, it's nonsense.[4]

---

[3] D. Boulton, *The UVF, 1966–73: An Anatomy of Loyalist Rebellion* (Dublin, 1973), 172.
[4] Ibid.

It may have been nonsense but it was attractive nonsense.

The UDA 'no-go' areas may have made policing the Shankill difficult, but the security forces actually had Spence in their hands two months before he was finally recaptured. The Paras raided a club in Brennan Street frequented by the UVF brigade staff and arrested about thirty men. They were all taken to the holding centre in Ladas Drive, where they were held for a while in a large room before being taken first one at a time and then in twos and threes into another room where military policemen sat behind desks. Each man was asked a series of routine 'screening' questions—name, address, reason for being in the club, who else did they know there, and so on—the sorts of questions used by the army to build up profiles of whole areas. Spence gave a false name and was released, as were all the other UVF brigade staff men present. Of course, one cannot be certain, but the inability to find Spence, even when he was lifted in the company of people who should have been recognized as other leading UVF men, suggests either extreme carelessness or a lack of desire to find Spence.

There are at least four possible explanations of why the security forces might have preferred him at large: three loyalist and one republican. The republican version is the claim that the British government actively encouraged the UVF to kill Catholics; releasing Spence was just part of that overall strategy. In one loyalist version, Spence was allowed to remain at large so that he could be followed and observed and thus unintentionally serve as a guide to the underworld of the UVF. Another loyalist theory is that security-force chiefs were concerned about the folk-hero status Spence was acquiring by his dignity and military bearing in the Maze. If allowed to remain at large, he might prefer freedom in exile to a return to prison. If he fled the country, he could be discredited as a coward who had deserted his people.

The third loyalist version is that security chiefs, worried by the growth of the UDA and the sectarian murder campaign, hoped that Spence, with his martial rhetoric and respect for the OIRA, might be able to offer a more amenable and predictable leadership to loyalists. If anyone did entertain that possibility, they were to be disappointed. After Spence's four months 'on the Road', the UVF men were no tamer or more moderate than before; there were just more of them. During the time Gusty was able to move around the clubs and pubs of west Belfast, a large number of new members were recruited.

Spence's defence speech at his trial for failing to surrender after his two-day parole is worth quoting as an example of his rhetoric and as an illustration of the way the UVF saw itself. He began by referring to his first conviction:

[This is a] political ploy to have another go at Gusty Spence and to defame my name. But unlike the farcical and political trial that I underwent in 1966, this time I shall have my day in court. My voice shall not go unheard. I am concerned only with my word, which means more to me than life itself. . . . [on the way back to prison] an incident happened over which I had no control. The world knows the rest. If I had been a party to the event which occurred I would not have allowed my family to suffer the anguish which they did. . . . This court must realise that certain men were not prepared to let me go back to the prison—members of the organisation to which I have the honour to belong—the Ulster Volunteer Force. After my kidnap there was no moral onus on me to report back.

He said that during his freedom he had worked for the betterment of Ulster:

I moved about the population quite freely and was heartily welcomed. . . . I am a soldier and I have been motivated purely by patriotism. If the intent of this charge was to defame me instead of merely observing the law, then I am convinced the Crown has failed miserably, simply because the people of Ulster have become more mature and politically aware. If I had had myself in mind I had only to leave the country never to be heard of again. In fact I stayed to do what I had to do.

Neatly returning to the narrow meaning of *parole* as 'word', he concluded: 'If this court decides that I have broken my word, then I must also suggest that so too have Westminster, Mr Heath, Mr Chichester-Clarke, Mr Faulkner and other unionist politicians when they gave their solemn word on very vital matters.'[5] Enough of the jurors were convinced to give him the benefit of the doubt and the jury failed to reach a verdict.

Military Mystique

Where the UDA began as an unruly mob and only gradually moved to a military structure and rank system, the UVF has always

[5] *Irish News*, 5 Dec. 1973.

seen itself as a military organization, and a major part of its self-image is its supposed military superiority over the UDA. One army search found a five-page typed document of 'Brigade regulations'. Among them was regulation 2(b):

All platoons and other such units shall assemble on parade once each week for the purpose of:—Roll Call, Pay Parade, Receipt and Transmission of Orders, and Training. (Such training to include:—weapon training, fieldcraft, interrogation procedure, military discipline, and foot drill).[6]

Were the matter at hand not the awful one of killing, this sort of document would remind one of children's games with their elaboration of roles and rules, and their almost fetishistic attention to detail, and yet all of it 'pretend'. In the Nissen huts of Long Kesh most of the UVF men (much to the amusement of the UDA prisoners) followed a military pattern of daily life with kit inspections and drills. For short periods one or two country areas may have organized and conducted themselves in a military fashion. But the general reality was much closer to the UDA's 'wee teams'. Indeed, even the most senior UVF figures find it hard to talk consistently in the language of brigades, battalions, and companies. As we will see with the story of Lenny Murphy, a 'company' was any self-identifying group of men who joined the UVF. In Belfast, this usually meant a group which drank in a particular pub. So Murphy's company might be accurately described as the 'Brown Bear' team, while the company led by 'Chuck' Berry was the Windsor Bar mob. Assembling on parade meant turning up at the bar.

The martial rhetoric was especially heavy in statements claiming responsibility for murders and in *in memoriam* notices for fallen comrades. To give an example of the former:

On Thursday, 2nd April an Active Service Unit of the Ulster Volunteer Force consisting of four men armed with automatic weapons executed PIRA Volunteer Laurence Marley at his home in the staunchly Republican area of Ardoyne.

Two Volunteers carrying an automatic shotgun and a 9 mm high powered Browning went to the house, Marley refused to open the door, the Unit opened fire, killing him.

Laurence Marley had served long prison sentences for IRA activities

[6] *The Times*, 11 Feb. 1974.

including blackmail, possession of arms and explosives. Upon his release he became re-involved with the organisation and this re-involvement cost him his life.

The Ulster Volunteer Force reserve the right to strike at republican targets where and when the opportunity arises.[7]

The following is part of the speech made at the funeral of Bobby 'Squeak' Seymour, an east Belfast UVF man who had been given four life sentences on the evidence of Joe Bennett before Bennett's evidence was thrown out on appeal. He was shot in his radio and video shop on the Woodstock Road by the IRA.

Among us there is anger and frustration and a terrible sense of loss. Above all, though we come with heavy heart to pay our deep-felt tribute to One of our Own, Volunteer Robert Seymour leaves us today. A young man who dedicated his life to his country has given all that any Soldier could ever give. As an exemplary Volunteer we acknowledge the stature of a basically quiet and unassuming man. Without fear he soldiered for our cause. Yes! Without fear! For those who really knew him can identify this as perhaps his only fault. . . .

Your memory will be with us as we go on. For on we must go. This Organisation will serve the needs of its People. It will be Vigilant and it will be Calm in the furtherance of our cause. . . .

> For they shall not grow old
> As we that are left grow old
> Age shall not weary them nor the years condemn
> At the going down of the sun and in the morning
> We will remember them.[8]

There were area variations but the command structure in the UVF seems generally to have been no tighter than it was in the UDA. Sometimes orders came from brigade staff, but often the instructions would be no more specific than 'plan something big for 4 April'. Individual groups would often devise their own 'moves'—a bank robbery or a murder—and have them sanctioned by brigade staff after the fact. But the looseness of structure meant that operations were only as 'surgical' and controlled as the skills and interests of the individuals in that particular group allowed them to be, which was often not much.

Part of the UVF's myth involved frequently criticizing the UDA

[7] *Combat*, Apr. 1987.
[8] Ibid., July 1988.

(or the UFF) for inefficiency. For example, one press statement appealed to all loyalist organizations to stop the sectarian killing campaign:

We call upon the UFF whoever they may be to desist from their present murder campaign and to channel their energies and resources into some form of constructive action ... the indiscriminate killing of Ulstermen on account of their religious beliefs can do nothing whatever to preserve the Protestant liberties and restore democracy to Northern Ireland.[9]

The 'whoever they may be' is wonderfully disingenuous. Any senior UVF man would know exactly who the UFF killers were; some of them had been in the UVF! But it manages to suggest that the tight discipline of the UVF places them so far above the grubby sectarian killers that they don't even know them.

Moves and 'Wee Jobs'

Most of the murders committed by loyalists in 1972 and the first half of 1973 were the work of the UDA, with the three UFF teams of west Belfast, south Belfast, and east Belfast being particularly active. But after July, the UVF began to catch up. In the late summer and autumn of 1973 the UVF mounted a very effective retaliation to the IRA's campaign of pub bombing, and it planted more bombs than the UDA and IRA combined. In Belfast there were sixteen pubs destroyed in as many days.

As an illustration of UVF activities of this period, one might analyse the killings of 1974, the year of the UWC strike and the unbanning of the organization. It was also the year of many UVF press statements condemning UFF sectarian murders! It should be noted that, because of the difficulty of always distinguishing UVF from UDA killings, this list will not be exhaustive.

On 9 January John Hugh Crawford, a 53-year-old Catholic, was shot dead at his upholstery business in Milltown Road, Belfast. Four weeks later Vincent Charles Clark, a 43-year-old Catholic, was shot dead as he left his friend's house in Westrock Gardens, Belfast, where he had been watching television. On 28 February the UVF bombed the Red Star Bar in Donegall Quay in the Belfast docks area. Hugh Harvey died and a woman lost both legs.

The next month a UVF team bombed the Conway Bar in

[9] UVF press statement, 11 Feb. 1974.

Greencastle. There were about 150 people in the bar when the bomb exploded without warning. Two men—James Mitchell and Joseph Donnelly—were killed and many others were injured. On the last day of March the UVF claimed one of its own when Jim Hanna, at one time the overall military commander, was shot dead as he sat in a car with his girlfriend on the Shankill Road. He was suspected of 'touting' for the security forces.

The Dublin and Monaghan car bombs in May have already been mentioned. They killed thirty people. In the same month the UVF bombed the Rose and Crown pub on the lower Ormeau Road in Belfast; six people died. A particularly pointless killing occurred in Bangor in July when two young UVF men shot dead a 16-year-old Catholic boy who had approached a Twelfth bonfire. On 4 October a Belfast UVF gang shot at two Catholic men as they walked to work on the Lisburn Road. Robert James Willis died. Six days later the Protestant Action Force (PAF) (the south-east Antrim UVF) shot dead Albert Lutton in Newtownabbey in revenge for the shooting of two Protestants earlier in the week. The next day the PAF claimed the murder of Jimmy Hastie.

The UVF, using the PAF name and a new one—the Ulster Protestant Action Group (PAG)—had a particularly active weekend in early November. First Patrick Armstrong, a young Catholic merchant seaman, was shot dead, apparently as retaliation for the bombs planted by the IRA in Woolwich and Guildford. Then two Catholics working on a lorry in a garage on the road to the airport were shot dead. The same evening a PAG gang entered a house on the Springfield Road and shot dead John McQuitty, who was watching television.

In almost none of these murders could any plausible claim be made that the victim was an active republican and in very few of them was such a reason offered. Given that a lot of the 'moves' of this period involved the IRA tactic of lobbing bombs into pubs, there was clearly little or no targeting of specific individuals. In so far as the killings were explained, they were usually presented as retaliation for some IRA act. That is, they were every bit as 'sectarian' as the UFF killings the UVF so roundly condemned. As one senior UVF man candidly told me: 'Of course, the hits then were sectarian and don't let anyone tell you otherwise. When we didn't know who the IRA were, the murders had to be sectarian.'

Internment of Catholics had been introduced in August 1971 as part of a response to the worsening security situation and was intended as a comprehensive 'rounding-up' of IRA men. The internment of Protestants was different in that it was used not to remove a group of people but to imprison individuals whom the RUC believed to have been responsible for particular crimes about which the evidence necessary for a conviction was not forthcoming. Some loyalists were detained for nothing more than association with people who might have been terrorists, but by and large the internment of loyalists was well directed against people who, while they may not have been guilty of the particular crime with which they were associated, were undoubtedly major 'players'.

The order in which UDA and UVF men were interned reflected the severity and timing of their campaigns. Three men who were not UVF activists were detained in January and February 1973 on suspicion of being UVF men. Some UFF activists were interned in the spring and autumn of 1973, but it was not until the end of the year that the security forces turned their attention on the UVF brigade staff. Tommy West and Bo McClelland were lifted but the editor of *Combat* escaped and went 'on the run'. As with the search for Spence, efforts to find him do not seem to have been terribly strenuous, as he visited his home and UVF offices quite frequently and remained in active command of the east Antrim brigade.

Going Public and Doing Politics

From 1966 the UVF had maintained a very low profile, preferring to have its men work through other organizations. However, the rapid growth and high profile of the UDA caused considerable pressure from the rank and file for a more public presence. UDA leaders, widely viewed as late comers to the struggle, band-wagon jumpers who strutted around the streets in camouflage jackets and bush hats, with insignia on their sleeves, 'like fuckin cock of the walk', were resented by some UVF men, who felt their own efforts were not getting due recognition. UVF men began to 'come out' of Tara and the various other groups they had been involved in and assumed a higher profile.

In the way he ran the UVF compounds in the Maze prison,

Spence played a very important role for the UVF in maintaining and embellishing the martial mystique. But not everyone liked his regime. Although many hero-worshipped him, some UVF men deeply resented being ordered around by what one wee hard man called 'a cunt in a cravat'. The strong and opposite reactions that Spence still provokes make it hard to evaluate his contribution to the development of the UVF—some exaggerate it while others deny that he ever did a useful thing—but there is no doubt that he was instrumental in getting a small number of senior people in the UVF to think politically. Between 1966 and 1973 Spence moved from being an uncritical unionist to being a self-consciously populist loyalist. In a dramatic borrowing of a phrase from the civil-rights movement, Spence was happy to counter-assert that the unionist working class had also suffered fifty years of unionist misrule. He frequently combined attacks on unionist politicians with pleas for negotiation between loyalist and nationalist para-militaries: 'Let the rattle of oratory and the volley of words be heard instead of bombs and bullets—we need the strategy of political policies in place of battle plans. Let us face one another across the negotiating table as opposed to no man's land.'[10] Here Spence's drawing on the traditions of the first UVF was having a radical effect. For all that those who attended to the history of the First World War glorified the sacrifice of Ulstermen, the deaths of thousands in the mud fields of Flanders was clearly an enormous waste, and the appreciation of the final pointlessness of such sacrifice was not absent from Spence's reflections on the past and effected his view of the present. It was the patriotic duty of loyalists to defend Ulster from republicans, but they should also be searching for a solution.

In early 1973 Billy Hull, who was always easy with a press statement, announced that LAW had held talks with all the loyalist paramilitary groups and was forming a common front. The UVF reacted angrily and announced that those members who had taken part in such talks had no right to represent the UVF. The 'active service branch of the Force did not intend talking to anyone. Their main aim was to eliminate the IRA and restore stability to the community.'[11] But other counsels prevailed.

[10] *Irish News*, 12 Nov. 1972.
[11] *Irish Times*, 23 Jan. 1973.

Some people came to command paramilitary units because they were more vicious and cruel than anyone else, but many arrived in leadership positions in the UDA and UVF because they were already figures of some standing in their communities. The almost complete collapse of the rule of law in many working-class parts of Belfast in 1971 and 1973 meant that such men became more and more involved in representing working-class people to such state agencies as the Housing Executive and in themselves making the sorts of decisions that would normally be made by a government department. It was a short step to thinking about electoral politics.

In the summer of 1973, at the same time as various UDA men were involved in Vanguard, some UVF men were promoting the Ulster Loyalist Front (ULF). Although it maintained the right of citizens to bear arms to protect themselves, it distanced itself from sectarian murder and suggested a number of policy points ranging from worker partnership schemes in factories to the return of jury trial and the release of all internees.[12] It had two elected representatives: Hugh Smyth, who was a city councillor and an Assemblyman, and Fred Proctor, a councillor (who later became a vocal critic of the UVF gangsterism and a DUP councillor; later still he joined the Unionist Party).

This first tentative move towards conventional politics was followed a month later by the declaration of a cease-fire. Although it maintained the right to defend loyalist areas, the UVF was temporarily ceasing aggressive actions. In fact, as was usually the case on all sides with announced cessations of hostility, its members continued to kill using flags of convenience: either 'Red Hand Commando' or, a new one introduced in the autumn of 1974, 'Protestant Action Force' (or Group). On 4 April 1974, in order to encourage the more moderate elements on both sides, Secretary of State Merlyn Rees announced the lifting of the bans on the UVF and Sinn Fein.

Strike

In his account of the UWC strike, Robert Fisk gives little space to the UVF and suggests that it played only a small and grudging part in its organization. McKittrick said: 'With its peculiar penchant for

[12] *Irish Independent*, 15 Oct. 1973.

considering itself superior to the other Loyalist groups, the UVF took little part in the Ulster Worker's Council strike ...'[13]

This is slightly misleading. Although Gibson annoyed other committee members by qualifying his support for this or that plan with the observation that he 'would have to check with brigade staff', he was involved in policy discussions, as was 'Big Bill' Hannigan, an ex-UDR officer who was officially a representative of the DOW but close to the rural elements of the UVF. The second-in-command of the RHC was a member of the organizing committee (and indeed is featured in a photograph of a celebration dinner a year after the event, as is John McKeague, who was not involved because he was in prison at the time).

If there was reticence at brigade staff level, rank-and-file UVF men were often as active as the UDA. In Monkstown, the strike was co-ordinated from the UVF club. The disastrous 'raid' on north Antrim pubs was the work of a mixed UDA and UVF gang. It may well be that the feud with the UDA over the shutting of a pub during the strike has misled commentators. In most areas the UVF were as committed to the strike as the UDA.

The success of the strike and the very obvious power that the paramilitaries were able to deploy in bringing down a government encouraged some UVF leaders to take political action further. Shortly after it ended, the UVF announced its political party. In a letter to individual volunteers (which was also printed on the front page of its magazine *Combat*), the UVF explained why it was forming the Volunteer Party. First the UVF had been denied 'the just right to express openly its political ideology' and had been branded as 'nothing but a bunch of hooded assassins, determined to wreck Ulster by the use of violence'. Secondly, politicians had misused the trust placed in them by loyalists and had allowed Ulster to crash into a state of anarchy.

Armed with this knowledge we felt that now was the opportune time to come out from the shadows into the bright sunlight and expose ourselves politically to the hostile pressures exerted by those politicians who had tried unsuccessfully to castigate us by use of lies, to prove for once and all time that the Ulster Volunteer Force is a creditable organization and an organization which can be trusted to act effectively and responsibly in any given type of situation.

[13] *Irish Times*, 1 Aug. 1975.

A curious aspect of the statement is its frankness about policy formulation. Although the author believes the UVF is capable of producing such a thing, he recognizes that it does not yet have a policy:

> another requirement is the formulation of a policy document which embraces all shades of opinion within the organization. In order to achieve this as quickly as possible we ask all interested personnel to submit to the Political Executive their proposals.[14]

Most parties begin with a policy and then recruit members. This one was beginning with members—the Volunteers—and hoping to discover that they already shared a political viewpoint. The two things that the VPP was clear about were opposition to independence and dislike of internment. On the former point, Gibson's election leaflet was clear:

> Some loyalists think U.D.I. would be 'OK.' Go it alone and save money by cutting down the social security, social services and increasing taxes and let those who don't work emigrate. This is very foolish because it would be against those who are in work as well as the unemployed. . . . We believe that in Ulster today there is quite enough suffering without making more. If poverty got worse and if the clamour for jobs got greater and wages failed to keep up with wages on the mainland, we believe that sectarianism and violence would get worse. Nobody wants that.
>
> U.D.I. means anarchy and anarchy means Civil War, the outcome of which would be too horrible to contemplate.[15]

The party argued that 'Internment and harassment have caused great suffering for ordinary working people for the last five years.' It proposed the release of all detainees who were members of organizations 'which have called effective cease-fires' and two-thirds remission of sentences 'for all people imprisoned for offences connected with the civil disturbances'.[16]

Not all Volunteers were happy with the VPP. Some felt it was a distraction from the thing the UVF did well: killing. Others, including a future chief of staff who was close to Spence, thought that a working-class unionist party was a good idea but hardly worth the effort when the chances of success were so slight in a field already overcrowded with competing unionist parties.

[14] *Combat*, vol. 1 (14).
[15] Note that Barr campaigned for Gibson, even though the VPP rejected his negotiated independence programme.
[16] VPP election leaflet, 1974.

At the first hurdle, the VPP failed. It applied to join the UUUC coalition of loyalist parties but was turned down. This was hardly a surprise, given that, since the end of the strike, the politicians had been moving as fast and as far as they could from the paramilitaries. Despite the rebuff, Gibson was keen to stand for west Belfast in the Westminster elections that came in October 1974. On 19 August it was reported that Johnny McQuade, a popular working-class loyalist associated with Ian Paisley, had decided not to stand as the agreed unionist candidate in west Belfast. The unionist politicians had no intention of allowing the gunmen to acquire the legitimacy that would follow from being the only group willing to stand against Gerry Fitt, and the DUP put considerable pressure on McQuade to change his mind, which he did. Gibson offered a meeting of senior Orangemen and Shankill loyalists a compromise. He would stand aside if Glen Barr, or some other young activist, was chosen instead of McQuade, whom he felt to be old for the job. The offer was rejected and Gibson remained in the ring.

Barr broke Vanguard ranks and campaigned for Gibson.[17] After much dithering in the west Belfast UDA, Harding Smith agreed to support Gibson and appeared on an election platform with him. He need not have bothered. Fitt was returned with 21,821 votes. McQuade came second with 16,265, and Gibson came fourth, with 2,690 votes, which was only 14.2 per cent of the total unionist vote. The next month there was a mass meeting of UVF leaders in the north Belfast Orange Hall and it was decided to close down the VPP. A number of changes in the leadership of the UVF saw the influence of the more politically minded 'old guard' reduced.

Ideology in the UVF

Before leaving UVF politics, I would like to add a cautionary note. A number of commentators whose knowledge of the UVF comes

[17] Barr was disillusioned with the UUUC because he was denied a chance to stand for the safe Unionist Westminster seat of Londonderry. The selection of candidates was supposed to be agreed by the three parties in the Coalition, and Barr expected to be the Vanguard choice, but, although Paisley supported him, the OUP nominated its own man and Bill Craig, who was still close to the Derry Unionists, did not object.

only from reading their published literature and their press statements have made the mistake of reading too much into them.[18] There seems little point in comparing this or that statement and trying to analyse the shifting position of the UVF in working-class politics. I do not mean that Spence, Gibson, 'Richard Cameron', and others were not serious in the things they said. Rather, I mean that, while the desire for a working-class alternative to the unionist parties was quite sincerely felt, the actual content of UVF policies at any one time was of no great significance, because relatively little systematic thought went into formulating those positions and there was little or no consultation with members, most of whom 'didn't give a shit about the politics'. While Gibson's views on detention and the dangers of UDI were probably widely shared, there was little other sense in which he was a spokesman for the UVF, because there was no UVF consensus of opinion for which he could speak. Although he was talking with the weariness and wisdom of a lot of prison-time hindsight, one senior activist probably has it right when he says:

We never had an overall goal. I never really knew what I was fighting for. If you was a journalist or that I might come out with some wee thing but I never really knew. A journalist would phone up and ask what we were thinking. We'd take down some book and take a few sentences out and jumble them up and give it to him as our policy.

I want to stress here that I am not saying that UVF men were less bright than the IRA; the UVF's politics were muddy because there was little scope and few resources to develop coherent politics.[19] And that was the case because there were already better-established political groups which represented many of the views held by UVF members.

There were no doubts on the fundamental question of all Ulster politics—the border. No one in the UVF was suggesting a united Ireland or anything like it. However, there was disagreement about the second most important question—relationships with Westminster. By and large most UVF men were unionists; that is,

[18] A general weakness of Nelson's otherwise excellent *Ulster's Uncertain Defenders: Loyalists and the Northern Ireland Conflict* (Belfast, 1984) is that it takes the UVF's politics far more seriously than did most UVF men.

[19] The issue of the 'space' for political innovation is discussed in detail below (see Ch. 9).

they wished to maintain a strong constitutional link with Britain. However, what form that link should take was not clear. John McKeague, the founder and leader of the RHC (soon to be fully merged with the UVF), was in favour of a sovereign Ulster government in a federal United Kingdom,[20] but his second-in-command shared Gibson's dislike for any form of independence. Beyond the constitutional issues there was even less agreement. At times, the UVF of Spence sounded socialist, and in another country many of its members would have been Labour men. At others, especially if accused of communism, it sounded rabidly right wing. But none of this should be surprising when one remembers that what UVF members had in common was that they had joined the UVF. Although they were recruited from a fairly narrow class background, some were rural and some were urban. Although few were committed evangelicals, some were more religious than others. Some were skilled well-paid workers and others were long-term unemployed. Some were thoughtful planners and others were hoodlums. Why should such a variety of people agree on policies beyond the simple constitutional issue?

The Feud with the UDA

Like any two competing organizations, the UDA and UVF have rarely been on good terms for long. Harding Smith's uneasy relationship with the UVF has already been mentioned.

During the UWC strike, the UDA and UVF, largely under pressure from women who did not want their husbands drinking all day, ordered that clubs and bars close. While most bars closed, a UVF pub on the Shankill remained open. UVF member Joe Shaw came in with some friends and was ribbed by the regulars about having allowed his 'local' to be closed. Later, well oiled, Shaw and some friends went back to North Queen Street and opened up the North Star bar. A UDA patrol arrived, tried to close it, and were showered with empty bottles. The UDA men retreated and returned with a shotgun. In what an internal UDA report called 'a fracas', Shaw was shot.

Andy Tyrie and Tommy West, chief of staff of the UVF, met to talk out what was turning into a nasty situation. They agreed

[20] *Newsletter*, 16 Nov. 1974.

that the shooting was an accident and that there would be no retaliation. Further, as the document put it in its best official style: 'Personnel of both organizations were ordered by their respective commanders that in the event of ill-feelings resulting in violence, weapons under no circumstances would be used. Fisticuffs would be permitted on a man to man basis.'

The March attack on the Catholic-owned Conway Bar in Greencastle has already been mentioned. An inexperienced YCV team pushed open the door of the bar, fired a few shots which killed a female customer, and then carried in a bomb. The bomb exploded prematurely, injuring a number of people, including the three bombers. Their driver panicked and drove to the Loyalist Club, which was used by UDA and UVF men. His report to his UVF colleagues and their noisy reaction caused the UDA men to ask them to keep it down, one thing led to another, and a western saloon fight broke out.

The next night there was another fight and on the third evening two UDA men who had been particularly prominent, Lieutenant Stephen Goatley and Volunteer John Fulton, were shot dead by the UVF. The murders were later 'explained' by the claim that Fulton and Goatley had been the 'UFF assassins' who had murdered Shaw. In reply to the UDA's view that these were murders, the UVF insisted that 'both men were given a fair trial by a joint UDA/UVF court and the sentence carried out as ordered'.[21]

Two weeks after its own people had botched the Conway Bar job, the UVF (or a security-force 'black propagandist'?) had the nerve to issue a press statement from its political wing condemning sectarian killings. The UDA was criticized for not doing enough to stop them and especially for bombing the Conway Bar and a Bangor bar bombing which killed reservist policewoman Mildred Harrison. A UVF man later pleaded guilty to that killing.[22]

The feud continued in Belfast. In a UDA attack on the Albert Bar in east Belfast, two UVF men were wounded. In retaliation, a UVF team took a UDA man out of the Oakley Bar and shot him.[23] In what sounds like sour grapes, the very small Londonderry UVF announced:

[21] UVF press release, 20 Mar. 1975.
[22] *Irish Independent*, 18 Mar. 1976.
[23] *Belfast Telegraph*, 19 Mar. 1975.

we are going to execute their UDA leaders because they have been guilty of the most violent sectarian violence, including the murders at the Top of the Hill Bar, the bombing of St Patrick's Hall, and the attacks on the Greencastle fishing boats, which they tried to blame on our Red Hand comrades.[24]

On the night of 30 March all hell broke loose in east Belfast with the UDA firing on the homes of ten UVF men in the space of just over an hour. One of those whose house was attacked was Ken Gibson. The next night there were shootings in loyalist pubs in east Belfast and a week later the UVF retaliated with bombs. The UDA issued the following press statement:

Brigade staff of the east Belfast UDA view with total horror and abhorrence the gutter-level bomb attacks on three UDA homes in east Belfast last night. In one incident in particular in St Kilda Street off the Ravenhill Road, the bombers were observed lighting the fuse and immediately opened fire at point-blank range before throwing the device into the house in which five children were sleeping. We ask the loyalist community to try to imagine the depraved mind of the UVF 'loyalist', planning and assembling a bomb to plant in a Protestant home ... while we reserve the right to and indeed will take retaliatory action against the UVF or any splinter group connected with them, we will not, repeat not, be drawn to the depths of depravity by bombing loyalist homes and endangering of innocent women and children.[25]

A week later two UDA men—Hugh McVeigh and David Douglas—disappeared. The immediate suspicion was that the UVF was responsible, but, in a extremely tense meeting with UDA leaders, UVF brigade staff denied it. In what was an attempt further to confuse or provoke ill-feeling, Eileen McVeigh got a phone call from a man falsely claiming that he represented a breakaway group of fourteen paramilitaries (six UVF and eight UDA) which was holding the two men and that only the end of the feud would lead to their release.

A UVF team plotted to murder north Belfast UDA leader Sammy Doyle, but never followed through. An attack on Sammy Smyth, sometime political spokesman of the UDA, was almost

---

[24] *Irish Independent*, 26 Mar. 1975.
[25] Statement phoned to BBC Belfast, 9 Apr. 1975. It is possible that this was yet another 'stirrer' from British intelligence. The UDA did not usually call their commanders 'brigade staff'.

successful. Nine shots were fired through the front door at him and his daughter.

The feud continued, despite the election to the Constitutional Convention which took place on 1 May. Eight UDA men walked into the UVF's London Bar in east Belfast, were refused drinks, and started a fight in which Ken Gibson had his wrist broken as he resisted being bundled into a car. A local UDA men was stabbed.

When I asked one participant why the feuding had gone on so long, he identified lack of management skills as a key factor:

The hostility, a lot of it was just bumming and blowing—our team's better than your team. I don't want to use the word but I would say that we didn't have the breeding. We didn't have the experience of handling men that could have sorted out those kinds of problems. We were just brickies and plumbers.

True, but there are two other things. First, political parties compete for votes and tell lies about each other, but violence is rarely used. Paramilitary organizations are in the violence business. Their members regularly kill. They have guns. When they fall out, they use them against each other. Secondly, loyalists had more of a problem than republicans. This seems largely a result of the stronger centralized structure of republican paramilitarism. Between December 1986 and March 1987 twelve people were killed and several more injured in a feud between the small INLA and the Irish People's Liberation Organization (IPLO). In the early days after the IRA split, Officials attacked Provisionals and there was retaliation, but most republican 'operators' are in one organization—PIRA—and it is strongly controlled from the centre. Loyalist paramilitaries are divided between two large organizations, neither of which has a strong centre.

Outside Belfast

Like the UDA, the UVF was strongest on the Shankill Road and in parts of greater Belfast such as Rathcoole and Carrickfergus to which Shankill Road Protestants had moved. 'See the first generation especially, they were never off the Shankill or the Newtownards Road. Put them on the M2 out of Belfast and they were lost.' Although the loyalist paramilitaries were concentrated in the big city, there were pockets elsewhere. One UVF group that was particularly active in late 1974 and early 1975 under the PAF banner was based in Dungannon and was responsible for more than thirty murders in the mid-Ulster murder 'triangle' formed by Dungannon, Portadown, and Armagh.[26] As we have already seen in the earlier discussion of sectarian murder, it is a mark of the difficulty of detecting and preventing that sort of crime that the group had committed so many before an accident delivered some of them to the police.

On the last day of July 1975 a van carrying five members of the Miami Showband from Banbridge to the Republic was waved down by the red torch of what appeared to be an Ulster Defence Regiment (UDR) or army patrol. The driver pulled in and the five were ordered out to stand by the side of the road facing away from the van. As the patrol was searching the van, there was a massive explosion, which instantly killed two of its members. Others started firing, killing three members of the band and seriously wounding the other two.

The two men caught in the blast were blown to pieces. An arm with 'UVF Portadown' tattooed on it was found some yards from its torso. Identification was made easy when the UVF claimed the two dead men—Wesley Somerville and Horace Boyle—and explained that they had been blown up by a bomb in the Miami Showband's van.

This was minimally correct but failed to mention that Somerville and Boyle were placing the bomb under the driver's seat when it prematurely detonated. It seems that the idea was to hide the bomb in the van during what would be taken as a routine 'stop and search' and have it explode once the band was on home soil, inside the Irish Republic. It would be assumed that the band was knowingly smuggling explosives and there would be no one alive to say differently. Apart from killing Catholics, this would allow political capital to be made of the ease with which explosives could be smuggled through the border.

With some luck and good detective work, the police rounded up Raymond Crozier and Roderick McDowell and they were

[26] Some senior members of this group are widely thought to be responsible for the upsurge of UVF activity in late 1990 and 1991.

convicted of their part in the shootings. Three of the gang were members of the UDR.[27]

I have already considered the IRA's claims to be 'unsectarian' in its killing. In early January 1976, and apparently in revenge for the Miami Showband murders, an IRA group stopped a minibus of workers at Kingsmill in Co. Armagh and asked each their religion. The lone Catholic was told to stand aside and the eleven Protestants were shot. Only one survived. Of the ten who died only one—an ex-sergeant in the Ulster Special Constabulary—had any contact with the security forces.

The Coup

In October 1975 a minor incident in Carrickfergus brought down first the south-east Antrim brigade of the UVF and then the brigade staff. A Volunteer was picked up and taken to the Carrick British Legion. Suspecting he was going to be 'court martialled', he asked the men who had brought him if he could go downstairs to collect his lighter and cigarettes. He made good his escape and went straight to the police, where, in return for protection from the UVF, he offered to tell all he knew, and he knew about the killing of McVeigh and Douglas. He was able to take the RUC to the graves, in a remote part of Co. Antrim near Gobbins Cliffs, Islandmagee. With the bodies and the testimony of the defector, the RUC was able to round up thirty-one east Antrim UVF men and, at the trial two years later, convict them of a number of serious offences.[28]

The discovery that senior UVF men had killed McVeigh and Douglas caused considerable dismay within the organization. One senior man told me of his reaction on hearing what the east

[27] M. Dillon, *The Dirty War* (London, 1990), has the wrong Christian names for Crozier and McDowell. James Joseph Somerville, Wesley's brother, was convicted in 1981 of a number of serious offences, including involvement in the Showband killings. Labour MP Ken Livingstone has claimed in the House of Commons that Capt. Robert Nairac, a British army intelligence officer murdered by the IRA in 1977, 'may have been in charge of the UVF gang, and that he deliberately blew up the UVF because they knew too much' (McKittrick, *Independent*, 2 Sept. 1987). This fanciful nonsense is based on the assertions of Colin Wallace and Fred Holroyd and, for the reasons given by McKittrick and by Dillon in *The Dirty War*, can be dismissed.

[28] *Irish News*, 12 Mar. 1977.

Antrim men were being charged with: 'I was shocked. Stunned. I just couldn't believe it. I was almost in tears. I had sat there and heard the buggers deny they had anything to do with it.' It came on top of a number of other reasons for dissatisfaction. First, there had been too many mistakes. Six UVF man had been killed that year, five by their own bombs. On 2 October, just before the Antrim men were lifted, there was a major 'offensive'. Units were instructed to plan something spectacular. The group led by Lenny Murphy (of whom more in Chapter 7) robbed an off-licence and killed two Catholic women. Four Coleraine UVF men blew themselves up and further increased the embarrassing 'own-goal' rate. The organization was again banned. Secondly, there were financial problems. Thirdly, there were a number of released detainees who had held senior rank, who were unhappy about their status, and who were capable of taking over.

The result was the one outright coup in the UVF's history. With the blessing of Gusty Spence, a group of armed men went down to the UVF's office and told the brigade staff that they were out of jobs.

A press statement phoned in to the BBC on the 21st put it formally:

At a meeting today Tuesday 21st called by battalion commanders throughout the UVF . . . it was decided unanimously that the present brigade staff be stood down because the policies they were pursuing were totally contrary to the principles under which the UVF was formed. This must not be seen as a split in the organization as the decision to stand down brigade staff was a result of a democratic vote.

For a brief period, there was some dissension, with the very small North Down UVF supporting Mid-Ulster and the PAF in rejecting the new brigade staff, but the change was generally welcomed by both loyalist politicians and the leaders of other paramilitary groups. The new leadership, which was largely the old brigade staff of the VPP era, was regarded as a more reasonable set of men, with whom business could be done.

The press statement was misleading in its suggestion that there was a formal democratic structure for electing and removing brigade staff. The UVF (and the UDA) was never a democracy in that sense. People 'emerged' as leaders because they took the initiative in organizing a group of men, and they held their positions so long as they had the active support (or fearful acquiescence) of their men.

You just knew when you had to go if you lost the confidence of your men. If your people no longer wanted you there, you just got the message and quit. That notion that you could never quit the UVF was nonsense. You could always quit. No man was ever shot out of brigade staff. When people started complaining you just knew whether you could ride out the storm or had to go. It was street psychology. You didn't need votes.

That speaker is undoubtedly right in his description of power as something amorphous and nebulous. One has it only so long as people continue to respect or fear you and it takes little for them to stop doing either.

Explaining Leadership Changes

Many journalistic accounts of the period try too hard to find consistent lines of explanation for changes in the leadership of the UVF. For a start, there was fairly continuous turnover as internment or court conviction took people out of circulation. Secondly, people were sacked for personal failings. The man who returned as chief of staff in the 1975 coup lost his job on both counts. He had made a great play of the need for the organization to shed its gangster image by controlling the 'homers' of its members, but was himself caught in the kidnapping and holding to ransom of a well-known Shankill Road publican. The west Belfast 'first battalion', the leader of which was also arrested in that affair, insisted that the imprisoned chief be sacked. Other people were removed for personal incompetence, suspicion of unreliability, or because they were on the losing end of a personal grudge. But even where there was open competition for positions (as occurred in the changes of 1974 and 1975), it is misleading to represent these, as they generally are portrayed, in terms of an enduring conflict between 'hawks' and 'doves'. Certainly there were (and still are) people in the UVF who wished to reduce the amount of ill-directed and random violence and increase the amount of community work and political action. One thoughtful activist said:

I've always tried to get the UVF to do more for their own people, the grass roots. I sometimes think that the people have suffered more from their own paramilitaries than from the other side. The nationalists have suffered more from the Provies than they have from the UDA and UVF and I suspect the same could be said for us. I have always tried to use my influence to point the organization away from violence.

The important point is that the speaker had nothing against violence *per se*; he merely questioned its usefulness. He admired the courage of those people who were prepared to kill and at times supported the military campaigns. He might be classed as a 'dove', but he could be extremely 'hawkish'. All the brigade staffs supported (albeit with differing degrees of enthusiasm) the political initiatives and higher profile of the 1974 UVF: 'Even the most bloody-minded and militant people liked to see Ken Gibson up there in his uniform speaking about this and that. Militants and politicos is all wrong.' Such a division may at times be appropriate in analysing the much larger and legal UDA, which had a significant trade union and community-action element in its leadership. One UDA brigadier told me: 'I always kept well clear of the military end of it. If you were in a room and people started talking about military things, then it was time to leave.' But almost all the UVF leadership were 'operators', and the disagreements only ever concerned the limits of the use of violence and its tactical value in this or that situation.

There was not more internal dispute between those people such as Gibson who wanted to use the UVF as a vehicle for the mobilization of a working-class loyalist political movement and those who wanted the organization to confine itself to using violence to combat the republican and nationalist threats to the continued existence of an Ulster state because flags of convenience allowed people like Lenny Murphy to continue to kill while the UVF maintained its public cease-fire posture. However, the blow-out of late 1975 left the Secretary of State little choice but to sign an order proscribing the UVF with effect from 4 October. The brief flirtation with legality was over. Some leaders saw value in returning to the underworld: '[the ban] was the best thing that could have happened to us. We were going to wrack and ruin. Too many cowboys were being allowed in and they were using our name to justify ordinary criminal acts. Underground we would find it easier to maintain discipline.'

An attempt had been made to acquire legitimacy through community action and the ballot box and it had failed. The theme will be further explored later, but in summarizing the mid-1970s for the UVF one can make the same point that was made in describing the aftermath of the UWC strike. Although many working-class Protestants were prepared, with varying degrees of willingness, to support the UVF in its role as avenger of IRA violence, few were happy to have those people as their political representatives. As we will see in the examination of the UDA's attempts to develop a coherent politics, Ulster Protestants had an implicit sense of a division of labour. Politicians did politics and para-militaries did muscle and there was little or no enthusiasm for a blurring of the boundaries. In failing to develop the VPP and related initiatives, and then being banned again, the UVF was forced back to its initial role.

The move towards greater political involvement and away from simple violence was undermined by the IRA. So long as the campaign of republican killing continued, there would always be strong pressure from less thoughtful members to retaliate. It was also not helped by the feud with the UDA. A large number of people (including some of those involved in attacks on the other organization) admitted that interparamilitary violence caused problems of credibility with its own people and, in the absence of status as a social or political force, the organization was pushed back to doing what it did best. Political maturation was also both encouraged and undermined by outsiders. In his accounts of the changes in brigade staff, McKittrick sees the hand of the Stormont and Westminster officials keen to wean the UVF off political murder; the arrest of east Antrim UVF men was seen as part of that plan. However, at the same time unionist politicians were doing their best to keep the UVF out of politics. Had the VPP been allowed to join the UUUC and Gibson been the agreed candidate, he would still not have displaced Fitt, but he might have done well enough to convince many Volunteers that the VPP should be supported.

There was also constant 'stirring' by the security forces, who used such black propaganda vehicles as the fictitious Ulster Citizens' Army to exacerbate the always considerable tensions within the UVF. One UCA leaflet produced in 1976 accused the UVF of the murder of more than forty loyalists and the attempted murders of eight more (including Vanguard leader Bill Craig, ex-Convention members Mrs Jean Coulter and Frank Millar sen.,

Grand Master of the Belfast Orange Order Thomas Passmore, and Fred Proctor).[29]

When in 1974 the papers carried a story, purportedly from a UVF source, claiming that their Coventry members were being instructed to carry arms, the official spokesman had to go to lengths to deny that the UVF was exporting violence to the British mainland. There was also a message phoned into the BBC which claimed that a UVF unit had tried to hijack a Belfast–Heathrow flight! On their own these irritants would have been of little consequence, but they were part of a continuing campaign to de-legitimate the UVF in the eyes of its constituency by stressing the erratic gangsterism of the organization.

To summarize, there were many obstacles to the development of a coherent and popular political line within the UVF. With that avenue closed off, the organization fell back on its original role: the use of violence to defend Ulster from republicanism.

The UVF in Quiet Times

In my conversations different people chose slightly different dates but most volunteered the observation that somewhere around 1977 changes in the political and security climates markedly reduced the popularity of the UVF. When the political violence continued to claim more than a hundred lives a year, it may seem curious to talk about relative peace, but one needs to bear in mind the contrast between the early and late 1970s. Although the IRA continues to the present day to be able to mount a successful campaign of assassination and economic disruption and had a notable success with the hunger strikes in 1981, there were a number of changes which collectively produced and represented increased stability.

First, there was a temporary end to ambitious political initiatives. Roy Mason, Secretary of State from September 1976 to May 1979, had a few rounds of talks with local leaders about possibilities for devolution but these came to nothing and he deliberately committed himself to eschewing political initiatives in favour of concentrating on law and order and economic regeneration. By the time James Prior's 'rolling-devolution' assembly and the Anglo-

[29] *Irish Times*, 15 Nov. 1976.

Irish accord were presented, the various changes to be described had already done enough to erode much Protestant support for paramilitary activity.

Security Policy

An important plank of Mason's law-and-order campaign was the increase in the proportion of the security forces that was locally recruited, or 'Ulsterization' (see Statistical Appendix). From its high point in 1972 of over 17,000 troops in the province, British army presence fell to 13,000 in 1979 and under 10,000 in 1984. The overall impact of the reduction was actually greater than that suggested by the numbers, in that troops were generally withdrawn from the greater Belfast area and concentrated on the border. The one area in which the army became more active was in under-cover operations, and Mason's standing in loyalist eyes was much enhanced by his introduction of SAS units into the province. One UVF man, then in the Maze, told me: '1977 was a watershed in loyalist violence because Roy Mason took the gloves off. You need to look at what point the security forces actually took over from the loyalist paramilitaries.'

An important part of security policy was the 'normalization' and 'criminalization' of policing. Although the trial of political cases by a judge sitting without a jury (the 'Diplock' courts, named after the judge who recommended the procedure) makes it clear that these are not normal crimes, the phasing out of internment and the 'special-category' status for political prisoners were part of a general attempt to present (and deal with) political violence as though it consisted simply of ordinary crimes. One element of that process has been the reduction in the amount of work done by the army or the UDR. It is now policy for all UDR patrols to be accompanied by a police officer (though it happens in only about 60 per cent of patrols). An ironic consequence of this has been to undo the initial recommendation of the Hunt report that the RUC, like other police forces, be unarmed. The reality of policing in Northern Ireland has meant that the withdrawal of the army has been accompanied by the increasing 'paramilitarization' of the RUC.

Although perceptions of the security forces in republican areas may have changed little, there was a major change in loyalist areas.

The army was now very rarely seen, and even the UDR was rarely active in 'safe areas'.

The RUC establishment was markedly increased. At the start of the Troubles there were just over 3,000 police officers. This had gone to 4,409 in 1972 but increased to over 7,000 in 1979 and 10,296 by 1984. That is, over the course of the Troubles, the police establishment had trebled. It is not only the relative *sizes* of the army and the RUC that have changed; there has also been a reversal of authority. After it all but collapsed in 1969, the RUC had been subordinate to the army. The Mason era, with the appointment of Kenneth Newman as Chief Constable, saw the restoration of 'police primacy'. The RUC was much expanded, better trained, and better equipped. Most importantly, the roles of the GOC and the Chief Constable were reversed and the Chief Constable was made overall director of operations.[30] The army was reduced to being 'in support' of the civil powers, and more and more of that 'in-support' role was given to the UDR, which had been formed to replace the B Specials. In 1972 it had 644 full-time and 8,117 part-time members; by 1979 it had been increased to a full-time complement of around 2,500 full-time and 5,150 part-time soldiers, an establishment that has since remained stable.

The impact of 'Ulsterization' and 'normalization' on Protestants was two-edged. On the one hand, more of the casualties of republican violence were local people and hence that support for paramilitarism which came out of personal experience of IRA violence was increased. On the other hand, the removal of the army from large parts of the province and the strengthening of the RUC were seen by many as proof that the worst was over and that responses to republican violence could be left to the police; hence overall support for private paramilitary initiatives was reduced. As one UVF 'lifer' suggested:

There was no need for us then. We weren't doing any fucking good; just getting in the way. I said we should grease our guns and put them under the floorboards and send a big cheque to the RUC benevolent fund and let them get on with it. Once they showed they was willing to do the business on the IRA, I couldn't see any point in us taking up police time.

[30] J. D. Brewer et al., *The Police, Public Order and the State* (London, 1988), ch. 3. For a good journalistic account of the RUC, see C. Ryder, *The RUC: A Force under Fire* (London, 1990).

Levels of Violence

How people come to feel threatened is a complex issue. Our responses to unrest are compiled in an unpredictable way from our own personal experiences, those of our family and friends, and from reactions to what we hear and read of what is going on. There is clearly no simple relationship between the amount of violence recorded and how unstable people perceive the situation to be. None the less, as background information to help us guess how people feel, the recorded incidence of various sorts of violent act is not a bad guide.

The peak year for Troubles-related deaths was 1972, when 467 people were killed. In the years from 1973 to 1976 the number varied between 250 and 297, but in 1977 only 112 people were killed and the annual figure remained around or under a hundred until 1982. Fatalities are one indicator of levels of violence; of all the 'results' of violence, they have the greatest impact on a small number of people. But if one is trying to describe the general climate or feel of a period, then other broader indicators are probably of more significance. As one can see from the details given in the Statistical Appendix, the number of shootings and bombings fell even more dramatically than the killings. In 1972 there were more than ten thousand recorded shootings and over a thousand explosions. By 1977 the number of shootings had fallen to around a thousand and bombings were only a third of that. Five years later there were only 547 recorded shooting incidents and 219 explosions. The violence was becoming more focused and concentrated.[31]

Even republican and nationalist critics of the loyalist para-militaries admit that much of their violence is a reaction to the campaigns of the IRA. Overall figures for shootings and fatalities include loyalist 'moves', of course, and it could be that the figures I have cited above show a marked decline, not because the IRA was slacking but because the UDA and UVF were, for other reasons, cutting back. I want to get the causal connections here as clear as possible. There were at least two reasons for the clear reduction in UDA and UVF violence. The first was the belief gradually spreading among loyalists that there was no longer the

---

[31] Sources of these data are given after the appropriate tables in the Statistical Appendix.

same pressing need for 'military' actions because the government was more resolute. The second was the decline in republican violence, which, as we can see from Figure A.1 in the Statistical Appendix, clearly precedes the drop in level of loyalist activity. Fewer loyalists thought violence necessary, and even those who remained committed to the armed struggle had lost some of the sense of urgency. The world was not about to end. There was more time to pick targets and plan jobs. A third and related reason for the decline in loyalist activity concerns the security forces in a more direct way: as well as improving its performance against PIRA (and perhaps because that success left it freer to concentrate on its 'second front'), the RUC was increasingly successful against the UDA and UVF. The long trial of the east Antrim UVF in 1976 was followed with notable successes against the UVF in north Belfast, in Ballysillan, and on the Shankill, where 1977 saw the arrest of the Moore–Bates gang (see Chapter 7). The UVF remained in business but with its horns temporarily drawn in.

Supergrass Trials

A major innovation of the 1980s was the 'supergrass' system. On 21 November 1981 Ardoyne IRA man Christopher Black was arrested. After two days of saying nothing, he talked, and made a large number of statements implicating himself and others in a long list of offences. He was granted immunity from prosecution. In the trial which began over a year later (and ran from December 1982 to August 1983) he gave evidence against thirty-eight accused and all but three of them were convicted.[32] Arrested around the same time as Black was Clifford McKeown, a Craigavon UVF man, who agreed to testify against more than twenty-five colleagues in return for immunity from prosecution for a number of serious charges, including murder. This was rather a false start, because McKeown changed his mind in July 1982 and refused to give evidence. However, the trial proceeded and eighteen men were convicted, mostly for quite minor offences. Although the police stuck to the letter of their agreement by not prosecuting him on the original charges, McKeown was convicted and sentenced to ten years for his part in an armed robbery.

[32] S. Greer, 'The Supergrass System', in A. Jennings (ed.), *Justice under Fire: The Abuse of Civil Liberties in Northern Ireland* (London, 1988), 73–103.

The supergrass trials were not entirely novel. Contrary to the myth of the case-solving detective so beloved of fiction, police work has always relied on 'information received'. Even where scientific evidence—for example of fingerprints and clothing fibres found on weapons—is vital in securing a conviction, usually some 'touting' is necessary to tell the police where to look for such evidence. What marked the Bennett, Allen, Gibson, and Crockard cases, however, was that the possibility of convictions rested almost entirely on the uncorroborated testimony of someone who was trading evidence for immunity from prosecution or a radical reduction of sentence.

That the RUC was willing to use what many legal experts regarded as a dubious legal procedure to secure convictions of UVF men should give the lie to the often-repeated claim that the state was soft on loyalist terrorists. The use of the uncorroborated testimony of Albert 'Ginger' Baker against his colleagues in the east Belfast UDA in early 1974 had failed to secure the desired convictions: Sir Robert Lowry, the Lord Chief Justice, decided that there were too many inconsistencies in Baker's evidence. But an informer had been successfully used against the east Antrim UVF men in 1976, when more than twenty people were imprisoned on the word of a former UVF man turned 'grass'.

Joseph Bennett

In December 1982 Joseph Bennett began his evidence against eighteen UVF men charged with seventy-two offences; many of them were brigade staff, very senior local commanders, or prominent officials of organizations reputed to have connections with the UVF. According to the story told in court, Bennett had joined the UVF in the west Belfast Orange Hall in March 1972. He was then living with his wife (who was dying of cancer) in the Coronation Park area of Dundonald. His first job for the organization was as an 'ATO', storing explosives, ammunition, and guns. He was raided and charged with possession of explosives, but while he was on remand his wife died, and he was given bail to attend her funeral. He absconded but did not go far; he lived in the Shankill Road area for eighteen months before being caught with guns and ammunition in March 1974 in a house in Mansfield Street.

He was sentenced to twelve years for possession. After three years in Magilligan prison camp, he was moved to the Maze, where he followed Gusty Spence as commander of compound 21. On his release in 1980 (with the by-then standard 50 per cent remission) he was offered a job by an east Belfast UVF man who ran a local pub and was invited by brigade staff to take over the running of the Sandy Row UVF.

In that capacity Bennett was supposedly involved in a large number of UVF crimes and in his evidence he gave details of these, in all cases minimizing his own part and maximizing that of the other men he named. Whether because he was actually a party to them or because he was in a position to pick up a lot of gossipy detail, he claimed knowledge of a number of shootings and bombings. He was also able to testify about the UVF's arms supply routes, implicating 'Nigger' Irvine in an arms-soliciting visit to European fascists and John Bingham in a trip to Toronto.

Although he seems to have been a proficient bomb-maker, Bennett was a womanizing thief who got in trouble with the UVF over money. He also stole £1,350 from the pub in east Belfast where he worked in March 1981. In that connection, he appeared at Belfast Magistrate's Court and was ordered to make restitution. According to his testimony, Bennett's failure to pay back money borrowed from the Shankill UVF led to a 'sentence of death', and he started to avoid the Shankill and mix with the UVF in Ballysillan in north Belfast, where he met John Bingham, then the commander in that area. In his evidence against Bingham he claimed to have seen him and others with an M60 heavy machine gun. A senior UVF man told me: 'That sentenced to death stuff is romantic crap. Mind, if I'd got my hand on the bugger I'd have killed him!'

Bennett was arrested in May 1982 after an armed robbery of a post office in Killinchy, Co. Down, in which the elderly postmistress, Miss McCann, was stabbed to death. He agreed to testify against his former colleagues in return for immunity from prosecution, money, and a new identity outside Northern Ireland.

Desmond Boal QC's trial defence was masterly and it took the form of attack. He was quick to point out the many ways in which Bennett had deliberately underplayed his own involvement in very serious crimes. His story about the post-office murder—that he had stood outside and only got involved when trying to break up a 'fight' between his accomplices and the old lady!—was feeble. Boal also listed all the other crimes in which Bennett had probably played an active part, which included very many of the UVF and RHC bombings of the period.[33] Among them was the murder of Jim 'Red Setter' Hanna on the Shankill in March 1974. According to Boal, Bennett believed Hanna had informed on him.

Despite admitting that his usefulness to the police 'would be measured in the number of men I put away',[34] and despite Mr Justice Murray finding that Bennett had lied in evidence about at least one matter, his uncorroborated evidence was enough for fourteen of the fifteen defendants to be convicted.

However, during the lengthy Bennett and Black trials, there was considerable adverse publicity, and even quite liberal jurists questioned the use of 'paid perjurers' (to the defendants) or 'converted terrorists' (to the RUC). By the end of 1984 senior Northern Ireland judges were having a change of heart. All the Bennett convictions were overturned on appeal. Lord Justice Lowry said it was 'probable in reality that some of the defendants are important members of the UVF' but that Bennett was not a reliable witness. Further, he decided against a retrial on the grounds that it would just give Bennett a chance to burnish his stories. However, only some of the convicted men were released. Others were remanded in custody to face new charges based on the testimonies of three more 'grasses': William 'Budgie' Allen, John Gibson, and Joseph Crockard.

William 'Budgie' Allen

Although the list of defendants contained fewer high status UVF men than the Bennett case, Allen's evidence allowed a large number—forty-seven people—to be charged for a total of 226 offences. Allen was himself of much lower rank than Bennett: a YCV on the fringes of the organization. As a preliminary to the trial he admitted fifty-two relatively minor terrorist charges and was sentenced to fourteen years. Among his offences were firing a shot from a passing car at people on the Falls Road; planning to murder a Cliftonville Road garage worker who was thought to be an H Block activist; planning to drive into the Markets area to

---

[33] *Newsletter*, 24 Feb. 1983.
[34] Greer, 'The Supergrass System', 86.

murder people at a hunger-strike bonfire protest (by the time they got there the fire was out and the crowd had gone); being part of a 'team' that picked up an errant UVF man for a knee-capping; and planning to murder a UDA man as part of a 1980 feud.[35]

In the second month of the trial the case collapsed when the judge rejected Allen's evidence as 'totally unreliable' and directed that twenty of the defendants be found not guilty. Four days later another sixteen men were released. Six defendants who either pleaded guilty or, according to the police, made statements of admission, were convicted for a variety of offences including murder. A year later, Allen was given a royal prerogative pardon by Tom King, the Secretary of State.[36] One of the highest ranking defendants, Frenchie Marchant, announced that he forgave Allen for the time he spent on remand, but the UVF as an organization was less forgiving and announced that Allen would be killed if his English hideout was ever discovered.

John Gibson

At the same time as the Allen case was proceeding, a number of senior UVF men were on trial in two other 'grass' cases. In October 1983 John Gibson, another Belfast UVF man, was arrested and charged with two murders, one the killing of John Gerard O'Neill in September the previous year. Nineteen men were charged on his evidence, which went back to events of the early 1970s. One of them, Fred Otley, was charged with conspiring with Gibson to murder UDA man Sammy Doyle. Another, a leading figure on the social and political wing of the UVF, was charged with being present at firearms lectures in 1972. He was released on £400 bail after testimonials from DUP MP Peter Robinson, Ulster Unionist MP Harold McCusker, and John Carson. When charged, one of the accused said: 'Hans Christian Anderson will never be dead while John Gibson is alive.'

Presumably because Bennett's immunity had both provoked public outcry and undermined his credibility as a witness, Gibson was first charged, convicted, and sentenced to life for 143 terrorist offences, which included four murders.[37] This at least meant that

---

[35] *Newsletter*, 9 Aug. 1984.
[36] *Belfast Telegraph*, 19 June 1985.
[37] *Guardian*, 15 Nov. 1984.

the RUC had one 'result' when Gibson retracted his evidence and the cases against the other accused had to be dropped.

James Crockard

Like Allen and Gibson, Newtownabbey UVF man James Crockard began by pleading guilty to a large number of terrorist offences and being sentenced. He was given 'life' and a further six-teen years for two murders, three attempted murders, and five conspiracy-to-murder charges. His promised evidence led to twenty-nine people being charged with ninety-two charges; one of those charged was a man who had just been released after the collapse of the Allen case!

Crockard had joined UVF in 1973. Although not sworn in until August 1974, he had scouted the Club Bar in south Belfast for a bomb attack in 1974. One of his other offences was the use of a home-made machine gun on a bus queue in the Ardoyne area; it fired only three shots before jamming. He also helped plant two bombs in Atlantic Avenue at Easter 1976 and robbed the Belfast Gasworks and the Maple Leaf Club in east Belfast.[38]

As in the Bennett case, skilful cross-examination by Desmond Boal QC undermined Crockard's testimony, and on 21 February Mr Justice McDermott decided that, although some of Crockard's evidence was 'probably reliable ... the burden of proof upon the Crown in any criminal case is a heavy one and my conclusion is that in this case Crockard's evidence has not measured up to that high standard'.[39] The cases against those men who had admitted nothing were dismissed. Unfortunately for them, eight had admit-ted their guilt and they received a variety of lengthy sentences.

The supergrass system failed to produce a large number of sound convictions, but, if the purpose was to keep a large number of active terrorists off the streets, it was a resounding success. Not only did some of the cases take a very long time to come to trial, but some people against whom a case failed were then rearrested on the supposed word of another supergrass. By the time the final set of charges against him were dismissed, one man had spent four-and-a-half years on remand—the amount of time he would have served if he had been convicted and sentenced to nine years.

[38] *Belfast Telegraph*, 21 Jan. 1985.
[39] Ibid. 21 Feb. 1985.

It is very difficult to judge the impact of the trials on the UVF. They were certainly a major distraction for the organization. Well over a hundred men were in prison for an average of two years and that imposed considerable financial strains on the organization. Money and time were spent in court which could have been spent elsewhere. However, the command structure was not seriously disrupted. The imprisoned leaders were replaced by close colleagues who were happy to relinquish their posts when the former brigade staff were released. Although there were fewer operations than in earlier years, the UVF continued to raise money and arrange assassinations.

Military Actions

Paramilitary violence is always less well directed than its planners and apologists wish. A recurrent theme of UVF (and UDA) press statements is apology for 'mistakes' of the past and the promise of greater selectivity in the future. However disingenuous such apologies might be, they do have the value of honestly describing the policy of the past. As a summary of how the UVF saw itself, we can do worse than return to one of its own lengthy statements of April 1974:

We believed, rightly or wrongly, that the only effective way to beat the terror machine was to employ greater terrorism against its operatives. . . . By bombing the heart of Provisional enclaves we attempted to terrorise the nationalist community into demanding that the Provisionals either cease their campaign or move out of the ghetto area. By bombing business premises and other such properties which we had reason to believe were terrorist meeting places or sources of revenue, we believed we could force the Provisionals out of business or at least cause a drastic reduction in their operational activity. By attempting to eliminate Provisional activists and 'backroom boys' . . . we hoped to crack their morale and destroy their chain of command.[40]

The article went on to say that the brigade staff had now formulated a distinction between clearly defined acts of resistance and indiscriminate acts of terrorism and that it would be concentrating on the former. But the record of violence since 1977 shows little improvement on the criticized previous policy. There has been one

[40] *Combat*, Apr. 1974.

very significant change: the virtual disappearance of the bomb. There have been problems with the supply of explosives and bomb-makers, but there was also a deliberate change of policy towards a more contained and better directed form of violence.

Despite the end of pub bombing, only a minority of UVF murders could be described as falling within their own terms of reference, if narrowly interpreted. To take those of 1989, in that year UVF men killed 26-year-old Ian Catney in Smithfield Market in Belfast. Although the INLA denied he was a member, two years earlier he had been attacked in the INLA–IPLO feud and his cousin was a spokesman for the Irish Republican Socialist Party (IRSP). In February Anthony Fusco, with no known republican connections, was killed in the same area. Just over a week later, Sinn Fein councillor John Joseph Davey of Magherafelt was murdered by the UVF. The two victims in March were a 63-year-old Catholic David Branniff, shot at home in north Belfast, and Jim McCartney, who was shot while standing outside a Catholic pub in west Belfast. Neither is known or plausibly supposed to have had IRA or republican involvement, although Branniff's son had been involved with the PIRA and had been shot by that organization as an informer. In May a Catholic joiner, Malachy Trainor, was shot at work on the loyalist Rathcoole estate. The UVF claimed he was in the South Down IRA, but the RUC denied any such connection. In September Patrick McKenna was shot while walking along a road in west Belfast. The UVF claimed he was a well-known IRA man. Local people denied any such connection.

In December a PAF team murdered Liam Ryan and a bystander at the Battery Bar in Ardboe, where Ryan worked as manager. He had been charged in the United States with smuggling arms for the IRA. Although the IRA denied he was still active, more than a year later *Republican News* published a photograph of an IRA honour party firing a salute over the grave of 'Volunteer' Ryan.[41]

Clearly, given what was said earlier about the various conflicting reasons all players have for hiding the truth, one cannot do more than speculate, but, of nine victims, one was a bystander. Of the remaining eight, two—Davey and Ryan—were legitimate

[41] *Republican News*, 14 Feb. 1991, p. 2.

targets in the UVF's own terms. A third and fourth—Catney and Branniff—had tenuous family connections with armed republicanism. My guess, and it is no more than that, is that the other four had no such connections.

One or two attempted murders, had they succeeded, would have tilted the balance further in the direction of legitimate targets. On 10 November UVF men attacked Sinn Fein councillor Brendan Curran at his father's home near Lurgan.

Note that this is not an exercise in moral arithmetic but an attempt to assess the effectiveness of the UVF's stated policy, and the general conclusion must be that, while the considerable reduction in killings from the early 1970s has seen a proportionate increase in the directedness of political violence, the outcome is still some way from the image which the UVF presents of itself.

Cultural Activities

In passing I have already referred to a major difference between the bases for legitimation for republican and loyalist paramilitaries. That Protestants and Catholics have been in conflict since the time of settlement means that both sides have traditions which justify the use of force for political goals. While republicans have maintained the 'physical-force' tradition, for loyalists it has been eroded because the state and its security forces have taken over from Protestant militias. This has meant far less confidence on the loyalist side in the correctness of paramilitarism. The UDA and UVF have to compete with the government and its far superior access to the sorts of symbols which can be used to legitimate the use of violence.

Many loyalists have been aware of the problem of legitimation and the 1980s have been a period of 'cultural production' as the loyalist paramilitaries and those elements of Orangeism that tacitly support them have set about trying to organize and publicize those symbols of their tradition that justify their actions. Interestingly, the UDA and UVF have gone in quite different directions in the search for symbols of tradition. The UDA's use of Ulster's Cruithin pre-history will be discussed in Chapter 9. The UVF has turned to a much closer period of Ulster's history and has put considerable effort into researching and publicizing Ulster's contribution to the British effort in the First World War. Most issues of *Combat* have at least one article about the original UVF and the 36th (Ulster) Division.

Politics and Community Work

The ambition of the VPP has not been repeated, but Hugh Smyth has continued to represent the Shankill on Belfast City Council since 1972. Like Johnny McQuade, Hughie Smyth is elected because of his constituency work and his personal ties with his electorate and not because he is associated with the fringes of the UVF. In 1979 his supporters constituted themselves into the Progressive Unionist Party (PUP) but it failed to export itself to other areas of the province. In 1984 Gusty Spence was released and for a while worked for the Progressive Unionist Party before setting up the government-supported Shankill Activity Centre as a site for leisure and training activities for unemployed young people. To put these sort of activities in context, they are the kinds of things that people like Smyth and Spence would have been doing had there been no Troubles and no paramilitarism on the Shankill. It is hard to argue that the UVF has been pioneering or innovatory in developing radical forms of social organization.

Conclusion

The Standard Bar UVF of Spence and McClelland was a small radical vanguard which grew rapidly in the chaos and crisis of the period from 1970 to 1974. It saw itself as a tight military organization and neither sought nor achieved the size or public presence of the UDA. Although the VPP was an electoral disaster, an enduring political presence on the Shankill was established and the UVF continues to attract the support of a small section of the urban working class. The UVF is similar to the UDA in being strongest in Belfast, but it has more support in country areas, where the name and tradition of the 1912 UVF remain more evocative. The main outlet for Ulster patriotism in rural areas is now the UDR, but the very small number of men who feel that more is needed are more likely to join the UVF than the UDA. Although the UVF's assassination campaign has been no better directed than that of the UDA, it has remained relatively free of the taint of racketeering.

Efforts to develop a cultural and social side to the movement have been moderately successful and, despite strenuous efforts to portray them as unprincipled gangsters, the UVF has managed to develop its symbolic use of the traditions of the original UVF. Although much smaller, the UVF's ability to draw on the historical resonances of its name suggests that it will endure even if the UDA disappears.

There is not much that the RUC and PIRA agree about, but both share the view that UVF men are gangsters, motivated primarily by a lust for power and a desire for personal gain. Doubtless there are some Volunteers so motivated, but my impression is that many (especially in the leadership) would be only too happy to retire. They believe the UVF is needed so long as PIRA continues to use force to change the constitutional position of Northern Ireland. As 'defenders of the Protestant people', the UVF has to compete with the security forces, and its ability to attract members, funds, and public support depends to a large extent on Protestant perceptions of their own security. The success of the security forces in reducing the overall level of violence and sense of instability has removed a lot of the perceived need for the UVF. As one recently released UVF 'lifer' put it:

Why should loyalist paramilitaries be operating now? The original rationale was to kill extreme republicans. The security forces are now prepared to use total force and to shoot to kill so what need is there for the organizations? I think they should be stood down and devote themselves to training every man and woman in Northern Ireland to defend themselves.

6
Friends and Relations

THERE are three things that foreign friends can usefully provide for a paramilitary organization: political pressure, money, and weapons. Republican terror groups have more of all three than their loyalist counterparts.

There is no doubt that the British government's actions in Northern Ireland—from the pressure for change on Terence O'Neill to the Anglo-Irish accord—have been heavily influenced by international pressure, especially that from the powerful Irish lobby in the United States. The civil-rights slogan 'One Man—One Vote' was aimed not at domestic audiences but at London, Paris, and Washington, and it was successful in mobilizing international support for the movement. The move to explicit nationalism also had its external dimension, with the IRA and sympathizers looking for, and finding, international support for its campaign for 'national self-determination'. Even this late in the twentieth century, nationalism remains a popular cause in most parts of the globe and the very high number of countries which have only recently become independent nation-states, often after protracted wars, makes it relatively easy to market the integrity of the 'national liberation struggle'. The IRA became very skilled at selective presentation of its own agenda. To a third world or eastern European audience, it would appear as a left-wing anti-imperialist war; to a US audience, likely to be frightened off by any hint of 'communism', it appeared as a conservative bourgeois nationalist movement.

Some of the IRA's international support is, and has been, extremely cynical—the 'mine enemies' enemy is my friend' school of international relations. Libya's Gadaffi may be a genuine believer in armed struggles for national liberation, but it is hard to believe that the generals of East Germany's secret police wanted anything other than to destabilize the British state.

Open support for the IRA is rare and is characteristic only of countries such as Libya, whose relations with Britain have long been close to war. Especially since the IRA began its attacks on 'soft' British army personnel in western Europe, most European countries have been active supporters of the Westminster government's policy on terrorism. However, the US case is different. While the official spokesmen of US governments have consistently supported Britain, there has often been niggling tolerance for the IRA at slightly lower levels of power, not open support but irritating ambivalence. Thus in 1979 the sale of handguns to the RUC could be blocked because some Congressmen argued that the police in Ulster oppressed the Irish people (this while the same country happily supplied such unsavoury Latin American dictatorships as that of General Manuel Noriega in Panama!), or a self-confessed IRA killer could remain in the United States because ways were found of evading and stalling extradition orders.

While the US government is no friend of the IRA—and the FBI has been diligent and successful in monitoring and destroying arms-buying attempts—there is a powerful lobby of Irish Americans, concentrated around the Boston area, which does openly support the IRA and which raises large amounts of money for it. In the late 1980s Noraid's contribution to the IRA's £4 million budget was only around 4 per cent. Local schemes such as tax exemption fraud, cross-border smuggling, and running drinking clubs are now the main sources of money, but the Yankee dollar was very important in the early days. Adams estimates that in the early 1970s Noraid raised about 50 per cent of the IRA's funds.

International contacts have also been good to the IRA for arms-purchasing. AK47 rifles, RPG-7 rocket launchers, and Semtex explosive are not readily available in Britain. They are fairly easily available to anyone who has the support of an east European government, an Arab state, or enough money to buy them on the extensive international 'terrorism and small civil wars' market.

The IRA is internationally popular, well funded, and well munitioned. In contrast, loyalist paramilitaries have always been short of friends outside Ulster and almost completely shunned outside Britain. Such links as the UDA and UVF have had will now be explored.

Fascists and Opportunists

An unintended consequence of the IRA's success in portraying itself as an anti-imperialist liberation movement—that is, as left wing—is the perception of the UDA and UVF as 'right wing', and the curious suitors such a depiction has attracted. Such racist and fascist movements as the National Party and the National Front (NF) have failed miserably in British domestic politics and have quite naturally looked for opportunities to attach themselves to causes slightly more popular than their primary concerns. The integrity of the United Kingdom is one such issue, and many right-wing groups have tried to win active support from the loyalist paramilitaries.

Links between loyalist and neo-Nazi movements are slight and depend quite literally on two or three individuals, but this has not stopped journalists fearlessly pursuing the truth and then burying it beneath hyperbole. The following is an example:

The links between the UDA and NF were even stronger [than those with the UVF]: NF/UDA involvement has been shown in a number of court cases, e.g. when two men were gaoled in Preston in 1975, nine gaoled in Lancashire in 1974, three convicted in Winchester in 1974, all on military-type charges.[1]

At best the story concerns events one remove from the case it wishes to make. It is also misleading. It does not show links between the NF and the UDA, but between the NF and British supporters of the UDA, which is a very different thing. It also exaggerates badly. The nine UDA men convicted at Lancaster Crown Court were found guilty of drilling and possessing a very few firearms. There was nothing in the court record to suggest that the men were NF activists. If the Preston case in 1975 is the trial of two men from Belfast—Wylie and Kinner—and three Liverpool Orangemen on explosives smuggling, there is no evidence that any of the men was active in the NF. The three men convicted at Winchester of involvement in an arms supply-line from Canada to Belfast through Portsmouth were John Griffiths of Leeds, John Gadd of Liverpool, and Roy Rogers-Forbes of Headingley. Nothing is known of Griffiths's politics. Gadd was a member of the NF and Rogers-Forbes was a member of the Monday Club, a fringe group on the right wing of the Tory party. Taken together this is not impressive evidence of NF–UDA links and is a long way short of the active partnership implied by the phrase 'NF/UDA involvement'.

[1] M. Maguire, 'The Loyalists and the Neo-Nazi Connection', *Hibernia*, 31 July 1980, p. 10.

Stephen Brady is cited frequently in such stories because he is one of the very few people who come even close to making the case for fascist and racist influence on loyalism. Brady, reputedly a Belfast-born Catholic, claims to have been a follower of Ian Paisley before he joined the UVF. According to one biography, 'Brady soon left Belfast for Britain where he joined the League of St George'.[2] Given the unlikelihood of a Catholic being in the UVF, where even marriage to a Catholic can cause colleagues to doubt one's steadfastness in the cause, I am not surprised he left Belfast. However, the membership claim is made only by Brady himself and is likely to be spurious; there is no evidence that he was ever active in the UVF. Brady became involved with a veritable spaghetti of European fascist groups and wrote a long letter to Andy Tyrie suggesting ways in which the UDA could develop such contacts. Note who approached whom. Tyrie did nothing more about the suggestion than two years later paying Brady's fare to Belfast to talk to him.

Stretching the point even further, Johnson offers as startling evidence the fact that David Kerr, local organizer of the NF in Belfast in the 1980s, was once election agent for Nelson McCausland, an independent unionist in north Belfast with no known ties to loyalist paramilitaries!

The best-documented fascist connections have been with the UVF. I have already questioned the extent to which *Combat* editorials in the mid-1970s represented anyone other than their author, but 'Richard Cameron' was sometimes to be found saying positive things about the NF. Indeed, his interest may explain why the first UVF political organization was called the Ulster Loyalist Front, a name which had no traditional Protestant resonances.

In 1980 Ed. Moloney reported that the UVF had been visited by a number of members of Column 88 (an extremely small British Nazi group) and had given them 'arms training'.[3] According to Joe Bennett's 'supergrass' testimony, he and Jackie 'Nigger' Irvine attended a neo-Nazi convention in Belgium in 1980. The intention was to buy weapons and chemicals for bomb-making, but the Nazis insisted as part of the deal that the UVF attack Jewish

[2] C. Johnson, 'The National Front and the Ulster Connection', *Fortnight*, 7 July 1986, pp. 7–8.

[3] E. Moloney, 'British Nazi Group Links up with UVF/Tara', *Hibernia*, 21 Feb. 1980, p. 8.

targets in Belfast. The UVF men made their excuses and left empty-handed. Nigger is reputed to have told the neo-Nazis to 'fuck off'.[4]

To summarize, the links between Ulster loyalism and British and European extreme right-wing groups are (*a*) very slight, (*b*) usually initiated by the racist right, and (*c*) fail to endure. Such ethnocentric tendencies as loyalists have are overridden by the British army's history of fighting Nazis and the fact that most European right-wing groups are distinctly Catholic. Very few members of the UDA and UVF will have fought in the Second World War but many are ex-servicemen of one sort or another. Both organizations (and loyalism generally) draw on the traditions of the British army and British Legion. So long as the language and the symbolism of extreme right-wing movements evoke Hitler, the Nazis, and the Third Reich, they will alienate those loyalists who claim descent from the UVF which fought against the Germans in the Battle of the Somme.

Let us put 'fascist influence' in perspective. In September 1987 local NF leader David Kerr stood in a by-election for the Newtownabbey District Council. He polled twenty-seven votes in an area that has regularly returned candidates with loyalist paramilitary associations. In early 1990 he announced that the Belfast NF office was shutting up shop.

True Believers: Scotland

One of the few places outside the province where there is considerable support for Ulster loyalism is Scotland, which is no surprise given the close historical ties between the two countries. Since pre-history, migration between Ulster and Scotland has been common. The Scoti from Ulster settled Argyll and became the Scots. The Scots returned during the Plantations and became Ulstermen. In the mid-seventeenth century there were some 70,000 Scots in a total Ulster population of only 250,000.[5] In the nineteenth century, Ulstermen, Protestant and Catholic, sailed to

---

[4] To present as complete a picture as possible, I should add that David Seawright, brother of George, was involved in both the UVF and NF in Scotland in the early 1980s, but he was not very important in either.

[5] W. Macafee and V. Morgan, 'Population in Ulster, 1660–1760', in P. Roebuck (ed.), *Plantation to Partition* (Belfast, 1981), 47.

Scotland in search of economic opportunity and by 1840 about 10 per cent of the population of Scotland were 'Irish' or of recent Irish descent.[6]

In a country that was not only minimally Protestant but also strongly Presbyterian, the arrival of such large numbers of Roman Catholics provoked considerable anti-Catholicism. The Orange Order had no impact on the highlands, where there were evangelical Protestants but few Catholics, but it spread rapidly through the industrializing lowlands of Scotland, where it offered an expression for anti-Catholicism and a fraternal organization in which men who lived hard and unrewarding lives, often new to the impersonality of the town and the factory, could develop a sense of fellowship, self-confidence, and self-worth. Like many fraternities, the Order allowed a form of 'ethnic closure' to be practised. In certain areas and occupations, you had to be in the Orange to work. The Irish immigrants were poor, ill-educated strangers to the disciplines of industrial life who entered the labour market at the bottom. The Orange Order was one expression of the relative advantages of the native Scots. Irish Catholics turned in on themselves, forming ghettos separated from their hosts by class, religion, and culture.

The Home-Rule Crises

The first Home-Rule crisis of the 1880s had considerable impact on the political life of western Scotland, as it had on Liverpool and Lancashire. Many of the Irish Scots became active in Irish political organizations; some were actually elected to Westminster as home rulers by constituencies in Ireland.[7] However, for reasons we need not explore, the same quarrels in the second decade of this century had far less impact. When Sir Edward Carson spoke in Glasgow, only 8,000 people turned out; Liverpool managed a crowd of over 150,000 at 7.00 o'clock on a Sunday morning.[8] Although the Church of Scotland's Glasgow Presbytery announced solidarity with its sister Presbyterian Church in Ireland, it was left to the Revd James Brisby (an Ulster *émigré* who ran an

---

[6] S. Bruce, *No Pope of Rome: Militant Protestantism in Modern Scotland* (Edinburgh, 1985), 26–7.

[7] T. Gallagher, *Glasgow: The Uneasy Peace* (Manchester, 1987), 42–84.

[8] Ibid. 72.

independent evangelical ministry in Bridgeton) to provide clerical legitimation for the Scottish branches of the UVF.

The Scottish UVF units were organized as 'athletic clubs' attached to Orange Lodges. There were seven in all, claiming one thousand trained men and as many again in training. At a rally in the centre of Glasgow on 28 March 1914 between four and five hundred Volunteers were presented with colours and heard the Marquis of Graham, in the course of a rousing denunciation of 'some brutes in parliament' who would put Ulster out of the Union, announce confidently:

Not only were there thousands of men in Ulster but there were thousands of men outside Ulster who would have nothing whatever to do with that obnoxious thing called Home Rule . . . When they in Scotland remembered what their own country had passed through for the sake of religious freedom their hearts warmed to those Ulstermen. What were these Volunteers for? They were out to back up the Ulstermen in their fight. They were men of the right stuff.[9]

The onset of the First World War turned attention away from Ireland, but the opportunism of the 1916 Easter rising in Dublin brought a minor revival of anti-Irish sentiment, ably expressed by Andrew Amos, the disillusioned Border radical in John Buchan's novel *Mr Standfast*, whose description of Ulster perfectly captures the grudging sense of Presbyterian common identity.

Glasgow's stinkin' nowadays with two things, money and Irish. I mind the day when I followed Mr Gladstone's Home Rule policy, and used to threep about the noble, generous, warm-hearted sister nation held in a foreign bondage. My Goad! I'm not speakin' about Ulster, which is a dour, ill-natured den, but our own folk all the same. But the men that will not do a hand's turn to help the war and take the chance of our necessities to set up a bawbee rebellion are hateful to Goad and man.[10]

The aftermath of 1916 also brought an increase in 'Irish' political activity, with a large number of Sinn Fein branches being founded and a lot of money being raised for the nationalist cause. But the partition of Ireland and the consolidation of the Free State and Northern Ireland governments allowed the Irish question to

---

[9] S. Bruce, 'The Ulster Connection', in G. Walker and T. Gallagher (eds.), *Sermons and Battle Hymns: Protestant Popular Culture in Modern Scotland* (Edinburgh, 1991), 231–55.

[10] J. Buchan, *Mr Standfast* (London, 1988), 64.

slide again from the front pages. The (as it turned out temporary) solution to the Ulster problem meant that, when relationships between Protestants and Catholics in Scotland again became fraught (as they did in the Depression), there was no amplifying resonance from the simultaneous instability in Ulster, which attracted little attention in Britain. Although there were briefly successful anti-Catholic parties in Glasgow and Edinburgh in the early 1930s, Protestant Action and the Scottish Protestant League petered out after discovering the hard truth that the fundamental conditions for enduring sectarianism were rapidly disappearing from Scotland. There is not space here to explain why sectarianism in Scotland and in Ulster followed such different careers,[11] but the extent to which they have diverged can be seen in the assimilation of the Hiberno-Scots.

In one of its last displays of hostility to the 'Irish' (which by now meant the Scottish grandchildren of the Irish), the Church of Scotland General Assembly in 1923 heard a report entitled *The Menace of the Irish Race to our Scottish Nationality*. The authors had no complaint about 'the presence of an Orange population in Scotland. They are of the same race as ourselves and of the same Faith, and are readily assimilated to the Scottish race.' But Irish Catholics

cannot be assimilated and absorbed into the Scottish race. They remain a people by themselves, segregated by reasons of their race, their customs, their traditions, and, above all, by their loyalty to their Church, and are gradually and inevitably dividing Scotland racially, socially and ecclesiastically.[12]

It was not actually the case that the newcomers could not be absorbed. Race turned out to be a far less enduring property than was thought in the 1920s. Many Irish 'customs' were those of socio-economic circumstance; as the Irish got richer they moved out of their ghettos and into the mainstream. For example, despite the Catholic Church's position on contraception, the Catholic birth rate declined to the average.[13] Which left only

---

[11] See Bruce, *No Pope of Rome*, and 'Sectarianism in Scotland: A Contemporary Assessment and an Explanation', in D. McCrone and A. Brown (eds.), *Scottish Government Yearbook 1988* (Edinburgh, 1988), 150–66.

[12] J. Handley, *The Irish in Modern Scotland* (Cork, 1964), 358.

[13] S. Kendrick, F. Bechofer, and D. McCrone, 'Recent Trends in Fertility

loyalty to their Church, and even that was negotiable. An increasing number of middle-class Catholic parents sent their children to state schools, and the rate of 'lapsing' from the Church was high: one estimate suggests that 16 per cent of the total population of Scots Catholics 'fell away' between 1951 and 1976.[14] With a very high rate of intermarriage, sectarian conflict and ethnic discrimination became difficult to sustain and gradually the numbers who wanted to maintain it declined.

The Troubles

The Troubles have polarized Scottish Protestantism. The upper classes and religious and political leaders have become more determinedly ecumenical and hostile to Orangeism. Ulster's problems are taken as a sign of what happens if you encourage sectarianism. At the other extreme, a very small number of Scots, often those with family ties to Ulster, have become active in illegal actions to support 'their people'.

Initially the Orange Order was militant. In 1971 Scottish Grand Secretary John Adam toured Orange Halls and enrolled ex-servicemen and men with National Service or TA experience who were willing to go to Ulster to fight. Reports vary of the numbers who signed up, but it was common for west coast lodges to produce fifteen, twenty, and twenty-five volunteers. If repeated throughout the Order, this would have meant some three thousand volunteers. Those I have talked to insist that they were in earnest and that it was only because the UVF said that it did not yet need them (the UDA had not yet emerged as a coherent force) that they did not go. But already there was a division between the Orange leadership and some of the rank and file. The latter thought they were being asked to ready themselves to fight alongside the UVF. The leadership believed they were compiling a register of people willing to aid the 'constitutional authority'.

There was a considerable increase in the number of Orangemen crossing to Ulster for the Twelfth of July marches. In 1970 the chartered MV *Manxman* took over a thousand Scots Orangemen from Ardrossan to Belfast. Two years later the *Scottish*

Differentials in Scotland', in H. Jones (ed.), *Population Change in Contemporary Scotland* (Norwich, 1984), 33–52.

[14] Bruce, *No Pope of Rome*, 222.

Daily Express headlined its Twelfth issue: 'Scots in Belfast Front-line: Ten thousand Scots Orangemen flooded into Belfast yesterday to join in the flag celebrations'. In a militant rejection of appeals for the demonstrations to be called off, Scottish Grand Master Thomas Orr said before sailing: 'We will march on Wednesday . . . no matter what happens. If it does erupt into civil war then I'm sure that many Scots will want to remain.'[15] In an emotional speech at the Finaghy field, Orr echoed the Marquis of Graham in repeating his assertion of support: 'We shall support you in any way and in every way we possibly can . . . I assure you, friends, our offer of help is no empty promise.'[16]

That help took a number of forms. Partly to counter the propaganda value of Catholic families being evacuated to the Republic, the Order organized some very small-scale 'evacuations' of Ulster Protestants. During the 1974 strike, the Order sent food to Belfast. A number of west coast lodges offered a social service of 'rest and recreation' for loyalists from particularly troubled areas. The murder of four Orangemen in Tullyvallen Orange Hall in Newtownhamilton, South Armagh, in September 1975 produced another brief bout of enthusiasm for aiding Ulster Protestants. There was excited talk about evacuating the Protestants of South Armagh, and one district lodge bankrupted itself buying camp beds and other emergency supplies for such an evacuation. The Scottish Grand Lodge sent to Belfast a delegation which had talks with loyalist politicians and paramilitaries.[17] The Glasgow County Grand Lodge established an Ulster Relief Fund (which still exists); it paid for some Protestants to be brought to Scotland for holidays but did little more (it is maintained now in case civil war breaks out in Ulster and mass relief is needed).

But, as the conflict went on, and as more became known about the activities of loyalist paramilitaries, the Order leadership worked to distance itself from the UDA and UVF. In the autumn of 1976 Roddy MacDonald—UDA boss in Scotland—declared in a television interview that he would be happy to buy arms and ship them to Ulster. Leading Lodge officials tried to expel MacDonald, but the three hundred delegates to a special disciplinary hearing of

---

[15] *Scottish Daily Express*, 11 July 1972.
[16] Ibid. 13 July 1972.
[17] *Irish Times*, 9 Dec. 1975.

Grand Lodge refused to agree that he had brought the Order into disrepute. Clearly their sympathy for what MacDonald was doing persuaded them to 'believe' his claim to have been manipulated and misrepresented by the media. Faced with considerable public pressure to dissociate themselves from the UDA, the five most senior Orange officials (including the Grand Master who had promised to do 'anything' to help Ulster Protestants) threatened to resign unless the annual general meeting a week later supported a motion 'which utterly rejected all support, be it active or tacit, of terrorist organizations, whose actions contravene the law of the land'. Grand Lodge supported the motion overwhelmingly.

MacDonald refused to do the honourable thing and resign, and his membership of the Order again became a public issue when he led a party of Scots to Belfast to help the UDA in the 1977 loyalist strike.

The UDA and UVF in Scotland

To understand the actions of some Scots, one has to remember the violence of 1972—over ten thousand shootings and a thousand explosions—and the apparent willingness of the British government to dismantle Northern Ireland and negotiate with the IRA. For working-class Protestants in Paisley and Renfrew, with family and close friends in Belfast, the response was a strong desire 'to fuckin well do something!' 'It was a disgrace the battering the Prods were taking over there. And what was our lot doing about it? Fuck all! Giving them tinned food was nae bloody use. The IRA was using guns and bombs. Were our people supposed to throw fuckin Spam at 'em?'

Initially the Scottish supporters did not themselves do much other than meet a lot and raise some money. When only unsuccessful operations become known to the police and reported in the papers, one can only guess at the flow of weapons from Scotland. My guess is that small quantities of arms, perhaps thirty or forty guns a year, trickled in the first few years. But many of these were old and of poor quality. The main purchase of one UVF cell, which led to them all being imprisoned, was of a fifty-year-old rusted-up revolver which had been found on the beach at Dysart.

The only time a Scottish group is known to have got a large

consignment of arms—when a young gunshop assistant murdered his manager and sold some seventeen rifles and handguns to Roddy MacDonald—they never made it to Belfast. Instead they were transported ineptly around Scotland, sometimes by couriers who had to be coerced, before coming to lie in a damp cellar where they stayed for sixteen months during which anyone who had touched them was arrested. In all some thirty men were convicted for their part in a series of crimes which were of no benefit at all to the UDA in Ulster.

What was of more use was the steady trickle of mining gelignite. Without the support of Semtex suppliers in Czechoslovakia and Libya or quarriers in Eire, this was the loyalists' best source of explosives. The typical story was of a UDA or UVF cell coming across a miner who either volunteered or was 'persuaded' to steal four or five sticks at a time from the coal face. This would be accumulated and shipped in a variety of ways to Belfast. In 1973 twenty sticks of gelignite were found in the cistern of a toilet at Stranraer station, presumably waiting to be taken on to the Larne ferry. The same year an anonymous tip-off lead the police to a house in Drongan, Ayrshire, where they found fifty sticks of mining gelignite. Whether it is a sign of increasing loyalist efficiency in collecting explosives or police efficiency in detecting them is not clear, but five years later the police intercepted a lorry on the M1 heading north to Stranraer and found 263 sticks of gelignite and 275 lb. of sodium chlorate, the basis for home-made explosives. Again, that the gelignite was of four different kinds shows the small quantities in which it was initially acquired.

Wallies and Grasses

Generally speaking the greater the public support for an activity, the larger the numbers involved, the more selective an organization can be (if it wants to be), and the higher the degree of commitment it gets from its members. The lack of Scottish support for paramilitary activity can be seen in the weakness of many UDA and UVF cells. Around a nucleus of two or three highly committed men there was an outer ring of associates who felt some sympathy for the plight of Ulster Protestants and were attracted by the glamour of being in a 'team' but who had little depth of commitment. The shift from fund-raising to gun-running and acts of political violence in Scotland itself was enough to cause such people to rethink their involvement. The leader of the Paisley UDA group, who tried to get his team to 'do something', frequently had to threaten and 'discipline' them. The lack of intense commitment can be seen in the willingness of many low-level UDA and UVF men to help the police with their enquiries. In 1979 some ninety or so people connected with the UDA in Paisley and Dumfries were arrested by the police; only two of them did not make a statement. With one or two notable exceptions, even most leaders of UDA and UVF cells proved only too willing to sing.

And it was not only after arrest that such co-operation was common. Although my records are not exhaustive, I have details of twenty-four major court cases relating to paramilitary activity and every one of them either originated with, or was much helped by, volunteered information. Although the circumstance of having to justify 'grassing' one's comrades encourages people to find honourable reasons for betrayal, I think we can take as genuine the professed reluctance to bring Ulster's troubles to Scotland. Helping the boys 'over by' was one thing, but bringing it home to Glasgow was another. On 10 March 1973 an explosion ripped a hole in the roof of the Apprentice Boys' Hall in Landressy Street, Bridgeton, in Glasgow. A few hours after the blast, the following letter was sent to the *Daily Record*:

Sir, I am writing to you because I feel that the troubles which have taken place in Northern Ireland over the last few years could be inflicted on us in Glasgow. I am sorry but I must remain anonymous—I would be killed if it was known I was informing against the Protestant cause. My main reason for doing so is that I have young children and have fears for their safety should the outrages which are happening in Belfast happen in Glasgow. I foned 999 about one o'clock this morning and told them that big Bill Campbell and another man, George—I don't know his second name—had taken explosives into the hall in Landressy Street. I know for a fact that yesterday afternoon the same two men collected about 20 sticks of gelly from a butcher's shop in Bridgeton.[18]

---

[18] *Daily Record*, 11 Mar. 1973. When I first quoted this letter, I did not notice what now seem like glaring inconsistencies of style. The author can use a future conditional but cannot spell 'phoned'! Whether other mistakes were tidied up by the sub-editor or the present mistakes were introduced to add verisimilitude cannot now be known; the original letter was given to the police. However, the journalist

According to the writer, the explosives had been destined for the Catholic chapel in Clyde Street, but they never made it: the gelignite was unstable and exploded while Campbell and Martin were at a meeting in the hall.

When, six years later, the same UVF group bombed two Glasgow pubs frequented by Catholics (the only offensive action taken in Scotland), the police were again much aided by advance information about the group.

Scottish opinion leaders united to condemn the pub bombings. In justifying what he described as exemplary sentences, Lord Ross said the trial had revealed an appalling picture of a gang of thugs intent on assisting violent men engaged in illegal and dreadful sectarian fights in Ulster. That was bad enough, but in addition explosives had now been used in Scotland:

To all decent-minded people here, the activities of the accused are seen for what they are—wicked, brutal and senseless. The accused have really chosen to wage war against society and society must be protected. This court always takes a most serious view of crimes involving arms and explosives and those involved can expect no mercy. . . . Others who may be tempted to continue evil work of this kind should realize that they will be liable to similar or even greater sentences.[19]

When similarly lengthy sentences were given to Paisley and Dumfries UDA men involved in gun-running, Orange Grand Secretary David Bryce, now well distanced from the martial bluster of the Marquis of Graham, John Adam, and Grand Master Orr, supported the judge:

The sentences will be a warning to other people who think there is something romantic about obtaining arms. We in the Orange Order certainly do not condone violence nor do we condone the gathering of arms. There is no place in our organization for people like those convicted or for anyone involved in paramilitary organizations.[20]

That the legal establishment shared Lord Ross's view is clear from the subsequent pattern of sentencing, which reached some sort of record when in 1989 UDA men from Perth were found guilty of (badly) making small amounts of handgun ammunition. The sup-

---

who handled the letter is confident that it was authentic. That it contains correct detail which would only have been known to an insider suggests it is genuine.

[19] *Scotsman*, 23 June 1979.
[20] *Glasgow Herald*, 17 June 1979.

posed ringleader and instigator, a man with no previous record, was given sixteen years for conspiracy to further the aims of an illegal organization, or, as a friend of his put it: 'for thinking about it. He'd have got less time if he'd fuckin killed somebody!'[21]

We should be clear about the extent of support in Scotland for these activities. When Roddy MacDonald claimed in 1976 that the UDA had 'thousands' of members, he was exaggerating greatly. Today there are a few hundred people who are involved in some minor way in actively supporting Ulster loyalist paramilitaries.

A New Generation?

The large Glasgow pub-bombing and Edinburgh gunshop-killing trials of 1979 effectively removed the first generation of loyalist activists in Scotland. A less flamboyant but more successful leadership took over and maintained a steady trickle of explosives and weapons through the 1980s, but since 1989 there has been a significant change in Scottish loyalist activity that, ironically, owes much to a republican initiative. As a response to the 1981 IRA prison hunger strike and the death of Bobby Sands and nine other republicans, a number of republican flute bands were started in Govan, Coatbridge, and Dumbarton, among other places. The bands and their marches gave opportunity for young loyalists to counter-demonstrate noisily, but they were also an encouragement to imitate. The traditional Orange flute band did little except rehearse, play, and drink too much. The Scottish republican bands consciously tried to educate their members in a political philosophy. They were 'consciousness-raising' as well as entertaining, and it was this aspect which attracted loyalists to follow suit.

In Fife in September 1987 a group of young men formed the Young Cowdenbeath Volunteers flute band and took as their uniforms and banners replicas of those of the 1914 14th battalion of the Royal Irish Rifles. At first hearing, this sounds like the sort of celebration of British martial tradition that the Orange Order should very much favour. But the uniforms presented a perfect ambiguity. The 14th battalion is what the 1914 Young Citizens' Volunteers (part of Sir Edward Carson's UVF) became when it

---

[21] For details and background to the case, see K. Farquarson, 'Scots Loyalty in the Killing Field that is Ulster', *Scotland on Sunday*, 9 July 1989.

was incorporated in the regular army, and the Cowdenbeath band had chosen its name so that its initials were YCV. Thus what superficially appeared as an act of military remembrance could also be seen as a sign of support for the present-day and illegal UVF. Grand Lodge of the Scottish Orange Order banned the YCV, and another band, the Greengairs Thistle, which wears the battle-dress uniform of the 36th (Ulster) Division. For good measure Grand Lodge decided that 'the initials YCV in a band's name be not acceptable' and that the YCV march 'Wild Colonial Boy' 'be banned and any tunes of a possible paramilitary connotation be discouraged'.[22]

By and large this generation of Scottish loyalists has taken the judiciary's exemplary sentencing policy to heart and confines its activities to fund-raising for loyalist prisoners' aid. However, even such perfectly legal activity is objected to by the Orange hierarchy. A number of attempts have been made to discipline members for supporting the Loyalist Prisoners' Aid (LPA: the UDA group) or Loyalist Prisoners' Welfare Association (LPWA: the UVF version) and the most recent has brought the Orange Order to the courts. In 1989 two members of Lodge 160 'Pride of Midlothian' of Edinburgh were suspended by Grand Lodge for collecting for LPA at a District Lodge dance. When Lodge 160 refused to expel them, Grand Lodge lifted its warrant (which, being translated, means 'kicked it out'). In an unprecedented recourse to secular authority, Pride of Midlothian applied to the courts for an interim interdict, which was granted.[23]

The final judgement in that case may take some time, but it seems very likely that a number of lodges will secede to the more militant Independent Orange Order over the issue of support for loyalism. While many members are willing to accept that displays of solidarity with fellow Orangemen 'over by' must be kept within the law, they see the present Grand Lodge policy of outlawing even legal acts of support for paramilitaries as fundamentally anti-loyalist.

Value of Scottish Support

Roddy MacDonald's heart might have been in the right place, but he was less than useless to the UDA: his attempts to buy arms put

---

[22] Minutes, Grand Lodge of Scotland, 2 Sept. 1989.

[23] For details and background, see I. S. Woods, 'Boys of the Boyne', *Scotland on Sunday*, 1 July 1990.

many UDA men in gaol and his willingness to talk to the media embarrassed the Orange Order into disciplining UDA supporters. The Bridgeton UVF cell was similarly unhelpful. But even more effective Scottish paramilitaries have been regarded with something like disdain by their Ulster colleagues. One experienced Scot complained that, although he was listened to respectfully, as soon as his back was turned they said 'what the fuck does he know!' and ignored him. For many loyalists, Ulster begins and ends on the Shankill Road. Ulster 'country boys' are described as a 'bit odd'. Non-Ulstermen, even ones who spend a lot of time in the province, remain outsiders.

Scottish fund-raising has been of considerable value. How much Scottish loyalist support for the UVF and UDA is worth is not clear and one can only estimate. I would guess that about £100,000 a year is raised through dances, collections, and the sale of loyalist merchandise. Although less than half of what a single bank raid might raise, it is none the less a handy sum. More important than the money raised or the small amounts of arms that are brought from or through Scotland is the morale-boosting consequence of knowing that the loyalist cause has some support outside Northern Ireland. Scots bands get especially warm welcomes on the Twelfth parades in Ulster because they are a signal that Ulster Protestants are not entirely without friends.

True Believers: England

Not surprisingly, given that it was the point of disembarkation for many Irish migrants, Liverpool, and such neighbouring industrial centres as Preston and Manchester, have always been the most Orange part of England. Through the second half of the nineteenth century and well into this, Liverpool had a history of sectarian violence, and in the 1930s there was a Protestant party which held council seats for the strongly Protestant wards of St Domingo and Netherfield.[24] As happened in Glasgow, the Troubles brought radical polarization, with a small number of Orangemen becoming involved in various support activities while

[24] On Protestant politics in Liverpool, see P. J. Waller, *Democracy and Sectarianism: A Political and Social History of Liverpool, 1868–1939* (Liverpool, 1981); F. Neal, *Sectarian Violence: The Liverpool Experience, 1818–1914* (Manchester, 1980); R. Henderson, *George Wise of Liverpool* (Liverpool, 1967), and *Seventy Five Years of Protestant Witness* (Liverpool, 1973).

Protestant church and civic leaders did their utmost to distance themselves from Liverpool's sectarian past.

As with Scottish support, it is difficult to assess English contributions to the loyalist cause when generally only failures come to public attention. However, if we assume that English police forces are moderately successful in prosecuting paramilitary activity, we can take the cases that come to light as some guide to the quality and extent of English support.

In 1975 the *Daily Mail* was contacted and offered the story of 'The First Lancashire Volunteers', a supposedly trained 'army' of men ready to fight in Northern Ireland. Photographs of nine men (one an ex-B Special) engaged in various military postures appeared in the paper and all nine were arrested and sentenced to between two and three years in prison. Although defence counsel had an interest in minimizing the seriousness of their offence, we can accept his view that no serious terrorist group sells its story to the press for £150 (and gets cheated of the money by the paper!).

Another case involving the English UDA was considerably more serious, but none the less had a farcical element. A key witness against Roy Rogers-Forbes, John Gadd, and John Griffiths, all charged with smuggling arms through Southampton and Portsmouth, was a Mrs Louise Davey, an English-born woman who claimed to have been a 'Captain' in the UDA in Belfast in 1973. She testified that, when she was living in Belfast, and after having given some information to British troops, a man came to her flat with a gun and insisted that she come to UDA headquarters to answer some questions. She claims to have knocked the gun from the man's hand with her handbag and made good her escape. She moved to Devon, where she was contacted by John Gadd, who announced that he and Tommy Thompson, a Liverpool man and supposed Commander of the UDA in England, were coming to stay on their way to doing some business in Plymouth and Southampton, business which the Crown would show to be gun-running. Quite what credence should be given to her evidence is not clear. Defence counsel attempted to show that she was a pathological liar and there were parts of her story that made little sense. She claimed to have been petrol-bombed four times in Devon. She had a photograph of her 17-year-old daughter, dressed in black, posing with what looked like a pistol. On the back was written: 'Training with a Browning automatic.

Yes, as well as my ability in the Irish gaelic language, now I can also use a gun. I have to as the main leader of the East Belfast Tartan Gang of Young UDA members.'[25] As we have already seen, loyalist paramilitaries differed markedly from their republican counterparts in having little use for women members. It seems barely credible that Mrs Davey held rank in the UDA and even less likely that her daughter was an east Belfast 'Tartan'.

However, Mrs Davey clearly knew Gadd and Thompson, and shopped them by writing to the Crown, which says a great deal for the lack of discretion on the part of the English UDA.[26] They were to pay dear, with Gadd being sentenced to ten years, Rogers-Forbes to seven, and Griffiths to five.

The evidence in the Southampton case led to the arrest and charge of Tommy Thompson in June 1975 for conspiring to contravene the Firearms and Explosive Substances Act. Like MacDonald in Scotland, Thompson had been unfortunately public about his role and had appeared in a BBC film about the UDA in Liverpool.

Those trials brought to an effective end the first phase of support for UDA, and developments since have paralleled those in Scotland. There has been a major rift in the Orange Order, with a number of lodges leaving and joining the Independent Orange Order; again the issue was how far one should go in supporting paramilitaries and it came to a head over the dedication of a UVF banner. The members of a north Liverpool lodge insisted that the banner denoted the original 1912 UVF and hence was not encouragement of an illegal organization. Grand Lodge insisted that the present UVF was the organization the militants had in mind. That the group who left (or were expelled) have held fund-raising events for the UVF's LPWA suggests that no one was being fooled. As with Scotland, English money for the UDA and UVF (probably less than that raised north of the border) is handy but not crucial. What is more important is the fillip that such 'foreign' support provides.

Perhaps one should not make too much of it, but it is interesting that in both Scotland and England such support as there is for paramilitarism has shifted from the UDA to the UVF. Although I

[25] *Guardian*, 27 Nov. 1974.
[26] Ibid. 5 June 1975.

have not interviewed enough people to be sure of the reasons for this swing, it is probably a result of the poor image the UDA has recently acquired for gangsterism and the greater symbolic power of the UVF's name and historical connections.

True Believers: Canada

Apart from small pockets in Australia and South Africa, the main source of support for loyalism outside the United Kingdom is Canada. Ontario is to Ulster Protestants what Boston is to Irish Catholics. Large numbers migrated there in the last century and Toronto remains a favourite North American destination. Orangeism is strong (there is even a Mohawk Lodge) and, in so far as Ulster loyalists have many friends outside Britain, they are to be found in the Toronto area. In the early days of the Troubles a number of leading UDA and UVF men raised money in Ontario.

In 1972 a group of five Toronto businessmen decided to ship arms in grain containers from Halifax, Nova Scotia, to ports in Scotland, Wales, and Northern Ireland. This operation was closed down by the Royal Canadian Mounted Police[27] and the UVF replaced it by a smaller but simpler operation. Guns and parts of guns were wrapped in tin foil to fool X-ray machines and posted to large European cities where post offices would be too busy to check all parcels. For a number of years the postal service provided a small but steady trickle of weapons. Three such parcels were detected in April 1979 at the Wellington Street Post Office in Glasgow. Two of them were addressed (with a false name in one case and a slightly modified name in the second) to members of the Maryhill UVF team. Their misfortunes were compounded when their leader decided to 'grass' the lot.[28]

Another Canadian supply route was stumbled upon when Canadian Billy Taylor was involved in a high-speed chase with the Toronto police. Investigation showed that Taylor had been buying guns in various parts of the United States and planning to ship them to Belfast via Liverpool in hollowed-out lead-lined car engines. In reporting the story the Belfast *Newsletter* (unionist in

[27] *Daily Record*, 31 July 1981.
[28] *Glasgow Herald*, 31 July 1981, has a summary of the case.

sympathies) achieved a new high in misleading reporting: 'His lawyer said Taylor had started discussions with an Irishman, John Bingham, in the early 1980s, which led to the gun-running scheme. Bingham was later shot and killed in Northern Ireland after two gunmen kicked down the door of his home.'[29] By describing one of the most senior UVF figures as an 'Irishman', the report manages to suggest that the weapons were being smuggled for the IRA!

As I have already noted, the only hard evidence about arms supplies concerns those occasions when routes have been discovered by the police. We cannot know what part of the total amount of material moved is represented by the cases where the smuggling has been discovered. The fact that the UVF does have Ingram sub-machine guns (a weapon Taylor was collecting) suggests that some consignments got through. How many we cannot say, but it is perhaps not terribly important, given that the loyalist paramilitaries seem to have as much weaponry as they 'need' for their task.

Opportunists: South Africa

In 1989 a new foreign connection came to light when three members of the Ulster Resistance (UR) movement were arrested by French police in a hotel room in Paris, where they were meeting a South African diplomat and an American arms dealer.

UR is the most recent and smallest of the paramilitary organizations. It was launched by Ian Paisley and Peter Robinson of the DUP and Alan Wright of the Ulster Clubs at a private meeting of some two thousand men at the Ulster Hall in Belfast in November 1986. UR was yet another of Paisley's 'third forces', raised with the customary martial bluster and the promise to use 'all means necessary to defeat the Anglo-Irish agreement'. The intergovernmental accord marked a radical development in British policy towards Northern Ireland in that, for the first time, it gave Dublin an institutional role in the running of the province (even if that role was confined to asking questions and raising problems). While constitutional nationalist politicians were keen supporters of the accord, unionists abhorred it and started a series of protest. A

[29] *Newsletter*, 9 Jan. 1990.

year after the accord, with the 'Ulster Says No' campaign achieving little, Paisley decided to raise the stakes with UR.[30]

The movement failed to recruit a mass membership but organized some active groups in the rural areas of Fermanagh and Armagh. Not surprising, given its patrons, it recruited well among Free Presbyterians (two of the three men arrested in Paris belonged to the Free Presbyterian Church in Co. Armagh) and other rural conservative Protestants.[31] Paisley and Robinson soon lost interest in UR and, when reports of illegality began to surface, both denounced their former soldiers.

UR members took part in a joint bank raid in Portadown with the UDA and UVF, and the money was used to buy a very large consignment of weapons supplied by a South African source. The same imperial diaspora which has beached Scots and Ulstermen in Canada and Australia has also sent many to South Africa. There is also a contemporary link, in that some South Africans and Ulster Protestants see parallels between their respective positions: a small pool of enlightened civilization surrounded by the hordes of darkness. However, South African interest in Ulster stems from self-interest rather than fellow-feeling. The South African contacts made it clear to the UR representatives that they would be happy to trade arms for something other than money.

The Shorts company, based at two sites in east Belfast, is one of the world leaders in missile technology and its work-force is overwhelmingly Protestant. In October 1988 two men walked into the paint shop and removed a model of the new Javelin missile aiming system. They missed a fully operational version of the aiming unit for the new Starstreak missile which had been there hours earlier.[32] A few months later, parts of a Shorts Blowpipe missile went missing. In early April, shortly before the Paris arrests, a Blowpipe was stolen from a TA base in Newtownards; one of three UR men in Paris was a member of the TA in Newtownards. As a result of the international embargo which has denied South Africa purchase of the most modern weapons, the

---

[30] For a good review of the UR, see McKittrick's story in *Independent*, 24 Apr. 1989.

[31] As a mark of the rural nature of UR, the two men who were sentenced on 22 Sept. 1989 for possession of a UR arms cache (part of the great South African delivery) were both from small villages in Co. Armagh.

[32] *Independent*, 24 Apr. 1989.

state-owned Armscor has developed mastery of copying and making its own substitutes (which it sells to other 'pariah' nations). The Blowpipe is an old missile and of little value to Armscor, but the Javelin would be useful and the Starstreak, which is still in development, would be invaluable.

Despite initial police reports that the missing missile parts were all models or inoperative, UR claimed to have two working Blowpipes and a set of plans for Starstreak. Given the poor record of security at Shorts, this is always possible. The Paris arrests brought to an end what might have blossomed into a very fruitful relationship for UR, but, before that link was broken, South Africa had provided a major consignment of arms.

Conclusion

At the start of this chapter I suggested that foreign friends were useful for political influence, money, and weapons. It is clear that in comparison to the IRA, the UDA and UVF are short of all three. Not only does the IRA have rich and influential supporters abroad but, more importantly, it has the Irish Republic. Since partition, the long-term aspirations for the Irish government and the IRA as regards Northern Ireland have been the same: its destruction. The Dublin government supported the civil-rights agitations, gave funds to arm nationalists in the north, and has been a constant critic of first Stormont and then British government actions in Northern Ireland. Although successive Dublin governments have condemned the IRA and have been ahead of Britain in some punitive actions (banning IRA spokesmen from the mass media, for example), the territory of the Republic continues to offer the IRA a haven which is relatively safe. It is not clear how Adams arrives at the specific number of '200 terrorists and 400 associates and family members'[33] resident there, but he is right in the general point that Dundalk, just across the border, remains a harbour for active IRA men. Although terrorist suspects can be extradited from the Irish Republic to stand trial in Britain, the recent record of extradition applications is one of apparently unassailable cases being rejected on trivial technicalities.

The value of the border for smuggling will be discussed later.

[33] J. Adams, *The Financing of Terror* (London, 1988), 226.

The support of many nationalists in the south for 'the armed struggle' no doubt produces considerable financial support. The border is of great practical assistance in allowing attacks to be launched on troops. But the greatest value of the Republic is simply the consensus of goals. However much government rhetoric tries to separate its desire for a united Ireland from the IRA's armed struggle to achieve that goal, that Northern Ireland's neighbour continues to wish it deceased remains an important source of comfort for those who wish its Protestant inhabitants deceased.

Although the extensive support in the west coast of Scotland and the much smaller pockets of support in Canada and England provide Ulster loyalists with money and small amounts of guns and explosives, there is a cost in that success in those two enterprises makes it impossible for supporting political influence to be exercised. British public opinion is firmly on the side of the government. The government is firmly opposed to the UDA and UVF. Any organization that openly supports the UDA or UVF, or that fails to discipline its members who support the UDA or UVF, will lose popularity and credibility with those British people who support the government. The few friends the loyalists have can help them with money and they can help them obtain weapons, but the more they succeed at those enterprises, the less able they are to exert any political influence.

7
Murdering Gangsters

ABOVE all else the success of a paramilitary organization rests on victory in the propaganda war. Loyalist paramilitaries compete with the security forces of the state for legitimacy, and that competition is concerned with image. The UVF and UDA wish to be seen as disciplined bodies of men, trained, organized, and willing to make the highest sacrifice to preserve their country, worthy successors to the 36th Division and the B Specials. Their opponents wish to portray them as murderous gangs of thugs and robbers. This chapter is concerned with the two aspects of paramilitarism that are potentially very damaging to its image: uncontrolled viciousness and racketeering. Killing (or the threat of killing) and fund-raising are both central to the operations of any paramilitary force, but both have to be tightly directed if they are not to undermine public support for the organization.

Lenny Murphy and the Moore–Bates Gang

Lenny Murphy was the son of a working-class Protestant Belfast family who had a history of difficult adolescent behaviour. When only 12 he was caught shopbreaking and given two years' probation. On leaving school he again got into trouble and another two years of probation. With the start of the Troubles, Murphy joined the YCV, the junior wing of the UVF.

He quickly showed a callousness and a hatred of Catholics that went beyond what was common, even in the hardest teams. A common feature of a lot of loyalist murders of the early 1970s was the 'rompering' that preceded them. Victims, often drunks picked up as they tottered home or people stopped at 'no-go' barricades, were taken to some secluded place, where they were tortured as an accompaniment to what passed for interrogation. The assumption (not in every case unreasonable) was that any Catholic knew something about the IRA, and sufficient brutality would release that knowledge.

On the night of Friday, 21 July 1972, at the height of the

Troubles, Francis Arthurs left the Catholic Ardoyne in a taxi which was stopped on the Crumlin Road. He was bundled out of the vehicle, hit on the head, and taken to the Lawnbrook Club, a UVF haunt just off the Shankill Road. After the drinkers who were not UVF men had left, Arthurs was brought out and beaten by most of the men in turn. He was also stabbed repeatedly. Only after more than an hour of this treatment was he shot dead. Lenny Murphy was one of those who was involved in the gang beating.

He was also, according to Dillon, involved in three more sectarian murders over the summer.[1] One of them, that of Thomas Madden, was particularly gruesome. Madden was suspended from a wooden beam in a lock-up garage and stabbed and cut repeatedly. In all there were 147 stab wounds on his body. The fact that he was first stripped and then very slowly and methodically wounded suggests that his assailants enjoyed causing pain.

Murphy's reputation as a remorseless killer was consolidated by his supposed murder of an accomplice. In January 1973 Murphy and Mervyn Connor stole a motorbike in the Glencairn estate and travelled to east Belfast to visit Edward Pavis. They had been ordered to kill Pavis because he was believed to be a gun dealer willing to sell to the IRA. The murder went without a hitch, but some months later the pair were picked up by the detectives. Apart from some contestable witness identification, the RUC had nothing that would stand up in court, so they offered Connor a deal to testify against Murphy. Unfortunately, they did not offer him enough protection. Indeed, security seems to have been worse in Crumlin Road prison than outside it. According to the story reported by Dillon, Murphy was able to leave the hospital wing where he was working and had access to poisons, go to Connor's cell, and force him first to write a note confessing that he alone had murdered Pavis and then to drink cyanide.

Without Connor, the Pavis case against Murphy collapsed, and in June 1973 Murphy walked free—as far as the hall of the courthouse, where he was detained under the Special Powers Act and taken to the Maze. He was sentenced to three years in prison for two escape attempts during his remand.

---

[1] M. Dillon, *The Shankill Butchers: A Case Study of Mass Murder* (London, 1989), 20–1.

On 13 May 1975, while the UVF was still legal, Murphy was released and returned to the Shankill Road, where he gradually put together his own 'team' of killers based at the Brown Bear bar. It included Billy Moore, a taxi-driver, Robert 'Basher' Bates, and Sam McAllister. One of their first actions was part of the 'big push' of 2 October that resulted in Secretary of State Merlyn Rees renewing the ban on the UVF. As their contribution to the mayhem, Murphy and Moore joined two other UVF men in a robbery of a Catholic-owned off-licence. Murphy led the shooting and personally killed three of the five people who died in what was intended to be a quiet civilized robbery. Two of the men involved were lifted by the police and talked about their own involvement, but neither named Murphy or Moore.

The Butchering

The 1975 coup in the UVF leadership was described in Chapter 5. Undermined by incompetence and misfortune, the brigade staff that had been in control for a year was replaced by a group of more experienced, older men who were a little more political. I made the point in describing those events that it was a mistake to present them as a tug of war between 'hawks' and 'doves'. However, there is no doubt that the new leadership wished to present itself as more responsible, more thoughtful, and more directed in its actions than the one it had replaced. In particular, it followed the by-now usual pattern of insisting that, in future, random sectarian murder would be replaced by attacks only on armed republican targets.

None of this rhetoric made the least impression on Murphy and his gang, who seem to have acquired a reputation that allowed them to do much as they liked. And what they liked to do was to 'stiff a Taig'. On 25 November, Murphy, Moore, Benny 'Pretty Boy' Edwards, and Archie Waller picked up Francis Crossan, who was walking from a drinking club in the Ardoyne towards the city centre. Crossan was repeatedly beaten in Moore's taxi, and was then dragged into an alleyway off Wimbledon Street in the Shankill Road area, where Murphy cut his throat with one of Moore's knives.

A small point of detail underlines the part the media plays in myth-creating: the 'Butchers' tag neatly fitted the team's methods, but it was an exaggeration to say that Moore had worked as a butcher. He had actually worked as a labourer in a meat-packing factory, where he is reputed to have asked one of the butchers to show him how to dismember a carcass.

A point of some significance in understanding Murphy and his team (and some other loyalist teams) was their willingness to kill Protestants. Murphy was a murderer first and a murderer of Catholics second, as the killing of Noel 'Nogi' Shaw shows. The new UVF leadership was determined to enhance its reputation by clamping down on petty crime and extortion. An old lady who lived on the Shankill was robbed by three young men who tied her up; she was left tied for twelve hours. The UVF brigade staff asked Murphy to find out who was responsible and 'knee-cap' them. Murphy suspected that the three were members of the Windsor Bar UVF team led by Anthony 'Chuck' Berry, and, without voicing his suspicions, he consulted Berry about the problem. Berry agreed that firm action should be taken. Roger McCrea, Edward Bell, and Stewartie Robinson were lifted and taken to the room above the Brown Bear, where they were threatened and beaten into confessing their part in the robbery. The three were then taken to a garage, where they were adorned with placards saying 'Shot for crimes against the Loyalist People'. But, just as the punishment shooting in the back of the knees was to take place, Robinson made a run for it and was shot dead by Archie Waller. Murphy ordered that the knee-capping of the other two go ahead and threatened that, if they said anything about Robinson's killing, they would be killed.

Robinson's body was dumped in a nearby alley. Murphy was quizzed by brigade staff about Robinson's death and denied any involvement. The leader of the Windsor Bar team was not satisfied and, when he learnt from Robinson's colleagues the identity of the killer of one of his men, he insisted that Waller be shot. Three men from the Windsor Bar came across Waller sitting in a car just off the Shankill Road and shot him dead.

Murphy was not prepared to allow that challenge to his position to go unanswered and he arranged to have two of the three killers lifted and taken to the Lawnbrook Social Club. Only one of the two, 19-year-old Noel 'Nogi' Shaw, was found. He was brought to the club, kicked, and beaten by a large number of men and, after being tied to a chair, pistol-whipped by Murphy, who finally shot him through the head and ordered the audience to clear up the mess.

After Christmas, and once the possibility of repercussions over the Shaw killing had died down, the gang went back to work. In January and February three Catholics were picked off the streets and brutally murdered. One of them, 55-year-old roadsweeper Thomas Quinn, was beaten and taken to Forthriver Way in the Glencairn estate on the western outskirts of the city, where he had his throat slit.

Apparently in response to the IRA's killing of ten Protestant workers on a bus at Kingsmill (which was itself retaliation for the UVF's murder of the Miami Showband members), Murphy planned an attack on workers going to Corry's Timber Yard in west Belfast. The mission was a great planning success; unfortunately, the two men who were murdered were Protestants. On 2 March Murphy made his first serious mistake. With Bates and two other men, Murphy was stopped by an army patrol on the Shankill shortly after two Catholic women in a car were shot at on the nearby Cliftonville Road. For some reason, only Murphy was detained. When it was clear that it would be difficult to link him to the attempted killing but that a pistol had been found in a hedge on the route, Murphy was released from custody and a surveillance team put in place. When he went back to search for the pistol (a valuable commodity for a team working largely without the sanction of the UVF's brigade staff and hence without access to the main armouries), he was again arrested.

According to Dillon, the RUC officers in charge of the investigation were confident that Murphy was the Butcher they were hunting, but they were unable to put together a case strong enough to ensure conviction for attempted murder, and the prosecuting counsel settled for a plea bargain in which Murphy agreed to admit the lesser charge of possessing a firearm.

To confound the detectives, who were confident they had the Butcher locked up for six years, Murphy and a confidant who was never convicted of his part planned to keep the gang working. Supplied with knives and hatchets by the person that Dillon calls 'Mr "A"', the gang continued its work through 1976, claiming five more victims.

The gang was also involved in a much more ambitious job which involved its only use of explosives. James 'Tonto' Watt, one of the UVF's best bomb-makers, was asked to prepare a device which would be planted along the traditional route of the IRA's Easter Rising celebration parade in west Belfast. Unfortunately, the planning was slightly awry. Since the division of the IRA into Official and Provisional sections, there had been two commemorative parades and the bomb went off during the wrong one. Instead of killing leading Provisionals and their supporters, the gang killed a young boy who had come out to watch the Official IRA march. There may have been unintended benefits from this mistake. As a UVF man put it to me: 'They got it wrong but it was still a republican parade and it set the Stickies and the Provisionals against each other.'

The feud between the UDA and UVF has already been mentioned. The Brown Bear Bar gang shared the dislike of UDA men and was responsible for killing two of them. On 20 December 1976 'Big Sam' McAllister had an argument in a pub with a UDA volunteer, waylaid him outside, and beat him to death. Despite UDA insistence that McAllister be severely punished, UVF brigade staff ordered only a token shooting: a couple of shots in the arm from a .22 pistol. He was so little discomfited by his wound that only a month later he joined Bates and Moore in killing UDA man James Moorehead, apparently for no reason other than that he walked into a bar where they were drinking.[2]

One can only speculate how long the gang might have continued to murder had it not been for the extreme resilience of the last of its victims, who survived horrific mutilation on the night of 10 May 1977. Gerard McLaverty had been lifted by the gang, taken to a disused doctor's surgery on the corner of Emerson Street and the Shankill, and severely beaten and frequently stabbed before being left for dead. He survived. Because the methods used had always resulted in the victims' deaths, the members of the gang took no precautions against recognition, and McLaverty had good sight of some of his assailants. In this, the third week of May, the second loyalist strike was in progress, and the RUC detectives knew that many loyalists would be out on the Shankill. They took McLaverty up and down the road until he spotted one of his assailants—Big Sam McAllister—standing outside a pub. McLaverty was also able to remember that he had been abducted in a yellow Cortina and the RUC knew that Moore

[2] Ibid. 160–1.

had such a car. With two of the gang identified, the rest followed very quickly, and under interrogation they all confessed, although each minimized his role in the various killings, claiming that he had just given the victim a 'kicking' or a 'good dig' while the others had inflicted the fatal wounds.

On 20 February 1979 Moore, McAllister, Bates, Edwards, and six others were convicted of nineteen murders. Moore and Bates, who pleaded guilty to eleven and ten killings respectively, were given actual life sentences. The judge said: 'I see no reason whatever, apart from terminal illness, why either of you should ever be released.'

One can only speculate what impact the newspaper reports of the gruesome details had on the reputation of the UVF. Just as there are Catholics who are so sectarian that they cheer any 'Prod' death, so there were loyalists who approved of the Butchers on the grounds that every dead 'Taig' is one threat less. However, most working-class Protestants would take the view that the UVF brigade staff itself periodically proclaims: that killing is an unfortunate necessity and is justified by the 'cause'. Uncontrolled killing, killing in which the assailants take obvious pleasure in their work, disgraces the cause. There can be no doubt that very many decent Shankill Protestants were horrified by the gang's catalogue of brutality.

Lenny's Return

Although everyone on the Shankill knew who Mr 'X' was, the strict British libel laws prevented Murphy being named in court or in the press reports of the trial of Moore and Bates. On 16 July 1982 Murphy left prison after serving his sentence for possession of firearms. Within twenty-four hours he had killed again. His victim was a complete stranger who just happened to walk into the Rumford Street club where Murphy was celebrating his release with some close friends. He moved back into extortion to raise some money and put a down payment on a large second-hand Rover, bought from a garage owner in Bangor who used to be in the west Belfast UVF. When the man later pressed him for the rest of the price of the car, Murphy killed him.[3]

His last killing was one of the very few which could in any sense

---

[3] According to C. Ryder, *The UDR* (London, 1991), 160, Murphy also shot a UVF man near Ballymena in September.

be described as a UVF-sanctioned murder. On 22 October 1982 a part-time UDR soldier Thomas Cochrane was kidnapped by the IRA. Murphy suggested that the UVF kidnap a Catholic and use him to bargain for the release of Cochrane. Senior UVF men agreed. Using a hijacked black taxi, Murphy lifted Joseph Donnegan from the Falls Road, took him to the loyalist club in Rumford Street, and tortured and killed him. Although Donnegan was dead, Murphy maintained the fiction of a possible swap and even contacted an SDLP politician about the possibility of an exchange. The IRA quite independently killed its hostage.

Murphy's time was running out. During his six years in prison the UVF leadership had changed considerably and he was short of influential patrons. Retrospectively journalists wrote that the men running the organization were well aware of the damage that had been done to their reputation by Murphy and of his uncontrollability. Like many other outsider views, this may have been an exaggeration. A man who was then a senior officer in the west Belfast UDA suggested that UVF brigade staff were still slow to appreciate Murphy's unpopularity.

The leaders who protected him were out of touch. They took the view that no one would touch Lenny and so that was OK. They never considered what ordinary members thought of torture killings. Murphy was a bad bastard who should have been stopped by his own people.

He was stopped, but not apparently by his own people. On the evening of 16 November, when Murphy made his regular visit to his girlfriend in Glencairn, he was shot dead by gunmen who machine-gunned him from the back of a blue Marina van that pulled up in front of his car. He was hit by twenty-six bullets and died instantly. A full sixteen hours after the shooting, the hit was claimed by PIRA.

As so often before, I have to admit that I do not know who killed Murphy. The *Irish News* reported that loyalists were responsible.[4] Dillon writes that the actual shooters were PIRA men, but that they were aided in the planning of the murder and in disposing of the weapons by UDA man Jimmy Craig and members of his 'team'.[5]

---

[4] *Irish News*, 7 Dec. 1982.
[5] M. Dillon, *The Dirty War* (London, 1990), 450–1.

Craig's involvement in Murphy's murder will be discussed in detail in Chapter 10. Here I would like to quote an interesting nugget of moralizing from an interview with a senior UDA man:

It was either loyalists who fingered [Murphy] to the IRA or who done it themselves and let the IRA claim it but either way it was bad because there shouldn't be that sort of collusion. If the bugger was so bad he needed killing, he should have been killed by his own organization. That was their job. Helping republicans kill someone, even a psychopath like Murphy, is just not on.

Not only would it have been more ethical for the UVF to have done it itself; it would also have enhanced its reputation among loyalists if it had been seen to be policing its own delinquents.

Explaining Cruelty

Criticisms of another author writing about the same subject may read like sour grapes, but Martin Dillon's *The Shankill Butchers* has become so popular that the weaknesses of its explanations need to be confronted. As in his first book, written with Lehane, *Political Murder in Northern Ireland*, Dillon follows good descriptive detail with poor explanation. There the mistake was to search for underlying political tensions to explain what were actually personal disputes. In trying to understand Murphy, Bates, and Moore, Dillon falls back on some very badly digested ideas from the study of abnormal psychology. The murders are explained by Murphy's personality problems and his influence over his gang, core members of which shared his lunacy. In brief, Dillon believes that Murphy, Moore, and the others would have been killers had they been transferred in adolescence to any other society, and he makes not terribly well-argued comparisons between the Butchers and such serial killers as the Moors murderers and the Yorkshire Ripper.

In evaluating Dillon's explanation, we should admit that terms such as 'sociopath' and 'psychopath', although they sound like technical terms from a well-developed set of theories, actually mean very little more than 'people who behave very oddly and do things we would not do'. Why they do them remains very much a mystery and to suggest, as Dillon does, that Murphy's abnormality may have had its origins in the problems of growing up a loyalist with a 'Catholic' surname is just wild guessing. It also overlooks the two UDA Sammy Murphys (one in Sandy Row, the other in west Belfast) who did not develop Lenny's penchant for close killing.

Secondly, we should question the value of the comparison with such serial killers as the Moors murderers or the Yorkshire Ripper. Hindley and Brady and Peter Sutcliffe (and many of the US parallels) were sexual perverts. There is no suggestion that Murphy, Bates, or Moore were sexual deviants or that there was any element of rape in their killings. The well-documented serial killers worked either on their own or in pairs.[6] They did not work in large gangs or perform for audiences. The subtitle of Dillon's book—'A Case Study of Mass Murder'—is misleading because this was not a case of one or two people murdering over and over again. It was a case of a large number of people being variously involved in a lot of murders. This may be of no consequence for the morality or even the political impact of the murders, but it is surely of some importance when comparisons are being used to generate explanations. That large numbers were involved in various roles suggests that the explanation in the case of Murphy's gang lies in the dynamics of the group rather than in the personalities of the individuals.

Norris's work as a forensic psychologist shows his serial killers to have been the products of severely disordered childhoods. From what little is known of the biography of Murphy's gang, their lives up to their involvement in the Troubles were quite conventional. Indeed, if one could leave aside their killings, their lives were surprisingly ordinary, and even Murphy's history of adolescent criminality was not that unusual for an urban working-class child.

Before one follows Dillon down the 'abnormal psychology' road, it is worth getting the killings in the right perspective. Were they that unusual that they need to be explained by disordered personality? Here Dillon seems to have missed the import of something he mentions in an early footnote. The first killing of the Troubles described as a rompering was, according to Dillon, the work of an east Belfast RHC gang led by John McKeague.

---

[6] For a good psychological study of serial killers that is based on lengthy interviews with the killers, see J. Norris, *Serial Killers: The Growing Menace* (London, 1988).

The body of the victim was badly burnt in a manner which suggested a substantial amount of torture before death.

McKeague . . . was believed by Military Intelligence to have been responsible for the murder of a young Protestant boy in Belfast in the mid-seventies. The boy's body was dismembered, burned over an open fire and dumped in the Lagan River . . . McKeague in some respects pioneered the 'rompering' process but it had a more bizarre application in the Shankill area.[7]

As dead men can be safely accused of anything, one has to remain agnostic about the authorship of those particular killings, but there is no doubt that there were many victims of loyalist romperings in the early 1970s.[8] One victim recovered from fearsome injuries received in a UDA club in east Belfast. He was stripped, tied to a bed, and repeatedly burnt with cigarettes and cut with a razor. Some teeth and fingernails were pulled out with pliers. He was shot in the head and left for dead, but survived to claim criminal damage compensation.[9] As well as the east Belfast gang responsible for that case, there were UFF murder gangs in south and north Belfast who sometimes inflicted gruesome injuries on their victims before killing them. For example, SDLP politician Paddy Wilson and his companion Irene Andrews were repeatedly stabbed before having their throats cut.

We also need to be wary of making too much of Murphy's use of knives. Dillon sees Murphy's choice of weapons as (*a*) a sign that he was more vicious than other killers and in a different way; (*b*) evidence of a desire to shock and terrorize; and (*c*) a device for involving the gang members in the actual moment of murder, thus binding them closer together. There may well be something in all of those suggestions, but people who knew Murphy suggest a more prosaic reason figured higher in his thinking than any of the above. In those days there were many police and army patrols on the streets at night. Any serious murderer calculated and tried to improve not only the odds against being caught but also the punish-

---

[7] Dillon, *The Shankill Butchers*, 19.

[8] As a general warning to future students of political violence in Northern Ireland, it should be noted that, while Dillon and Lehane, *Political Murder in Northern Ireland* (Harmondsworth, Middlesex, 1973), was ground-breaking in making public the fact and scale of loyalist sectarian murder, its attributions of any particular murder should be treated with extreme caution.

[9] *Belfast Telegraph*, 19 Dec. 1975.

ment likely to result from being caught. To have a loaded gun invited a charge of conspiracy to murder. To carry an unloaded gun brought only a possession charge. Knives could be explained away and might carry only a suspended sentence.

My point is that Murphy and his cohorts may have been extreme but they were not unique. That they were as comfortable brutalizing Protestants as Catholics might be thought to require a psychopathic explanation, but one can always justify killing 'touts' and traitors on one's own side (and republicans have done as much of that as have loyalists). And even the killing of people just because their faces did not fit or they were in the wrong place is not much more than taking to an extreme the territoriality of adolescent gangs. Although the punishment is traditionally a 'good doing' rather than murder, simply being on another gang's turf is taken as a serious offence.[10]

To continue the process of laying the foundations for explanation by putting these killings in the right context, we should also remember that ordinary people are quite capable of great cruelty in the right circumstances. Heskin summarizes Stanley Milgram's famous electric-shock experiments.[11] The subjects of the research were paid to take part in what they were told was a study of the effects of punishment on learning. Each was introduced to a partner (who was actually a knowing member of the research team) and lots were drawn to see who would take which part. The ballot was rigged so that the subject always became the 'teacher' and controlled the electric-shock device.

The learner was strapped to a chair with an electrode on his arm. The teacher was sat at an impressive-looking control desk with thirty switches which delivered to the learner shocks at 15-volt intervals graded from 'Slight Shock' to 'Danger—Extreme Shock' and 'XXX'. As an illustration of 'Slight Shock', the teacher was given a 45-volt tickle. In fact this was the only genuine electric shock in the whole experiment. The rest was acting.

The teacher was instructed to give the learner shocks of increasing severity whenever mistakes were made. The experiment was arranged so that mistakes would frequently be made and the

---

[10] On the extremely flexible notion of 'insult' to be found in adolescent urban male gangs, see D. Matza, *Delinquency and Drift* (New York, 1964).

[11] K. Heskin, *Northern Ireland: A Psychological Analysis* (Dublin, 1980), 87.

teacher would be put in the position of having to cause pain or refuse to continue with the experiment:

At 150 volts, the learner showed his pain by shouting 'Experimenter, get me out of here! I refuse to go on!' At 180 volts he shouted that he found the pain unbearable and at 270 volts gave an agonised scream. At 300 he pounded on the wall separating his room from the teacher's and thereafter made no further response. Under these conditions 62.5 per cent of subjects carried on shocking the learner right up to 450 volts.[12]

Even when the learner was giving his extremely convincing performance of great pain in the *same* room as the teacher, 40 per cent of the subjects carried on to administer the most severe shocks. In a third variation, the teacher was required to force the learner's hand down on to the plate which delivered the shocks. Even with that degree of intimate involvement in the punishment, 30 per cent carried on to inflict the worst pain.

To put it simply, most people in the experiment were prepared to cause what they believed to be severe pain to a fellow human simply because they had been paid to take part in an experiment. When the part of the subject was reduced to a subsidiary role, compliance rates were even higher. Ninety per cent stayed with the experiment to the end.

The point of reporting the Milgram experiment (and it has been repeated with similar results) is to disabuse us of the comforting idea that there is a clear division between normal decent people and 'psychopaths'. It may well be that Murphy, Moore, Bates, McKeague, the members of the various UFF teams, the IRA 'interrogators' who tortured a suspected tout with electricity before shooting him,[13] and the many others who in the last twenty years have inflicted grievous pain on their victims are indeed markedly different from the rest of us, but the widespread nature of the phenomenon suggests otherwise.

Without wishing to pretend that I fully understand why some people are capable of inflicting enormous pain on fellow human beings, I would like to suggest an alternative approach to explaining the Butchers. First we should recognize the commonplace nature of violence in urban working-class culture. Many working-class men regard physical force as an appropriate 'manly' way of

[12] Ibid. 88.
[13] *Irish News*, 28 Feb. 1974.

settling arguments, competing for status, and revenging slights and insults. As the biographies of 'hard men' like the Krays, Jimmy Boyle, Paddy Meehan, and John McVicar readily demonstrate, violence is just a part of life in certain social worlds.[14]

Secondly, one should appreciate the dehumanizing nature of enduring group conflict. When one 'people' has a long history of conflict with another, it develops invidious stereotypes so that its members are no longer seen as fully human. In an excellent discussion of group identities and boundaries, Randall Collins makes the important point that, in most pre-modern societies, the recognition of others as 'fellows' was restricted to those of one's own people: 'within those boundaries, humanity prevails; outside them, torture is inflicted without a qualm'.[15] For some loyalists, Catholics are not people, they are 'Taigs', and Taigs deserve all they get. And, contrary to the view of such republican propagandists as Kelley, this is every bit as true for the other side. There is as much callousness and indifference to suffering in the IRA's willingness to blow people to pieces so small that they have to be collected in little plastic bags or in the 1990 innovation of tying victims to the driver's seat of vehicles loaded with explosives and making them drive to their death. For the IRA, soldiers are not people: they are 'legitimate targets'; retired policemen are not people: they are agents of an imperialist oppressor; wives, children, and girl-friends of ex-police reservists are not people: they forfeited that status when they married or were born to agents of the occupying power; and anyway they are Protestants and Protestants aren't really people. Enduring group conflict allows each side to see the other (and those of their own side who fraternize with the enemy or who fail fully to support their own people) as having forfeited the right to be accorded the privileges of humanity. Every brutality of one side justifies the other in revenging it with an even more callous act, and where there is no evidence of brutality, it will be supplied by rumour. Even if it was not true that 'they' cut off the victim's penis and left it in his

---

[14] For graphic depictions of the violence of some working-class cultures, see J. Boyle, *A Sense of Freedom* (London, 1977), and J. Pearson, *The Profession of Violence: The Rise and Fall of the Kray Twins* (London, 1985).

[15] R. Collins, 'Three Faces of Cruelty: Toward a Comparative Sociology of Violence', *Theory and Society*, 1 (1974), 417.

mouth, one can believe it because that is the sort of thing that 'they' would do.

These two observations concern the tendency to violence between groups. For reasons which we do not understand, some people are more violent and vicious than others. In most circumstances they will be controlled by social pressure, and the opportunities for them to act on their anti-social desires will be limited. If they resist the social pressure to conform and insist on acting on their violent impulses, they will be punished. What has happened in Northern Ireland is that political conflict has reduced the social pressures which would have confined Murphy's expression of his viciousness to the occasional knife fight and perhaps a few killings, each punished by long terms of imprisonment. Only if he had been able to follow the example of the Krays and acquire a fearsome aura of violence and live largely within a criminal subculture, would he have avoided being shopped. The social environment can permit, encourage, or inhibit the acting out of anti-social tendencies.

What explains Murphy and the UFF murder teams of the early 1970s is the circumstances which not only allowed them to act out their anti-social tendencies but also rewarded them for doing so. When there was a 'good reason' for killing, when it could be publicly justified, and it became more and more common, then what one could do, and had to do, to be a 'hard man' was to kill and kill a lot. As one convicted murderer told me: 'It's like a game. If he killed one, you had to kill two. If he did three, you did four. To be top, you know. The man.' The rewards were considerable. Murphy's actions and the reputation they brought him allowed him to achieve a quality of life that might otherwise have been denied him. No one 'took liberties' with him. He was well paid. Because they feared him, people gave him 'respect'. His reputation attracted women. In sum, the political climate created a reward structure that encouraged some hard men to seek power and status based on their willingness to commit brutal acts.

This point reminds us of something missed by Dillon and that is that people's patterns of behaviour do not spring ready formed from their personality or childhood experiences (or whatever else is thought to be the wellspring of motives) but develop gradually. Any form of career, be it murderer or chartered accountant, is usually the end result of a number of very small decisions, some so small that at the time they do not even appear as decisions. Mostly we drift into a particular line of action, often led by our own unwillingness to make a bold decision. Here the difference between what we know about our feelings and what we know of others is vital. We know how we really feel, but we have only his word about how he feels. We do not know that he may really feel frightened, hesitant, revolted. Young men in a group brag and strike postures. The desire to be accepted by the group leads one person to endorse the sentiments offered by others and even to 'trump' them. In order not to lose face, one is pulled into doing something that one *claims* one is willing to do but privately one fears and loathes.[16]

You know, we'd be blowing about this and that. How we'd do this and that to the buggers for what they'd done. All fuckin bravado. I was scared shitless but it never occurred to me that they didn't want to do it either. It was only later, after you'd done the job and were back at the house shivering that you might admit it. Even to yourself. It was only in prison that we talked about it and I realised the other guys were as feared as I was.

Although I have already suggested that there is no great difference in the brutality of many IRA men and the Moore–Bates gang, there is no doubt that the IRA has a better image than the loyalist paramilitaries. The reason for the propaganda advantage is not that IRA men are nicer than UVF men. The Provisionals have too many atrocities to their name for that, and many of them are quite happy killing close-up. The difference is in the nature and availability of targets. If there have been fewer cases of republicans repeatedly stabbing their victims, it is surely because of the very different circumstances in which republicans find victims and not because they are more pleasant people. When the most favoured targets are security-force personnel shielded by armour plating, concrete walls, and barbed wire fences, the sniper's rifle, the culvert bomb with a wire to a control point in the Republic, and the mortar are the most effective weapons. When circumstances require, there seem as many republicans willing to kill in an intimate manner. One practised murderer specializes in shooting his victims from behind in the head at such close range that he must often be covered with blood and brains.

[16] Matza, *Delinquency and Drift*, 52–3.

As a final observation I return to self-image. Although atrocities do hurt the reputation of, and support for, the IRA, they are more readily excused because violence itself is not at odds with the nature of the organization. Despite the humane face of Gerry Adams, 'physical-force' republicanism has long glorified in the cleansing power of blood. Being allied to the state and the government, the loyalist tradition has less of a legitimate place for uncontrolled uninhibited violence. When the avowed purpose is to maintain law and order against cowardly rebellious Fenian scum, the enjoyment of killing discredits the organization that cannot discipline its members.

The Colour of Money

Organizations need resources. Most voluntary associations rely on membership subscriptions or something like them. However, when the need or the desire for money outstrips the ability or the willingness of the members to pay up, other sources are required. In this section I want to look at the various ways in which loyalist paramilitaries have funded their activities and the consequences of those choices. In particular I want to examine the implications of different sources of funding for internal cohesion and external image, or organizational discipline and popularity.

Subscriptions. When, in the early 1970s, the UDA was first accused of using illegal means to raise money, Tommy Herron indignantly asserted that nothing could be farther from the truth and that the UDA was funded solely by the subscriptions paid by its legion members. It certainly was not the case when Herron said it and had not been for more than the first few months of the organization's life.

Drinking clubs. Private drinking clubs proliferated in the early days of the Troubles. In part there was a reluctance to go out at night into main shopping areas and thoroughfares; in part people just wanted cheap drink and the company of like-minded people. Drink has always played a major part in the life of the paramilitary organization. Public houses provide the best public meeting-place where men can be away from the prying eyes and anxieties of their wives and children. Spence's team met in the Standard Bar. In the

early 1970s the UVF brigade staff could often be found in the
Bayardo Bar, round the corner from the office above The Eagle
chip shop on the Shankill Road. Vigilante groups used old tin halls
and empty houses as their headquarters and many were gradually
transformed into clubs. With so much time (and money) spent in
pubs and clubs, it made sense to have the profits ploughed back
into the organization. Surprisingly, the government did not mind
and licences were readily available, as was the labour to renovate
and police such clubs. Some were no more than an ordinary
terraced house; others were elaborate. One club had been a
cinema. With falling audiences, the owners tried to run a bar in
the foyer, but this was not a great success. A paramilitary group
offered to buy it, but the owners sold it to a publican who spent a
lot of money renovating it. Just before it was due to open, it was
badly damaged by fire. Surprise, surprise; it was then sold to the
paramilitary group.

Despite their barely disguised connections with paramilitary
organizations, the clubs had their licences renewed without difficulty. The Loyalist Club in north Belfast's York Road had its
application rejected because of a history of persistent fighting, but
it was the exception until the early 1990s, when the government
introduced a number of laws designed to limit paramilitary funding. Recently a number of clubs have had their licence applications
rejected for what is euphemistically described as 'inadequate
book-keeping'.

As the Mafia quickly discovered, the best way of using illegal
earnings to bring in more funds is to invest them in legitimate
businesses. Apart from the clubs, loyalists have not been terribly
successful at creating legitimate enterprises and some clubs have
even been so badly run that they have lost money.

Black taxis. In the early 1970s public transport in Catholic west
Belfast was often disrupted. Buses represented a readily accessible
part of 'the state' to attack. They are also big and burn well, which
makes them excellent barricades. In one estimate, by 1974 330
buses had been destroyed at a cost of £4.5 million. The local
solution to an often suspended transport service was the purchase
of large numbers of clapped-out London 'black taxis'. Rather than
take one person to his destination, these operated more as buses,
taking large numbers along pre-defined routes, picking up and

dropping off on the way, and usually at fares lower than the cheapest bus.

Once the idea had caught on in the Catholic Falls, it was imitated on the Protestant Shankill and Shore Roads. There was even co-operation across the divide when the government tried to clamp down on the black taxis by insisting that they were properly insured. The Falls Road taxi organizers helped the loyalists arrange insurance. Although republican and loyalist organizations deny it, the police are convinced that the taxi operations are a major source of funding for the IRA and UVF. In 1988 McKittrick estimated that seventy drivers were paying the UVF £29.20 a week, which amounted to more than £100,000 a year.[17]

Armed robbery. In September 1972 leaders of the UDA and UVF met to discuss the recent spate of armed robberies and issued a press statement denying that either was responsible: 'We will not tolerate the terrorizing of people. Consequently we warn the gangsters responsible that from today we will take special steps to apprehend them and warn all concerned that they will be severely dealt with.'[18] This was disingenuous hokum. The UDA and UVF have always raised money from armed robbery. Even the pre-1969 UVF did it. It got easier in the lawlessness of the early 1970s, when the murder rate and civil disorder kept the police stretched and when many people were afraid to give evidence. In 1971 there were two thousand armed robberies and one can guess that half of them were the work of loyalists. When armed robbers entered, a surprisingly large number of people developed bad eyesight and poor memories. By 1972 both the UDA and UVF were regularly robbing banks, post offices, and building societies. In case any-one needs convincing, reports of court cases can be checked. In January 1973 four UDA men from south Belfast were con-victed for robbing a publican of over £1,500. Five months later another four were convicted of robbing the Northern Bank on the Woodstock Road in east Belfast of £13,000. A member of UVF brigade staff told me:

There was a lot of people not happy about robbing banks and Post Offices. I wasn't happy about it but after a while we realized that we

---

[17] D. McKittrick, *Dispatches from Belfast* (Belfast, 1989), 147.
[18] Joint UVF–UDA press statement, 14 Sept. 1972.

needed to do 'appropriations' and we thought it was better taking it off the British government because they weren't doing the job and that's why we had to step in. Anyway, the banks and post offices got their money back. For a while we thought about giving them IOUs saying they get their money back after the war. We read that Che [Guevara] did that.

When large sums of money are needed, robbing banks is still the preferred option. The large joint UDA–UVF–UR arms buy discussed in Chapter 10 was funded with £250,000 stolen from a bank in Portadown.

Extortion.   The OIRA pioneered an extremely lucrative form of tax fraud. As a concession to small businesses operating on thin margins, small building contractors and one-man firms which have a good record of paying tax can apply for exemption from having income or value-added tax deducted from money owed to them by the main contractor on a building site. Instead of tax being taken off before the sub-contractor is paid, the whole sum is paid and the sub-contractor is supposed to settle his tax bill in full at the end of the financial year. Misuse of the system was easy. A *bona fide* certificate and identity cards were bought. Workmen getting paid £200 a week gave £50 to their 'patrons' (saving on the £66 tax they should have paid to the government). As there was no record of their employment, they could claim unemployment benefit and add perhaps £50 or £60 to their income.[19]

The certificate dodge was largely an OIRA racket and a little too sophisticated for some of the UDA men, who preferred more straightforward extortion.[20] But the profits to be made from both were too large to allow political differences to interfere with business. The UDA gave the OIRA permission to work building sites in mixed and even Orange areas in return for the freedom to operate its 'security-firm' extortion rackets in nationalist areas.

Robbery is simply illegal and unwelcome to the victims, but protection rackets are more ambiguous and offer scope for the actor to disguise the nature of what he is doing. The UDA came into being through vigilante activity and it saw itself as the pro-

[19] J. Adams, *The Financing of Terror* (London, 1988), 206–7.
[20] For reasons that are not at all obvious to me, the OIRA has always produced the most sophisticated means of fund-raising. In 1991 a court case showed it to be involved in counterfeiting currency.

tector of the loyalist people. As soon as UDA groups started creating 'no-go' areas and insisting on their need and right to police those areas, then policing in the more general sense of maintaining order became an issue. Often people would turn to the local UDA boss to have some problem solved. In return, the grateful recipients of advice and protection would make a donation to the organization's costs. In June 1973 there were stories of the UDA extorting money from businessmen in east Belfast. A group of publicans held a news conference in which they insisted that they had asked for and welcomed the protection the UDA gave. One publican said that the UDA had helped stop looting and robberies and that without its help he would have had to close.[21] But it is not a long way from solving people's problems and receiving a donation to hinting that, unless businessmen make a donation, they will have problems.

Stories of extortion surfaced regularly and ever more frequently in the early 1980s. An additional aura of respectability was conferred on some of the activities by the creation of 'security' firms. Some of the UDA fronts did actually provide conventional security, but many of their customers signed up because they were made aware of the likely costs of not doing so. The police became sufficiently concerned about this source of revenue to persuade the government to outlaw it, and from January 1988 it became a criminal offence to operate a security firm without a licence from the Secretary of State. It also became an offence to employ an unlicensed security firm.

Small shopkeepers and pubs and clubs were obvious and lucrative targets for 'protection-money' demands, but, for the UDA at least, the most lucrative enterprise was threatening building contractors. From the late 1970s the building trade in Belfast has been booming, first with slum clearance projects and then with the rebuilding of the commercial centre of the city. The extortionists justified their actions by portraying builders as businessmen getting rich from the hardships of ordinary people. If they could afford to leave behind the Troubles and drive home in their

[21] One has to allow for the corruption of some businessmen. In 1980 a printer on the upper Newtownards Road was sentenced to a year in prison for torching his own shop. In financial difficulties, he had tried to burn it down once and only caused slight damage; he approached the east Belfast UDA and asked them to do a proper job for him. Which they did. *Belfast Telegraph*, 21 Feb. 1980.

BMWs to their comfortable bungalows in north Down, why shouldn't they make a contribution to the 'war effort'? If they had to be encouraged to make such a contribution, so what? They were still getting more than their due while the men who defended Ulster languished in prison.

That many paramilitaries actually felt such resentment (rather than claiming it later as a rationalization for their acts) seems clear. It comes through from time to time in their attitudes towards members of the security forces. Although they are generally very sympathetic to those who have been selected as PIRA targets, one can find in *Ulster*[22] and in *Combat*[23] complaints about the high salaries being paid to RUC men and prison officers. UDA and UVF men made great sacrifices to defend Ulster and they got paid nothing. So why shouldn't they 'expropriate' the funds needed to finance their armies?

Although building sites provided easy targets for extortion, they did cause problems. Demanding protection money from a builder working in the middle of the Shankill was easy enough, but what did one do when he finished that job and started work on a site at the bottom of the Road, next to the republican Unity Flats? Now PIRA or INLA would want their cut and arrangements would have to be made. While there might be very good business reasons for negotiating with the enemy, it gave excellent ammunition to those critics who wished to portray loyalist paramilitaries as plain hoodlums, and it gave great scope for internal suspicion of the motives of men who did 'deals' with the enemy.[24]

Drugs. Since 1988 there have been two new lines of business in loyalist paramilitary fund-raising: drugs and pornography. Stories had been circulating for a few years before the murder of Billy McClure by the IPLO in March 1990. Martin O'Hagan of the *Sunday World* reported that McClure, who had UVF connections, had been involved in drugs-dealing with the IPLO. He also reported that Ulster Resistance, which has had trouble breaking into the more traditional forms of fund-raising, had imported a large amount of narcotics through Larne and sold it on to

---

[22] *Ulster*, Oct.–Nov. 1989.
[23] *Combat*, 25 Oct. 1989.
[24] See Ch. 10 for the career of Jimmy Craig.

criminals.[25] There was also a court case in January 1988 in which a van-driver at the Royal Victoria Hospital in Belfast admitted stealing pure cocaine and heroin from the hospital pharmacy in order to supply people in the UVF.[26]

Not surprisingly, it is hard to gauge the accuracy of the general claims about paramilitary drug-peddling. There is no doubt at all that loyalist prisoners have access to 'soft' drugs and thus, one may presume, that the leadership of the UDA and UVF knows about and either tolerates such a trade or is not sufficiently powerful to stop it. A senior UVF man killed in 1988 was reputed to be a supplier of 'blow'. Equally, I find persuasive those senior loyalists who insist that they are fundamentally opposed to the distribution of cocaine, morphine, heroin, and 'crack'. Although the RUC reported the shooting of three Chinese men in a north Belfast take-away as a punishment for failing to pay protection money, the UVF commander who sanctioned the shootings insists that they were involved in supplying hard drugs.

A difficulty in judging the conflicting accounts is that a para-military tag is often used for everything a person does, even when an act is not part of his work for the organization. Furthermore, people continue to be described by the labels 'UDA' and 'UVF' long after they have left or been expelled from the organizations. Given the large numbers of working-class loyalists who have been involved, it is likely that many of those now involved in drug-dealing will once have been involved in the UDA or UVF. What we need to know is the extent to which the organizations are now sanctioning and profiting from the distribution of drugs. The RUC says 'a lot'; the UDA and UVF say 'not at all'. The truth may lie somewhere in between, but I have no independent way of knowing.

The Problems of a Cash Economy

Legitimate enterprises keep detailed accounts and have them regularly certified by qualified accountants. Illegal organizations have to deal in cash with poor (if any) records of transactions. This causes a lot of problems. The easy money to be made is always a temptation to turn a little 'homer'. In an interesting case in June

[25] *Sunday World*, 3 June and 27 July 1990, and subsequent issues.
[26] *Newsletter*, 18 Jan. 1988, reported fully in *Republican News*, 21 Jan. 1988.

1988, a snooker club owner testified that three men had introduced themselves to him as the local UDA and demanded £5,000. 'I said I had an arrangement whereby I paid to the welfare of the UDA and if they were demanding money from me they had better square it with their headquarters first. Wallace then said "Fuck headquarters" and Coard said "This is our patch".' The demand was later halved and finally cut to £500. The owner arranged to pay in six days' time and meantime contacted the police and had video cameras fitted so that, when his extorters returned, they performed for the cameras.[27]

It is hard to be sure who was on the 'take'. The UDA and UVF accuse each other of being nothing but a bunch of gangsters. Such rivalry and mutual denigration is repeated within each organization, so that one area group will challenge the honesty of others. In the course of my interviews I have heard almost every leading paramilitary figure accused of personally enriching himself at the expense of his organization; the accusation is made especially often of people who have been deposed. In some cases the charge is reasonable, but the routine way in which it is deployed makes one suspicious of its application in many instances. One man acutely made the point that, as soon as a major figure dies, everyone accuses him of fraud: 'Fuck, if I get killed they'll say I took the money and that's yer own people!' Because it is always possible that someone is sticking to the money, and because the accusation is difficult to disprove, it can be frequently made, which creates a climate of mistrust and envy. A senior UVF man described his area's banking system:

We had an elderly man who was our treasurer. He was kept out of the way, never went to meetings or that. He ran a small shop and buried the money in that. Another man bought this wee shop and put a few tires in the window. Never did anything. He'd maybe fix the odd flat now and then but that's how a lot of the money was banked and moved about, through wee businesses. We didn't have a problem because our man was so tight but in some places there was a lot of trouble with all that loose cash and people dipping.

A UDA brigadier from the early 1970s said: 'I never handled big sums of money. There was no central brigade kitty. When we need money to buy toys and sweets, like, I instructed the company

[27] *Belfast Telegraph*, 7 June 1988.

commanders to raise so much by such a date.' Although the UDA brigadier was protecting himself against accusation, his system, like that of the UVF commander, relied on the integrity of the individuals who handled the money. The combination of the need for secrecy, the ease with which large sums of cash could be raised, and the lack of strong internal discipline created a climate in which many failed to resist the considerable temptations to enrich themselves. This naturally caused resentment among the rank and file and among the surrounding population. However, it is interesting to note that, within the organizations, feelings about personal financial gain are tempered by estimates of the worth of the person involved. A newspaper's tolerance of creative accounting in a journalist's expenses is related to the value of the story—a good story justifies more padding. Likewise a bit of high living will be tolerated if it is, in the new management jargon, 'performance related': 'I don't mind buying some fucker a car if they're doing something. But what are these guys doing? I'm not buying some cunt that's not doing nothing a new car.' The 'something' which they should be doing is killing IRA men. So long as an individual or a team is active and justifying its funding, resentment is less. But, as periodically happens, when other parts of the group's operation go wrong, when murders are botched, arms are lost to the police, volunteers blow themselves up or are arrested, or simply when there is not enough activity, then the perpetual suspicions become a cancer of complaint and undermine the solidarity of the group. A cycle of decline sets in as disillusioned good men withdraw and are replaced by hoodlums.

The UVF and Rackets

Racketeering within the UDA in recent years will be discussed in detail in Chapter 10. The UVF has always prided itself on being more principled and disciplined than the UDA. Every UVF man I have interviewed has asserted that, in comparison to the crooks in the UDA, most UVF men were straight. If there is a real difference, it may be explained by the greater strength of the UVF outside Belfast. The rural areas were known for their financial probity:

There was less trouble with money in the country areas. The country men were always different. They were fine at the shootings and bombings—

they liked the military things—but they hated robbing banks. Wouldn't do it. Raised all their money from themselves.

The city UVF men certainly robbed banks and they did extort. In April 1986 a small shopkeeper had his shop burnt during loyalist disturbances. He is convinced that it was no coincidence that he was not paying the UVF while other businessmen around him were. In May 1990 a Belfast court was shown taped evidence of a UVF man from Tyndale Grove (a strongly UVF area of North Belfast) extorting from three firms—two Protestants in North Belfast and a Catholic firm in Mallusk.

None the less, the evidence of fewer criminal cases as well as a smaller amount of plausible rumour suggest that the UVF has less of a problem than the UDA. UVF leaders themselves see this as a consequence of having kept to a minimum the circumstances that tempt members to enrich themselves. Perhaps of more importance has been the smaller size of the UVF, which makes internal control easier.

A Proletarian Movement

The point I am about to make is to an extent speculative. I do not have the evidence that would allow me to assert it with confidence but there is an important point of contrast between the loyalist paramilitaries and the IRA. For the reasons that I will elaborate in the final chapter, the IRA is able to recruit across a far wider spectrum of the class structure. Although it is primarily a working-class organization, it has some support from the university-educated middle classes and hence access to the accounting, legal, and business skills required to 'launder' its funds. The UDA and UVF are almost entirely without such resources and have thus had to raise and handle money in a much cruder fashion that creates more opportunities for homers and for internal envy, dissension, and disarray.

8

Security Forces and Terrorists

WHEN asked why they got involved, loyalist paramilitaries always mentioned, with varying degrees of fluency, the state and the security situation. They became volunteers because 'the Taigs was running up our street', republicans were destroying Northern Ireland, the IRA was killing Protestants, and the government was not acting with sufficient resolution. Whether the motive to paramilitarism is defence, prevention, deterrence, or revenge, it is related to the actions of the state. At its simplest:

There would be no need for the UVF if the government was doing its job properly. None of these lads would be in the Kesh now if the politicians had done what they should have done. We had to step in to fill a vacuum. It was a matter of survival.

The idea of 'filling a gap' is central both to the motives of those who joined and to persuading people outside the paramilitaries to support the volunteers; the success and survival of the UDA and UVF are thus intimately connected to the operations of the security forces. At one extreme of the range of possibilities, there may be little space for paramilitary initiatives because the security forces are seen to be doing the job. At the other, there may be considerable support for vigilante activity because the sense of being abandoned is widespread. Potential for paramilitary activity thus depends on the balance between a sense of threat and perceptions of the competence of the security forces. In the brief description of changes in the security climate around 1977 I suggested that support for the UDA and UVF declined when Protestant satisfaction with the security forces increased.

There is a second 'equation' which is vital to understanding the fortunes of paramilitarism and that is the response of the state, not to the enemies of the state, but to its supposed defenders. The second UVF of 1920 did well, not just because there was popular Protestant demand for it, but also because the government tolerated and in places encouraged and legitimated it. In this chapter I explore the operations of the security forces in this second equation: their relationships with the UDA and UVF. Have the army and police treated the loyalist paramilitaries as wayward but useful adjuncts to state policy or as enemies of the state?

There is no shortage of claims that the British government, largely through the Special Air Service (SAS), has encouraged the UDA and UVF with guns and information, and even at times taken part in joint operations with loyalist paramilitaries. Raymond Murray in *The SAS in Ireland* usefully brings together in one volume all the evidence for that case.[1] At the outset I want to differ from Murray and those whose allegations he repeats, not so much in my conclusions but in my caution about coming to conclusions. Too many of those who have written about the security forces in Northern Ireland have been happy to settle for a level of proof that will convince only those who already share their views. Too rarely are the motives of those who make allegations of security-force collusion questioned, when, given the secrecy with which such work would be carried out, good evidence will always be in short supply and the plausibility of any story will rest on the credibility of the teller.

Another introductory caution needs to be entered. Evaluating the record of the security forces is not easy when all sides have political capital to make from shaping public perceptions. There is a curious consonance of interests between loyalist paramilitaries and republicans, in that both wish to present the UDA and UVF as simply the security forces off duty. Republicans wish to show that, far from being neutral keepers of the peace, the RUC and UDR are active in the oppression of the Catholic people. In particular, such sources as *Republican News* want to show that the sectarian assassination campaign of the UDA and UVF is indistinguishable from the work of the state's forces. The UDA and UVF have an interest in pressing the same suit, but for the quite different reason that they want to claim legitimacy by showing that they have had within their ranks men who have served their country in more 'official' capacities. Thus one finds an article in the UDA's *Ulster* saying that, of forty-one lifers in Compound 17 of the Maze, four were RUC men, five were in the UDR, nine were regular army (these were men who had completed their military service before getting involved in the UDA), two were

[1] R. Murray, *The SAS in Ireland* (Cork, 1990).

prison officers, and six were Territorials.[2] That two of the major parties to the rhetorical conflict share a common interest in slanting perceptions of the RUC and UDR should make us wary in interpreting the evidence.

There are a number of different sorts of overlap between the paramilitaries and the Crown forces. The security forces may co-operate actively with loyalists by training, arming, and joining them in murders. If they are not taking an active part, army and police personnel may still offer a great deal of low-level assistance, from providing information to turning a blind eye, and in such ways make the jobs of the UDA and UVF men easier. In a third type of overlap, loyalists use the security forces by infiltrating them and taking advantage of the resources that are available to the state. Each of these possibilities will be discussed in turn.

Active Participation

In 1974 the Republican Press Centre claimed that the members of the UFF were 'in reality members of the British army assassination squads'.[3] With sixteen years of hindsight to draw on, and considerable knowledge of the UFF, I am sure that there is little or no truth in this claim. We know that British soldiers have murdered in circumstances that allow of no reasonable defence; the 'pitchfork' killings of a Catholic farmer and his labourer near Newtownbutler in Co. Fermanagh in October 1972 are a case in point. Although these were blamed on loyalist paramilitaries, they were the work of soldiers of the Argyll and Sutherland Highlanders who had almost no contact with local Protestants. There have also been a large number of killings of republicans, uninvolved Catholics (and even Protestants), in which members of the security forces, with varying degrees of plausibility, claim that their use of fatal force was justified. Many of these are documented by Murray. Here I am concerned with the narrower range of cases where it has been claimed that members of the security forces worked with loyalists to commit serious crimes.

The most frequently cited case concerns the role of Captain Robert Nairac in the murder on 10 January 1975 of John Francis

---

[2] *Ulster*, Sept. 1984.
[3] *Irish News*, 22 Feb. 1974.

Green at a remote farm just over the border in Co. Monaghan. Green was a leading IRA man who had escaped from the Maze by changing clothes with his brother, a Catholic priest. He was shot and killed in what appears to have been a very well-planned operation. At the time the speculation was that Green had died as the result of an internal IRA feud, because of some personal dispute, or at the hands of the UVF (who claimed the killing). However, Captain Fred Holroyd, who served as an intelligence officer at the same time as Nairac, claims:

I can only relate that Robert Nairac said quite plainly that he had been involved in the killing. He then produced a photograph of the dead man, lying in his own blood—a colour Polaroid, showing Green's corpse, with a black uncurtained window in the background. I took the photograph from him and asked if I could keep it. I was a keen collector of all such memorabilia. . . . Nairac seemed none too happy with this. But he did not ask for it back. . . .
  He told me that he had killed Green, together with two other men, who I assumed were S/Sgt B and the Sergeant Major, as they worked as a team. They had crossed the border without interference, and driven down the country road to Gerry Carville's farm. . . . They waited for their moment, kicked in the door and then emptied their guns into his [Green's] body.[4]

Does this story sound plausible? Do SAS assassins—when sober and in an office rather than drinking in a pub—tell other officers who are little more than acquaintances about their killings and do they show off photographs? And if, as Holroyd says, Nairac was 'none too happy' about handing over the photograph, why did he not insist on retaining it? If Nairac had shown the photograph and then put it back it his pocket, the story would have a truer ring.

  David McKittrick, who was initially sympathetic to Holroyd's claims, assessed the evidence of the photograph in 1987:

Mr Holroyd originally said that the photograph was not available for inspection, but the Royal Ulster Constabulary obtained it from his ex-wife in Zimbabwe. The *Independent* has examined the original photograph and obtained a copy. It does not match Mr Holroyd's description of it. There is no window in the picture, and since flash was used, it is unclear whether it was taken in daylight or at night. But it is clear that the photograph was taken many hours after Mr Green's death and not by his

---

[4] F. Holroyd and N. Burbridge, *War Without Honour* (Hull, 1989).

killers . . . forensic evidence indicates that the photograph was taken about 18 hours after the victim's death.[5]

The picture was taken by the Garda and circulated to border stations. A copy was sent to the RUC and an RUC officer recalls passing it to Holroyd. McKittrick further says that he has seen the page of Holroyd's scrapbook which dealt with the Green killing; it makes no mention of Nairac. On the back of the picture, Holroyd had written 'John Francis Green—murdered by the PIRA during the Jan. 75 truce'. He subsequently added beside the photograph: 'later found to have been shot by the UVF'. Now it might be, as Holroyd asserts,[6] that the RUC cobbled together a replacement photograph, but why they should have bothered when the original could have remained 'lost'? Although it is obvious that the RUC made this material available so that McKittrick would contest Holroyd's story, McKittrick has an inestimable record of being honest, sceptical, and well informed. Dillon, who has no obvious record of a pro-state bias, concludes a detailed assessment by agreeing that there is no substance to the Holroyd accusations about Nairac.[7]

In the circumstance of claim and counter-claim, assessment of the evidence will hinge on our measure of the character of the witnesses, and there must be doubts about Holroyd's credibility. During his tour of duty, his marriage broke down. Following complaints from his wife, Holroyd spent a month under observation in an army psychiatric hospital where it was concluded that he was not mentally ill, simply under too much pressure. He was transferred to a less stressful posting in Britain and resigned his commission the following year. A man who had until then invested his entire sense of identity and self-worth in his army career, Holroyd has since 1976 been pursuing a campaign to clear his name and establish that he was victimized because of his inside knowledge of 'dirty tricks'. Although his vast sense of grievance does not mean that he is wrong, his entirely uncorroborated evidence is that of a man who has a very large axe to grind and a particular interest in documenting dirty tricks.

[5] D. McKittrick, 'Unravelling the Truth in Ulster's Dirty War', *Independent*, 2 Sept. 1987.

[6] Holroyd and Burbridge, *War*, 78.

[7] M. Dillon, *The Dirty War* (London, 1990), 189–97.

Since the Green allegations were made, Holroyd and Colin Wallace have expanded their claims about Nairac to suggest that he 'ran' the Portadown UVF, arranged the Miami Showband killings, set the Miami bomb to go off early so that it would kill the UVF men who 'knew too much', and was allowed by his masters to be killed by the IRA for the same reason. This is fanciful nonsense and rests entirely on the truth of the highly contestable allegations about the killing of Green. The connection between Green and the Miami killings is ballistic. The same Star pistol was used in both; whoever killed Green had some connection with whoever killed the Miami members. If Nairac had something to do with the first, he had something to do with the second. But there is absolutely no reason to suppose that Nairac had anything to do with the Green murder apart from the fact that such journalists as Duncan Campbell report Fred Holroyd saying that Nairac told him he had something to do with it. If we do not believe Holroyd on the Green murder, then we must dismiss all the other allegations. It is worth noting that the allegations about Nairac and the Miami killings were not made by Holroyd at the same time as the claims about Green but were added only after the RUC had made public the ballistics information. If Holroyd had been as well informed as he claims, he could have made all his allegations at once.

Green and the members of the Miami Showband were killed by the mid-Ulster UVF, and Dillon's account is reasonably correct.[8] There is no mystery, nothing missing, that needs the involvement of a Robert Nairac to make it complete. Holroyd's Nairac story is believed, not because it is well supported by the evidence, but because many critics of the security forces suppose that such things were and are going on. The SAS was operating in the province and the SAS murders IRA men. Add the belief that loyalist paramilitaries are inefficient bunglers who cannot assassinate without assistance from the security forces and one has a recipe for belief despite the absence of evidence.

The Larne UDA and John Turnly

In evaluating the Holroyd claims, McKittrick makes a very important point. When people have been convicted for crimes they

[8] Ibid. 161–222.

committed at the behest of or with the assistance of the security forces, they might use the fact of state patronage in their defence; the Littlejohns are a case in point. In 1987 McKittrick estimated that there were eight hundred loyalist prisoners in jail for terrorist offences, 234 of them lifers. Several thousand more have passed through the jails.

Of these thousands, fewer than half a dozen have attempted to claim that the security forces were involved in their offences. None of the claims has stood up to scrutiny. . . . loyalist paramilitary sources have never, either publicly or privately, claimed to have worked with the security forces in assassinations.[9]

Perhaps the closest to such a claim was that made by Robert McConnell of the UDA, after being convicted but before being sentenced for the murder of John Turnly. Turnly was an affluent Protestant businessman from Ballycastle, Co. Antrim, who crossed the sectarian divide and joined the nationalist SDLP. He was an SDLP member of the 1975 convention and a Larne councillor from 1973. In 1977 he moved from the SDLP to the Irish Independence Party (IIP). In June 1980 he was murdered by the UDA.

Two weeks after the Turnly killing, a UFF team murdered Miriam Daly, who, with her husband James, was active in the National H Blocks Committee, a republican organization that campaigned against prison conditions. In October another H Blocks activist was murdered by the UFF when Ronnie Bunting and Noel Little, leading figures in the INLA, were shot dead in a house in the Andersonstown area of Belfast. In January 1981 another member of the Committee, Bernadette McAliskey (née Devlin), was the target when she and her husband were shot and seriously wounded by a south Belfast UFF team.

The campaign against the H Blocks Committee was the most successful period of the UFF's history; leading republicans rather than ordinary Catholics were their victims. The tidiness of the Daly and Bunting–Little killings encouraged the usual claims about SAS assassination squads, and for once the claims were based on more than the assumption that, unassisted, loyalists were incompetent. After he had been sentenced for the killing of

[9] *Independent*, 2 Sept. 1987.

Turnly, Larne UDA man Robert McConnell delivered a statement to the court:

In or around the month of April 1980 I was working as a fish salesman in the Larne area. At that time, although not a member, I had links with a loyalist paramilitary organisation. I was stopped one day near Cushendall by a van containing a number of men. I became satisfied subsequently that these were all members of the SAS and I had dealings with them on that and a number of subsequent occasions. . . . On the occasion when I first stopped and after they had satisfied me who they were they asked me to place a listening device in a bar in Cushendall where they said Gerry Adams and another man were waiting to meet with some others. I went into the bar and fixed the device to the underside of a stool near where Adams was sitting doing a crossword. . . . I agreed to meet [the SAS men] again and do things like that again if the need arose. They knew that in the course of my business I was going in and out of republican areas and during a series of subsequent meetings with them they discussed with me republican leaders and, in particular, Turnly, Miriam Daly and Bernadette McAliskey. They said they had information that over a two-year period the Republicans had a plan to escalate tension in the Province by civil disorder, large-scale importation of arms and explosives and by certain actions which would arouse the sympathy of republican people with the ultimate objective of starting a civil war. We realise now that this involved the hunger strikes. We were told by [an SAS man] that Turnly was important in this regard because of his experience of imports and exports and because of his experience of dealings with the East. . . . During this period weapons, uniforms and information on how to obtain intelligence gathering equipment was supplied by [an SAS man] who would contact me by telephone and arrange for me to pick up various items on lonely roads at the dead of night.[10]

McConnell's earlier confession to the crime (and those of his co-accused) made no mention of SAS involvement and this raises the question of why he should wait two years (and until after he had been sentenced) to tell his story. Dillon offers various possibilities but the most likely explanations are (*a*) that it was true and McConnell waited until he was sure that his silence was not going to be rewarded with a short sentence before spilling, and (*b*) that the UDA wanted to claim legitimacy for its campaign against republican activists by showing that agents of the state encouraged them in it.[11]

[10] McConnell's statement to the court, 11 Mar. 1982.
[11] Dillon, *The Dirty War*, 305–8.

Even if we believe McConnell, it is worth noting the very limited nature of what is being claimed. The SAS men are supposed to have supplied arms and encouraged the UDA men to target Turnly. But the Larne UDA was not short of the necessary weapons, and, as a prominent Protestant republican, Turnly would have been an obvious target without any army encouragement. There is no claim that the SAS assisted in the killing, even to the limited extent of making sure there were no police checkpoints in the area.

Dublin Bombs

Another loyalist action which is sometimes attributed to the security forces is the car bombing of Dublin and Monaghan during the 1974 strike. Murray begins with the orthodox assessment that these were the work of the UDA and UVF in Portadown (they were actually the sole work of the UVF), but then adds the claim made by Holroyd that the gang 'had links with an MI6 officer through a Royal Ulster Constabulary detective sergeant'. He also reports Colin Wallace as saying that 'the explosives used to kill nineteen people in the indiscriminate bombing of a main Dublin street . . . might have been supplied by British Intelligence'.[12] Although a number of different reporters are cited by Murray in his two-page account of this case, it seems clear that Holroyd and Wallace are the common 'authorities' being used by all the versions, and neither offers any evidence. Holroyd's claim is based on his general observation of a link between the SAS and loyalists in Portadown, and Wallace is actually saying only that giving explosives to loyalists is the sort of thing one might expect British Intelligence to do. For obvious reasons I cannot be more specific, but my own information about the mid-Ulster UVF of this period reveals no strong links with the British army or British intelligence and, though they might be expected to claim it, those interviewed have all denied such assistance in the bombings.

The Londonderry UDA

In his catalogue of SAS crimes, Raymond Murray cites the case of the murder of Michael McHugh in January 1977 'by two members

[12] Murray, *The SAS*, 109; it was actually a UVF job.

of the UDA, one of them a British Army agent.... Because of the agent it might be described as an undercover British Army murder.'[13] It might, but not with any great conviction. McHugh was a Sinn Fein activist who claimed to have been threatened a number of times by the army and by members of the UDR. However, as Murray says, he was killed by two Derry UDA men, one of whom pleaded guilty to the crime in November 1987. William Bredin confessed after being arrested with eight others after a tip-off from an informer. The second man was out of the country and, because there was no evidence to warrant arrest, he was never charged. Murray offers no evidence for the claim that he was a British army agent apart from the fact that on the night of the murder he had an army map with McHugh's lane and house marked on it; not the most compelling of evidence. Although Murray does not explicitly connect the McHugh killing and the attack on the Top of the Hill bar in Derry, he clearly believes the 'second UDA man' was responsible for both, and the military precision of the attacks is the main reason for supposing security-force links.[14] We are back to the assumption that UDA and UVF men were incapable of doing a job well unless the SAS helped them. This is actually a curious assumption; Murray himself describes a number of cases of SAS incompetence, and the record of the mid-Ulster UVF shows the considerable competence of some loyalist operators. If I have correctly guessed the identity of Murray's 'second Derry UDA man', it is certainly true that he was very fit, militarily skilled—his diving skills allowed him to fire-bomb a fishing fleet—and an able organizer. He might have had those qualities because he was a 'British agent', but, more mundanely, he had them already as an ex-serviceman. Like many UDA men, he had been in the army and it was precisely because he had those skills that he was asked to lead the military side of the UDA in Co. Londonderry. This does not mean that he was not a Crown force agent (a close colleague described him as 'a bit odd, very close'), but it offers a perfectly good alternative to Murray's explanation, which is no more than the presumption that 'competent paramilitaries must really be SAS men'.

In my conversations with paramilitaries I was only offered one

---

[13] Ibid. 187.
[14] Which he calls 'Brow of the Hill'.

new claimed instance of security-force participation in a serious crime and that concerned an afternoon in the early 1970s when a group of UDA men was interrupted by a squad of Paras while assembling a bomb in the Jolly Roger. The sergeant asked them where they were planning to put that. When the UDA men sheepishly failed to speak up, the sergeant announced that his men had a good place for it and took the bomb to the Shamrock Club, where it went off, causing considerable damage. His men had recently had a lot of trouble from drinkers at the Club.

Aid and Toleration

Security-force assistance for the paramilitaries, short of actual participation in the planning or commission of murders, can take a number of forms. In the early 1970s the UDA and UVF were helped by the desire of the security forces to blame everything on the IRA. The bombing of McGurk's Bar remains a classic example. To add veracity to the false claim that the bomb was an IRA own goal, a captain in the Royal Regiment of Fusiliers assured newsmen that he had seen the crater in the centre of the pub before it was obscured by demolition work.

On 13 May 1972 a car bomb exploded outside Kelly's Bar on the Whiterock Road. Sixty-three people were injured, some seriously, and one was later to die. As the first casualties were being taken to hospital, loyalist gunmen opened fire from flats on the ridge in Protestant Springmartin. IRA men moved into Ballymurphy and fired back at Springmartin. The army fired on Ballymurphy. In all seven people—six civilians and one soldier—were killed in the shooting. The interesting feature of the incident was the report given by the army to the press that the car which contained the bomb had been driven up to the pub by two IRA men, who went inside for a drink. In fact, the car had been stolen from a pub on the Shankill Road and the army knew it.[15]

So long as influential sources of opinion played down the extent of loyalist violence, public pressure to have the perpetrators 'made amenable' (in the police phrase) remained low, which one can presume was a benefit to the paramilitaries.

---

[15] For a Ballymurphy account of the incident, see C. De Baróid, *Ballymurphy and the Irish War* (Dublin, 1989), 154–61. See also *Republican News*, 14 July 1972.

There could also be the turning of blind eyes. According to what Jim Hanna of the UVF told Kevin Myers,[16] in the gunfight that followed the Kelly's Bar bomb, an army patrol helped Hanna and two other UVF men get into Corry's Timber Yard, which overlooked the Catholic Ballymurphy estate. The soldiers were present when one of the UVF shot and killed a Catholic. When a major heard of the incident he ordered his men to withdraw, but they did not arrest the UVF men, who were allowed to hold their position.

The RUC and Albert Baker

One of the most cited sources of claims of security-force assistance is Albert 'Ginger' Baker, who deserted from the Royal Irish Rangers in July 1971, after only a year in the army. He joined the UDA in east Belfast and there took part in a number of robberies and murders as a member of what he called 'the No. 1 Assassination team'. In the spring of 1973, possibly because he was suspected by his UDA colleagues of being a British army plant, he returned to his regiment in England, where he was court-martialled and discharged from the army. On 31 May 1973 Baker walked into a police station and told the duty sergeant he wanted to confess to four murders and eleven armed robberies. In August he was charged in Belfast and in October he pleaded guilty and was sentenced to life imprisonment with a minimum of twenty-five years.

The RUC had arrested three members of the east Belfast UDA in December 1972. In January 1973 they were charged with four of the murders to which Baker later pleaded guilty. Another four men were charged with the same killings. It was early 1974 before the cases came to trial and when they did they rested entirely on Baker's claims that the seven men had assisted him in various ways with the murders. Sir Robert Lowry, the trial judge, decided that Baker's evidence was 'manifestly unreliable'.

Baker insists that the RUC offered him a deal to shop the leading figures in the east Belfast UDA and tutored him in his evidence. He believes he was promised 'special-category status', but when he was sent to an English prison he received no such

[16] *Hibernia*, 12 June 1975.

consideration. Whether it was the protest of an aggrieved man or the irrational act of an unstable person is not clear but, while at Albany high-security prison on the Isle of Wight, Baker grabbed a prison officer and held him hostage in return for a helicopter to fly him to the Irish Republic. The sorry fiasco ended when four other prisoners jumped him. According to Murray, Albert and his brother believe that the prisoners were SAS men who were going to throw him out of the helicopter![17]

Since then Baker has become a professional writer of letters protesting about his prison conditions and claiming that the security forces were active supporters of the UDA in east Belfast. His allegations have been given considerable publicity; in the late 1980s the Labour MP Ken Livingstone used the House and a volume of his memoirs to repeat Baker's claims of high-level security-force support for the UDA.[18]

Even when presented by a sponsor, Baker's claims are not impressive. Although he told Livingstone that the UDA had close links with the intelligence services, he could only name one other UDA man and say that he had an intelligence contact. Baker was able to name a number of RUC officers who, he claims, gave weapons and information about republicans to the UDA, but the bulk of his allegations to Livingstone are nothing more than the assertion that the RUC knew who the UFF killers were and did nothing about it. Here his memory fails him. The RUC did do something about it. They arrested many of them and detained them for over a year before failing to get convictions. Some of those they could not plausibly charge, they had interned.

There is no doubt that the east Belfast UDA of this period killed a lot of Catholics. There is also reason to suppose that one or two RUC officers gave loyalists weapons and information. There is no reason to believe Livingstone's dramatic claim that: 'if only a quarter of what Baker told me is true it would be enough to demolish both the government's policy and its record in Ireland'.[19] Dillon makes a very important point about the very small base on which the allegations were built and the circular way in which they are presented so as to add unwarranted plausibility to them:

[17] Murray, *The SAS*, 101.
[18] K. Livingstone, *Livingstone's Labour* (London, 1988), 128–30.
[19] Ibid. 128.

One of the comments made by Baker in the course of his meeting with Ken Livingstone was that he was in contact with republicans in prison. I believe this is how some of his allegations made their way to the outside world. Republicans would have been keen to circulate his claims; in turn those claims circulated by the Provisionals reached Ken Livingstone and were put as genuine questions to Baker. When the theory came full circle, it was being addressed to Baker as though the allegations were not his and he was being asked to corroborate them. As a result, when someone not sufficiently acquainted with Baker's claims reads the transcript of the interview with Ken Livingstone, Baker appears to be confirming widely held suspicions or allegations which have their origins elsewhere, when in fact the prime mover or prime conspirator all along was Albert Walker Baker.[20]

Dillon could have made the point even more strongly. Livingstone's book presents an edited version of his interview. The longer version which Dillon prints shows that the bits that Livingstone leaves out are patently leading questions. Despite their lack of substance and the fact that, on the only occasion they have been put to the test of a public trial, his evidence was dismissed by a court, Baker's claims continue to be repeated as if they were well substantiated.

In the course of my interviews I have been told many small stories of security-force actions that suggested, if not encouragement, at least indifference to the loyalist paramilitaries on the part of lower-rank soldiers and RUC men. To give just one representative example: in 1973 soldiers in Belfast stopped three armed UDA men and, instead of arresting them, handed them over to UVF men, who questioned them and then let them go.

By far the most common form of assistance was the passing of information about republicans. Random sectarian murder is easy. All one has to do is stop a lone figure, ask him his religion, and then shoot him. If the area is unambiguously of one religion or another, one does not even need to ask and the victim can be shot from a cruising car. But to plan the murder of a particular individual, one may need to know a lot about his habits of movement, the interior layout of his house, his appearance, his car number and type, and so on. This is the sort of information routinely collected by the RUC, the UDR, and the army, and given to their officers so that suspects can be followed, watched, and sometimes apprehended. The focus for suspicion of collusion between the forces of the Crown and the loyalist paramilitaries then is the passing of intelligence. In December 1972 MP Ivan Cooper was complaining that the UDA was using official photographs, provided by an RUC officer, to single out people in the Kilrea–Ballymoney area for attack. In 1975 a leading UVF spokesman asserted that the UVF had British army photographs of IRA suspects.[21]

A recent court case gives an excellent illustration of the way in which the sectarian geography of Northern Ireland and the isolation of the security forces encourage contacts between the paramilitaries and the army. Joanne Garvin and her sister were part-time UDR soldiers at Girdwood Barracks in north Belfast. Inevitably Garvin lived in working-class loyalist areas of the city: first in the Shankill and then in the Tyndale district of north Belfast (a strong UVF centre). The woman with whom Garvin shared a house was going out with a UVF man and was frequently in loyalist clubs. When the boyfriend was jailed, the friend started visiting the NAAFI barracks at Girdwood with Garvin and met Corporal Cameron Hastie of the 1st battalion, Royal Scots.

Garvin travelled to and from work at Girdwood in taxis. She told the police that she thought at least two of the men who regularly drove her were paramilitaries. One driver several times gave her car registration numbers and asked her to have their ownership checked on the army 'Vengeful' computer. He said that the cars had been seen following black taxis. Garvin at various times gave numbers to Hastie, and to two UDR men, who ran them and gave her names and addresses, which she passed to the taxi-driver.

When the Royal Scots were close to the end of their tour of duty, a number of men talked about leaving information material for the UDA or UVF. Hastie gave Garvin documents, which she passed on to one of her taxi-drivers. Police notes of the interrogation of Garvin show a clear awareness of what she was doing:

We put it to her that she knew that, by passing on photographs of republican terrorists, this would enable the loyalists to target and shoot

[21] BBC Radio Ulster, 15 Sept. 1975.

the republicans. She said she realised this . . . she just thought she would
give them to M because she hated IRA men.[22]

Even if inaccurate, such information was important to the paramilitaries because it reinforced their self-image as agents of the
state. They could assure themselves that, whatever senior officers
said for public consumption, lower ranks accepted the UDA's and
UVF's claim to be on the same side.

Reasons for Help

There were obviously many reasons why officers in the security
forces would leak information to the UDA and UVF, and it is
often difficult to untangle them. In the first place many officers
were and are either unionists or Unionists. Lt.-Col. George
Styles, who led the bomb-disposal officers in 1971 and 1972,
expresses his unionism in his usually robust way:

the ordinary law-abiding people of the benighted province [are] a credit to
the race that calls itself British. But weren't they always? I cannot understand the nonsense talked about letting the Ulster people leave the United
Kingdom. Their debt and homage to The Queen has been paid many
times over in blood and sacrifice. They are as much as part of the British
Nation as the Scots, the Welsh or the English.[23]

I do not want to suggest that most or even many officers who
regarded the unionist position as legitimate assisted loyalist terrorists, but some soldiers have been anti-republican to the extent
of being willing to help others to do what they would like to do
were they not constrained by their professional roles. As one
would expect, this is more common the lower the rank.

As the Garvin–Hastie case shows, the socially and geographic-
ally segregated nature of Northern Ireland means that an enemy's
enemy must be a friend. For British troops, safe billeting and
relaxed social interaction can only be had in Protestant neighbour-
hoods. Retired Colonel Peter 'Basil' Brush, the leader of the
DOW, frequently entertained British army officers. Soldiers drink
in pubs frequented by loyalists and even in loyalist clubs. In such
circumstances friendships can develop with loyalist paramilitaries

[22] *Independent*, 7 Nov. 1989.
[23] G. Styles, *Bombs Have No Pity: My War Against Terrorism* (London, 1975),
179.

which would be barely conceivable with republicans. For example, Kevin Myers reports Jim Hanna, by then the overall military commander of the UVF, having as close friends three officers of 39th Brigade Intelligence at Lisburn. Group photographs of Hanna and two officers were taken from Hanna's home after his assassination (reportedly at the hands of UVF colleagues who believed him to be passing information to the security forces rather than gathering it from them).[24]

While the patterns of social interaction might be the 'pull' factor in helping loyalists, there is little mystery in the 'push'. Of the 876 members of the security forces who died between 1969 and 1989, 847 were killed by nationalists.

Infiltration

So far I have been discussing cases of the security forces 'using' loyalist paramilitaries by assisting them to achieve their goals. We need also to consider what might be described as the reverse of that relationship: the manipulation or penetration of Crown forces by loyalist paramilitaries. The claims of infiltration are most commonly levelled at the locally raised UDR, and its history will be briefly summarized.

The British army was sent in to Derry and Belfast in 1969 because the local security forces—the Royal Ulster Constabulary and the B section of the Ulster Special Constabulary—were proving incapable of containing, without exacerbating, the worsening situation. The reforms of the RUC which followed the Hunt Committee's report and the shift to police primacy in 1976 have already been described. One of the key recommendations was the replacement of the wholly Protestant B Specials with a new local defence force which would be acceptable to the Catholic community. Reactions to the new UDR were interestingly mixed. Many unionists were suspicious of it, because its formation implied criticism of the B Specials, because it would be under Westminster control, and because its senior officers would be drawn from regular British army regiments. On the other hand, its members would be better trained, better equipped, and better paid. Some Catholic politicians—John Hume,' for example—

[24] *Hibernia*, 13 June 1975.

encouraged Catholics to join, while Bernadette Devlin, Eamonn McCann, and all republicans were critics from the first, regarding it as just the old USC with a new name.

Initially the UDR was successful in recruiting Catholics. In the first years 18 per cent were Catholics, but by 1978 this had fallen to only 3 per cent, where it has remained since.[25] No doubt some of that change represented minority disillusionment with the politics and composition of the force, but a lot of it was due to the IRA's campaign of intimidation of Catholics who supported the state by joining the security forces or the RUC or accepted positions on the bench.[26]

Loyalist paramilitaries encouraged each other to join the UDR and their involvement can be explained in two ways, both of which are equally true. Many joined the UDA and UVF because they wanted to protect their country and people from republican terrorists. They joined the UDR for the same reason: patriotism. UDA and UVF men also signed up for the new regiment because membership afforded weapons training, access to weapons, intelligence on republicans, inside knowledge of security operations against loyalists, and the high chance of being given a personal protection weapon firearms certificate.

Although known involvement in the UVF would have prevented enlistment, UDA membership was not initially regarded as an obstacle. A Shankill UDA company commander and one of the founders of the UFF was an NCO in the UDR. In late 1972 Brigadier Ormerod said that UDA men could be in the regiment. The complaints that followed his comments led to a fairly speedy reversal of the policy.

There are a large number of cases of UDA and UVF men using their membership of the UDR to facilitate serious crimes.[27] The case of the Portadown UVF and the Miami Showband killings has already been described. There was also the scandal of 5 UDR based at Magherafelt. A former loyalist paramilitary was 'born again' and went to the local police to confess his crimes. One

[25] W. D. Flackes and S. Elliott, *Northern Ireland: A Political Directory, 1968–88* (Belfast, 1989), 397.

[26] For details of the IRA campaign to intimidate Catholics out of the UDR, see C. Ryder, *The UDR* (London, 1991), 47–9. Catholic recruitment was not helped by almost all promotions going to ex-B Specials.

[27] Ryder, *The UDR*, 150–85, documents these.

concerned the murder in January 1976 of 71-year-old Samuel Millar. Millar came across three men changing number plates on a car that had been used in an armed robbery at a post office in September 1975. He subsequently became the chief prosecution witness in the case. Robert Davis, a full-time member of the UDR, and another man went to Millar's farm to persuade him not to give evidence. When Millar refused, Davis hit him with an iron bar and then reversed his car over the injured man. According to his own testimony, Davis hit him a number of times to kill him. The story then gets bizarre. A local Provisional saw the two men burying Millar near Lough Neagh. PIRA passed information to the police via the confidential telephone. When nothing happened, PIRA issued a public statement, which prompted security forces to mount a search operation.[28] As members of the UDR, Davis and a friend joined in the search. They drove to the spot, dug up Millar, dressed the body in a UDR uniform, propped it on the front seat between them, and drove it through two RUC check-points to a new burial site. There the matter would have rested had not Davis's friend 'got God'.

Robert Nelson, another member of 5 UDR, was sentenced to ten years for a number of UDA-related offences, including the 1975 raid on 5 UDR's armoury. One hundred and eighty guns were stolen but recovered three hours later from a slurry pit. Malcolm Allen, a member of 5 UDR in 1971–2, was also in the south Derry UDA and was convicted for his part in the armed robbery that led to the death of Samuel Millar.[29]

Clearly dual membership and good contacts gave UDA and UVF teams some general assistance in that they supplied them with general information, but most of those I interviewed did not think they were greatly helped by it. The following response is representative:

[28] Murray follows contemporary nationalist sources in seeing the initial lack of police action as proof of security-force indifference to loyalist crime, which it might have been, but equally well it might have been a sensible reluctance to walk into an IRA trap.

[29] The murder of Adrian Carroll in Armagh in Nov. 1983 is not discussed because I do not believe that this was the work of the four UDR men convicted. The details in Ryder, *The UDR*, and I. Paisley, jun., *The Case of the UDR Four* (Cork, 1991), convince me that the Carroll murder was what the UVF always said it was: a straightforward PAF murder.

Did it ever make much difference? There certainly wasn't a big conspiracy while I was active. It would have involved too many people. You couldn't have a conspiracy that big. One unit might help a wee bit with this or that move by telling you what the search priorities for the next week were but I can tell you, I was never shown in to a job by a squad of woodentops like a bloody cinema usherette with a torch. And we never had a promise of a clear run at this or that target. We never had contacts that good that you could be promised a safe run in or out. The tasking officers would always be changing the details of a patrol's work at the last minute anyway. If we'd half the help we are supposed to have had there would be a damn sight more dead Provies!

Arms

UDR bases contain armouries. Some UDR men are members of paramilitary organizations. Paramilitary organizations need arms. The next sentence is obvious. UDR bases have frequently been broken into by loyalists. Even before the Troubles, militant loyalists recognized the value of state arms depositories. In 1967 a UVF 'team' broke into the armoury of an army camp in Armagh and found that it contained only wooden replica rifles used in drill. But they got better. On 10 October 1972 the UVF relieved the armoury of the 11th battalion UDR (in Portadown) of 83 SLRs, 21 Stirling submachine guns, and a lot of ammunition: 'We got so much fuckin stuff we didn't know what to do with it.'

In 1987 the Laurel Hill, Coleraine, base of the UDR lost 140 rifles, 2 light machine guns, 30 pistols, and a large amount of ammunition when a UDR man smuggled two UDA men into the base in the boot of his car. The alarm was raised and the transit van containing the weapons was intercepted shortly after on the motorway heading to Belfast. 10 UDR battalion (Belfast) had all the weapons in the armoury of its Lislea Drive base stolen; some were recovered on the Shankill.

The Scale of Malfeasance

The above is all anecdote. It illustrates the sort of links that exist between the UDR and the UDA and UVF, but it does not give us any idea of how widespread this sort of illegality is. It would be possible simply to count the number of UDR men convicted for scheduled offences (although the Regiment's practice of forcing members who are charged to resign before their trial means that some links will be overlooked), but this would be meaningless without some point of comparison. Unless one wishes to use imagined human perfection as the baseline, one has to compare the criminality of the UDR with the criminality of some other groups in order to discover if the UDR (and the other security forces) are better or worse than one would expect them to be. In the choice of an appropriate comparison group, one has to be clear about background expectations. Some notion of the scale can be gained from recent figures published by the Irish Information Partnership and summarized in Table 8.1 which compare the convictions of the security forces and the civilian population.[30]

TABLE 8.1. *Conviction rates for scheduled offences, 1985–9*

Offenders	Total	Rate per thousand
Civilian population	2,662	5.9
RUC	6	0.9
UDR	29	9.1
British army	8	1.7

Source: Adapted from Irish Information Partnership, *Agenda: Information Service on Northern Ireland and Anglo-Irish Relations* (6th edn., London, 1990), table A7iv.

The first column gives the total of serious Troubles-related offences for the five-year period 1985–9, and the second column expresses these as the rate for a standard unit of population. The very small numbers of offences do not permit us to perform any sophisticated statistical tests of comparison, but there is a very clear story. While very few members of the RUC and British army were convicted for scheduled offences, the UDR rate is markedly higher than that of the rest of the population.

However, there is a major problem with this presentation. We know that most terrorist offences are committed by young men. The security forces are composed primarily of young men. To make the criminality rate for the general population more reasonably comparable with that of the security forces, the base population from which the 2,662 convicted criminals are drawn should be only 'young men'—a quarter of that actually used, and the number of convictions should also be reduced by taking out those

[30] Irish Information Partnership, *Agenda: Information Service on Northern Ireland and Anglo-Irish Relations* (6th edn., London, 1990), 249–51.

for offences committed by women, juveniles, and men over 35. The adjusted figures are shown in Table 8.2. This leaves the relative 'badness' of the three arms of the security forces the same but raises that of the comparable non-security-force population and gives us a more reasonable estimate. Now one could interpret the data as showing that, while UDR men commit more offences than the general civilian population, they are less likely to offend than civilian young men, a more reasonable line of comparison.[31]

TABLE 8.2. *Adjusted conviction rates for scheduled offences, 1985–9*

Offenders	Total	Rate per thousand
Male 18–35 civilian population	2,600[a]	23.0
RUC	6	0.9
UDR	29	9.1
British army	8	1.7

[a] Total estimated by removing known female and juvenile offenders.

Insiders and Outsiders

One can quibble about the actual numbers but certain conclusions can be drawn from the data. The UDR has a far worse record of scheduled offences than the army or the police. This seems relatively easy to explain. The soldiers of the regular army are far less involved in the life of Northern Ireland. They serve short spells of duty and their main loyalties lie elsewhere. They may 'take sides' sufficiently to slip a loyalist acquaintance the odd montage of republican suspects but they are unlikely to get involved enough to commit serious offences. The climate of violence of the early 1970s may have allowed some soldiers to feel justified

[31] To make the comparisons even more reasonable the denominators should all be changed to reflect the actual number of 'people who had an opportunity' to commit a serious offence. At present the number of crimes is being divided by the size of the, say, RUC force in an average year in that period. It should be divided by the total number of people who were in the RUC in that period, which is slightly larger, because of turnover. Similarly, the number of UDR officers who *could* have committed an offence while they were in the UDR is quite a bit larger than the establishment in an average year, because, as officers left, new ones joined. However, the numerator is so small relative to the denominator that such an adjustment makes little difference and I have stuck with the IIP method, after adjusting for age and gender.

in 'unorthodox' retaliation but the general decline in violence has undermined many of the justifications for overstepping the policing role.

The relative unwillingness of RUC officers to take revenge outside the law is significant.[32] The differences between the UDR and the RUC have two sources. First, the RUC is more selective than the UDR. Secondly, it is a predominantly full-time force. Of almost 13,000 men, only 1,600 are part-time reserve officers. In contrast, about 43 per cent of the UDR is made up of part-time soldiers. RUC officers become, by virtue of their jobs, far more isolated from their community and far more thoroughly socialized into the goals and norms of the organization. Although some RUC recruits may initially be strongly motivated by patriotic concerns for the preservation of the Protestant people, such loyalties tend to be replaced by bonds to fellow officers and to the force. One also has to note the very different circumstances in which they work, for such circumstances are a source of motives and justifications to act in this or that way. UDR men are much more likely than the RUC to be deployed in areas that bring them into frustrating contact with known republicans. Even with the gradual expansion of the police role, more UDR than RUC men will be found manning vehicle check-points in 'bandit country' and experiencing the situation of being sure who the IRA operators are but being unable to do anything legal about it.

The point about the competing loyalties of security-force personnel is an important one and should be pursued a little further. Although I have not tried to quantify this observation, my reading of the cases that clearly involve security-force personnel in illegal and active involvement with loyalist paramilitaries suggests that it is found most often in the lowest ranks, among those who served only a short time, and among what, for brevity, one might call the misfits. Albert Baker was in the army only a year before he deserted. Michael Stone, who killed three mourners at a republican funeral, was discharged from the army after only a matter of months.

It is difficult to come to any firm conclusion about collusion between the UDR and the UDA and UVF. On the one hand, one

---

[32] In the first twenty years of the Troubles, the RUC and RUC Reserve lost 173 and 90 officers, and 179 UDR soldiers were killed; there were more RUC than UDR personnel. For details, see Statistical Appendix.

has nationalist politicians and community leaders who see the UDR as a thoroughly sectarian force which allows loyalist paramilitaries access to the military resources of the state. On the other, one has unionist politicians such as Ian Paisley, in whose eyes the UDR is unblemished. As we have seen in the above statistical exercise, it is very difficult to find some sort of objective 'bad apple' count. The regiment does have a worse record of scheduled offence convictions than the army or the police, but, in the nineteen years since its formation, perhaps thirty thousand men and women have served in the UDR and only twenty-three have been convicted of murder or manslaughter. Considering the backgrounds of those recruits and the strains under which many of them serve, this is not evidence for the view that the UDR is nothing but the UDA and UVF in uniform. To return to comparisons, the record of the UDR is exemplary when set against that of armies and police forces in Latin America where, in the 1960s and 1970s, there was an almost complete collapse of law and order and the security forces became simply the enforcing arms of right-wing parties.

The Policing of Loyalist Paramilitaries

What is often entirely omitted from discussions of Crown force assistance for loyalist paramilitaries is a consideration of the many ways in which, and the extent to which, the security forces have policed the UDA and UVF. I will begin by looking at the attitudes of British army soldiers to loyalist paramilitaries.

From the start of the Troubles ordinary soldiers have shown ambivalence towards Protestants. Accounts of soldiers' attitudes to the Troubles show considerable initial sympathy with the Catholic minority. After internment and the start of the IRA's campaign, the dominant view was probably 'a curse on both your houses'. A corporal in 1 Para told Arthur:

On the Wednesday after internment, we came down from Ballymurphy along the Shankill Road and the pavements were lined with Protestants cheering us, throwing us packets of cigarettes, waving Union jacks. Our driver, a Jock, stopped the wagon and shouted at them, 'Don't you start, you bastards. Because its your turn next. It'll happen to you as well, because you're just as bad'.[33]

---

[33] M. Arthur, *Northern Ireland: Soldiers Talking* (London, 1988), 63.

In his brutally honest account of being a Parachute Regiment officer in Belfast in 1973, Clarke has an account of a raid on a loyalist club on the Shankill:

> Club raid. Fantastic. Fantastic. This is going to be fun. . . . It's difficult trying to keep the excitement to a quiet level. All the toms [Para 'squaddies'] wanting to be part of the action and in the raid group. . . . Hookey hits the door with a flying kick and bounces back into the street. Fury doubled, he and Brian attack it with crowbars and finally break in where the noise of screams from the women and yelling abuse from the men, mixed with flying bottles, glasses, chairlegs and whatever else is available, hits you like a wall. Some guy tries to crown me with a broken whisky bottle. I try to get my baton into a swinging position and eventually have to club him with my SLR. . . . Two of my men manage to get to the rear of the club and the physical resistance begins to falter under the viciousness of the onslaught. More soldiers come in from the street, but there's still a little fighting going on. I cock my rifle and the place goes quiet.[34]

For Clarke and his men the Protestant Shankill was every bit as bad as the Catholic Ardoyne, and this failure to differentiate was quite reasonable when one remembers Tommy Herron's war on the British army and the large number of security-force casualties caused by the UDA and UVF in the early years. One of Arthur's interviewees from 2 Para inadvertently testified to even-handedness when he glibly noted that their recruits from Belfast were the most vicious and said: 'They weren't sectarian; they would slap anybody round the head.'[35]

Army units were certainly willing to commit serious crimes against loyalists. Two Black Watch soldiers were convicted for setting up a leading UDA man by planting ammunition in his car hubcaps.[36] In May 1972 a plain clothes soldier leapt from a car and fired at four Protestants driving along Silvio Street, between the Shankill and Crumlin Roads.[37] Three months later there were a number of attempts, apparently by members of the Crown forces, on the life of William Black, a UDR man who witnessed undercover soldiers interfering with cars and reported them.[38]

[34] A. F. N. Clarke, *Contact* (London, 1983).
[35] Arthur, Northern Ireland: *Soldiers Talking*, 102.
[36] Murray, *The SAS*, 193.
[37] *Hibernia*, 30 Mar. 1973, pp. 16–17.
[38] K. Lindsay, *Ambush at Tully-West: The British Intelligence Services in Action* (Dundalk, 1979).

Suspicion remains strong that the murder of Tommy Herron was a security-force operation.

As we saw in the case of the east Belfast UDA connected with Baker, the RUC was quite willing to use lengthy remands to keep paramilitaries out of circulation. And, although they rate barely a mention in most accounts of internment, loyalists were detained under the various special powers.[39] When they were convicted, loyalists were sentenced as severely as republicans.[40] As we saw in Chapter 6, the supergrass system was used with as much enthusiasm against loyalists as against republicans.

Finally, the case of senior UDA man Brian Nelson (which is discussed more fully in Chapter 10) shows the price that loyalist paramilitaries paid for such assistance as they received from the security forces. In the ten years or more that Nelson was a double agent, many of the jobs we can infer he was involved in were botched and the main consequence of the intelligence material he collected was to convict the UDA men who had handled it.

Conclusion

It is no easy matter to shift from anecdote to some sort of objective evaluation of collusion between the security forces and loyalist paramilitaries. The very large numbers of UDA and UVF men who have been convicted for scheduled offences and imprisoned should disabuse anyone who wishes to argue that the state has encouraged the paramilitaries to act as surrogates in its war against armed republicanism. As one would expect, where the security forces have planted double agents, they have worked primarily to the detriment of the loyalist paramilitaries. A very very small number of junior and marginal members of the security forces

---

[39] K. Boyle, T. Hadden, and P. Hillyard, *Law and State: The Case of Northern Ireland* (London, 1975), 75, explains why loyalists were much more likely than republicans to be charged and convicted using the normal criminal courts, but none the less there were sixty loyalist detainees in mid-1974.

[40] In mid-1974 about 300 of 900 convicted terrorists were loyalists (Boyle, Hadden, and Hillyard, *Law and State*, 75). For a detailed discussion of the courts' treatment of loyalists, see K. Boyle, T. Hadden, and P. Hillyard, *Ten Years On in Northern Ireland: The Legal Control of Political Violence* (London, 1980), 82–6, which concludes that, 'Though there were a number of cases in which different sentences were imposed for apparently similar offences, we could find no evidence of any systematic variation.'

have actively aided the UDA and UVF. A very small number have given slight assistance in the form of weapons and information. Despite sharing a common enemy, recruiting from the same population, and living in the same areas, the security forces and the paramilitaries have not enjoyed a cosy relationship.

We should also note that contacts between paramilitaries and the agents of the state are not entirely to the benefit of the former. As data presented in the final chapter will show, the state is much more successful against loyalist murderers than it is against republicans.

Finally, there is a simple point that may get lost in the search for signs of the state helping loyalist terrorists. The greatest assistance given by the state was given inadvertently and pre-dated the Troubles and that was to recruit and train thousands of Ulster Protestants for the British army. The loyalist murder squads that have been successful have benefited far more from the military service and experience of their members than from any present Crown force assistance. The public and the government might not accept the UDA and UVF claim that they are simply serving their country, as they did in the regular army, but the military tradition and experience of the Protestant working class is much more important for the present paramilitaries than current and illegal assistance from the Crown forces.

Terrorists and Political Innovation

RIGHT-WING unionists feared the political potential of the paramilitaries and after the UWC strike did everything they could to put them in their place. Some left-wingers, nationalist and unionist, have harboured fantasies of the political potential of the UDA and UVF, seeing in their occasional criticisms of their unionist 'betters' the first signs of the shared working-class consciousness which would unite them with the OIRA in the overthrow of capitalism. In this chapter I will examine in some detail the political evolution of the paramilitaries and their electoral fortunes.

With one or two exceptions, the UVF was thoroughly 'military' and its Volunteers shared only a desire to save Ulster from republicans and a liking for action. The origins of the UDA gave it a quite different composition. As well as those attracted by the excitement or by the need to defend their areas against republicans, there were a large number of trade unionists and community leaders, often older men, who wanted to see the movement develop some sort of 'forward direction'. While their initial reasons for involvement may have been defensive and informed by little other than a wish to maintain the political status quo, they quickly came to see the possibility and importance of improving the position of working-class loyalists.

Barr and Independence

The origins of LAW have already been described. At the same time as Belfast workers were getting involved in it, a small group of shop stewards in Derry were organizing themselves. At first they were concerned to keep their industries working during the various 'days of action' called by civil-rights leaders in the first few years of unrest. The loose network of shop stewards and union activists was the framework for both the Derry UDA and the area's section of the UWC. The leader, Glen Barr, became vice-chairman of Vanguard and chairman of the 1974 strike co-ordinating committee. Although it was some time before he convinced others, he soon concluded that the only long-term solution to the conflict was negotiated independence.

At the three-day conference that followed the collapse of the executive, Barr failed to convince the other paramilitary representatives, but one year later at a dinner to celebrate the strike victory he spoke of readiness to form a provisional government to take over if the British withdrew.[1] The dinner provided a neat illustration of the lack of agreement. As Barr was speaking, he was slipped a note (it was not clear by whom), and he added that 'his leader' had reminded him that this was only a fall-back scenario for 'a doomsday situation'.

Barr parted company with Tyrie and the UDA in 1975 when Vanguard split. In the constitutional convention that followed the collapse of the power-sharing executive, Bill Craig promoted the notion of a 'voluntary coalition' with the SDLP. He was convinced that the convention was the last chance to retain some sort of devolved government in the province. Institutional power-sharing was not a possibility, but Craig believed that the various emergency coalitions that the British government had adopted in such times of national crisis as the Second World War offered a model. Formally the system of government would be the conventional one of rule by the largest party, but, if the unionists won, they would invite SDLP leaders to hold office on the basis of agreement with the policy of the governing party on major issues.

It is highly likely that voluntary coalition would have been stillborn: it is hard to imagine the SDLP being able to agree with a Vanguard government's security policy. It is also hard to imagine that the SDLP would even agree to the outline unless the 'real deal' was better than the public one—unless, for example, it had secretly been promised something like institutional power-sharing. Certainly the suspicion that coalition was just such a Trojan horse appears to have been a consideration in Paisley's rejection of the idea, as was his realization that attacking such an idea as a 'sell-out' would allow him to outflank Craig and secure for himself the leadership of the right wing of unionism. The Official Unionists, the Democratic Unionists, and a large number of Vanguard activists rejected voluntary coalition, and Tyrie agreed

[1] *Irish Times*, 30 May 1975.

with them. Barr, who was involved in promoting the idea as a Vanguard convention member, thought it was at least worth putting to the test of a referendum. Sammy Smyth was extremely critical. After the UDA tried to muzzle him, Barr withdrew.

Another Strike

Barr's return to the position of UDA political spokesman was a result of the embarrassment of the second UWC strike. The first had been initiated by loyalist workers and then sold to politicians, but the 1977 reprise was the brain-child of Ian Paisley and Ernest Baird (a Holywood chemist and political nonentity who had taken over the remnants of Vanguard when it had split). In October of 1975, Paisley said of the UDA: 'They have murdered Protestants as well as Roman Catholics in the most sadistic and inhuman ways and have sought to intimidate decent people who seek to carry out their business in a proper manner.'[2] Perhaps so, but he needed their muscle and persuaded Tyrie a general strike was a good idea. The smaller paramilitaries fell into line but the OUP rejected the proposal. Everyone agreed that the goal of the strike—pressing the government into more resolute action against the IRA and any action at all on the political front—was worthwhile, but many were dubious about the means and the chances of success.

The strike began on 3 May and the UDA attempted to repeat its tactics of three years earlier. Members blocked roads and tried to intimidate motorists into staying home. Centres for the distribution of milk and bread were set up in loyalist areas. In an office on the Albertbridge Road in east Belfast passes were prepared for issue to essential workers. By the third day of the action the milk and bread were going to waste and the passes were still uncollected. Although many people stayed at home on the first day, once it became clear that the police and the army would act firmly to prevent intimidation and to maintain public services, most people went to work.

The UDA commanders made a mistake they had avoided in the first strike. Then they were under firm instructions that they were to avoid confrontation with the police. If the security forces insisted on having a barricade removed, teams were to fall back

[2] *Protestant Telegraph*, 4 Nov. 1975.

and set up another barrier around the corner. This time, UDA men stood their ground and the RUC humbled them. Several hundred UDA men blocked the arterial Newtownards Road in east Belfast; the RUC's Special Patrol Group rammed them out of the way.

A senior policeman flipped up the visor of his riot helmet, strode over to Tyrie and asked him if he would now keep his men off the road. Tyrie yelled at him in these words, among others: 'If you want trouble, we'll give you it. We're not doing any more talking because you stand and the IRA shoots you, murders you, murders UDR men and you can pour four thousand troops into East Belfast to beat the Prods into the ground. We're having no more of it.'[3]

When Paisley (some say reluctantly) accompanied his most loyal supporters—the farmers of north Antrim—to blockade the town of Ballymena with their tractors, the RUC cleared the roads and arrested him.

If the revitalization of the RUC under Kenneth Newman was one difference from 1974, the refusal of the power-workers to run down supplies was another. Billy Kelly, the organizer of the 1974 shut-down, had promised the United Unionist Action Council (UUAC) (as the strike body was formally called) the support of workers in the generating industry, but he had not actually asked them. When workers at the main generating plant of Ballylumford in Larne were balloted, they voted 286 against the strike and 171 for it. When by the fourth day of the action there were still no power shortages, the pressure on the Ballylumford workers was stepped up; many were threatened by their neighbours. Early on a Saturday morning, Paisley and Baird picketed the power-station to persuade the men to stay out. That evening, four Unionist MPs picketed the power-station to persuade the men to stay in. Although it was a close run thing, they did.

When it became clear that the strike was in trouble, an intermediary approached Barr and asked if he would come back to help run it. Barr declined, but said he would help the UDA get out of it. Tyrie declined the offer, but Barr was right that the only options left were about face-saving and blame-shifting. A pastmaster at cutting his losses, Paisley won that contest by using the

[3] *Irish Times*, 12 June 1979.

UDA's intimidation as an excuse for withdrawing from the action. Tyrie was left holding the baby and pretending he liked children.

I only went to a certain level. Intimidation was very mild. As the power men did not come out, we would have had to resort to violence to keep people from work and there was no way we were going to do that. Look, the Protestant community will not be forced into anything they don't want to do.[4]

What they didn't want to do was support the strike, and on 13 May, ten days after it began, it was called off.

Mass mobilization needs a clear goal, a simple change, something stopped or started. 'Improving the security situation' was insufficiently tangible. A demand so vague that one would not know when it had been met could not be as effective a rally-point as 'Destroy the Executive'. And people were both three years wearier and three years more secure. This is not a paradox. As each year of the Troubles has gone by it has been harder to mobilize unionists. For many, anger and shock have been displaced by resignation. They are much more likely to be trying to live their lives 'despite' the Troubles than actively pursuing a solution. At the same time, every year that has gone by since 1972 has been a step further from the precipice.

The failure of the UUAC to revive the spirit of 1974 was a considerable blow to the morale of the loyalist paramilitaries, many of whom had spent a week standing around on street corners looking lost and forlorn. Worse than that, it showed that the spirit of 1974 had flown. So long as it was never tested, the UDA could use the success of the first strike to claim either popularity or power: the people recognize us as the true defenders of Ulster and, even if they don't, we can bring the place to a halt! The need for the government to take seriously any UDA threat to pull the plug again was removed by the failure of the attempt to repeat 1974.

Tyrie's response was to take it as a salutary lesson in the dangers of trusting politicians: the UDA had been humiliated because it had allowed itself to be used as 'muscle' for the ambitions of Paisley. In an attempt to find a new role for his organization, Tyrie invited back the old political wing of the UDA:

[4] *Newsletter*, 19 May 1977.

Glen Barr, Harry Chicken (who was described in Magill[5] as 'the UDA's major political guru'), Bill Snoddy, and Tucker Lyttle. Their remit as the New Ulster Political Research Group (NUPRG) was to produce a coherent political direction for the UDA.

Although Barr and Chicken already knew what they wanted, almost a year of weekly meetings was spent hammering out the details and almost as much effort was put into selling the proposals to every company of the UDA. They also sold the need for restraint in killing: in 1975 and 1976 there had been 114 and 113 loyalist murders; in 1977 and 1978 the numbers were 25 and 8. At the end of the process of consultation, they could claim to have a full mandate from the UDA to press the case for negotiated independence. Barr made it sound very obvious:

We need to create a system of government, an identity and a nationality to which both sections of the community can aspire. We must look for the common denominator. The only common denominator that the Ulster people have, whether they be Catholic or Protestant, is that they are Ulstermen. And that is the basis from which we should build the new life for the Ulster people, a new identity for them. Awaken them to their own identity. That they are different. That they're not second-class Englishmen but first-class Ulstermen. And that's where my loyalty is.[6]

The new entity would not be a holding position on the way to a united Ireland but a sovereign state within the European Community. The proposed constitution was heavily influenced by the US model. There would be an elected President, nominated from outside the party system, who would choose an executive from local academic and professional élites. The cabinet would be answerable to committees drawn from an elected legislature. There would be a detailed Bill of Rights and a judiciary responsible for safeguarding civil liberties. In November 1978 the policy was

---

[5] *Magill*, Dec. 1978. Chicken was invited by Tyrie to lead the Ulster Community Action Group (UCAG) as an umbrella for the community organizations that had sprung up in loyalist areas in the early 1970s. UCAG was funded by the Northern Ireland Office and linked to nationalist community groups through the Northern Ireland Association of Community Groups. UCAG was intended to stimulate and co-ordinate local groups, but it got bogged down in the role of advice centre. Whatever potential it had for promoting radical non-sectarian grass-roots politics was killed off when, in its first months in power, the Thatcher government decided to cut back drastically on funding for 'quangos'.

[6] P. O'Malley, *The Uncivil Wars: Ireland Today* (Belfast, 1983), 319.

published as *Beyond the Religious Divide* and immediately attracted favourable responses from people across the political spectrum. An early supporter was Paddy Devlin, one of the SDLP leaders closest to the working-class trade-unionist background of Barr and Chicken.

The publication of the report was followed by a year of speaking engagements. The NUPRG members travelled to the United States and were well received by a number of US politicians. They addressed meetings in Dublin, Holland, and England as well as innumerable gatherings in Northern Ireland. But, although Barr and Chicken won the admiration of many disinterested commentators, they failed to convert any of the major parties to the idea of negotiated independence. When all was said and done, unionists wanted either full integration with Britain or a return to Stormont and nationalists wanted either a united Ireland or (as a temporary measure) institutionally guaranteed power-sharing in a devolved government. The NUPRG had not only to contend with external critics; there were also rumblings within the organization. One brigadier objected to giving brigade funds to support the political work. Others resented the prominence of Barr and Chicken. A few senior figures were critical of their policy.

The Rise of John McMichael

One such critic was John McMichael. McMichael rose through the ranks of the Lisburn Defence Association and then took over the whole of the south Belfast brigade. Although no intellectual, he was more articulate than many UDA commanders. He became slightly involved in the Ulster Community Action Group (UCAG) and was then secretary to the NUPRG. He made little contribution to the discussions and appears to have been there as something of a 'minder'. Unlike the other members of the think-tank, he was active on the military side of the organization and was responsible for planning and approving many of the UFF's assassinations. Despite McMichael's apparent agreement with the NUPRG's positions, he privately caused dissension by, as one man put it, 'poisoning Andy's mind about us'. Being a close friend of Tyrie, he was able to voice his suspicions of the UDA's political direction, and he was especially critical of the Northern Ireland Negotiated Independence Association, a committee formed to connect the

NUPRG to other small groups committed to that direction. He is widely suspected of alienating Tyrie's affections with the whispered observation that there were 'too many Taigs' involved, and he did his best to kill any possibility of cross-divide support for the Association by trying to have it named the *Ulster* Negotiated Independence Association.

Without any dramatic or very public split, Barr and Chicken withdrew from the UDA, with Barr diplomatically claiming ill health. John McMichael became the UDA's chief political spokesman. The change in direction became clear in 1981 with the formation of the UDA's Ulster Loyalist Democratic Party (ULDP). As its name—not only 'Ulster' but also 'Loyalist'—made clear, the new party represented a step back from the NUPRG position. In response to criticisms that the UDA was a 'Prod Sinn Fein', the ULDP offered a more limited independence within the United Kingdom. As McMichael explained it:

We found that although people feel anti-Westminster and anti-English they still have a great affection for the monarchy. So it would be independence within the EEC and the Commonwealth, which we think would be acceptable to many Roman Catholics.[7]

The ULDP also differed from the NUPRG in being a political party. Barr and Chicken knew that the unpopularity of the UDA would prevent those associated with it winning elections; their ideas could only succeed if taken up by another party. McMichael believed he could win elections.

Legitimation, History, and the Cruithin

Anyone who reads the UDA's magazine *Ulster* will be struck by the amount of space it gives to Irish pre-history. John McKeague's *Loyalist News*, in so far as it published much other than snippets of gossip, political commentary, and bad songs, was much closer to the Paisley pattern of the *Protestant Telegraph* in filling space with articles about Calvin and Knox, Protestant martyrs, the 1859 revival in Ulster, and the evils of the confessional and the convent system. In my explanation of the popularity and political success of

[7] Ibid. 333.

Paisley,[8] I argued that Paisley's evangelical Protestantism was an important part of his appeal, even for those who are not personally committed to that religion. The Ulster farmers of north Antrim shared Paisley's evangelicalism. Many Belfast working-class Prods were at best rare church-goers, but evangelicalism still played an important part in their childhood socialization. It was there on every corner of the terrace streets between the Shankill and the Crumlin Roads, where gospel and mission halls are more frequent than corner shops. It was there in the ritual and rhetoric of the Orange Lodges. Even the most thoroughly secular loyalist knew that evangelicalism was part of what it meant to be a Protestant. Conventionally, right-wing Ulster unionists drew on the evangelical vision of Ulster history for legitimation. For the Orangeman, 'History' began in Scotland and was transferred to Ulster, first with the settlers and then with the Scottish troops of 1641 who brought Presbyterianism with them. It was refined in the 1859 revival and in the Victorian era. This was a useful history for Paisley, who was able to present himself as the embodiment of all that was virtuous about the past, but it was no help at all to anyone looking for a radical alternative.

In keeping with its claims to the tradition of the name, the UVF has sought its legitimation in the Ulster martial tradition of the Somme. To find a background for its policy of negotiated independence, the UDA promoted a new history for loyalists: Ian Adamson's story of the Cruithin, which, surprisingly, is mostly true.[9] The Gaels were not the first inhabitants of Ireland. They displaced the pictish 'Cruithin', who moved to what is now Argyll. The Cruithin gradually became the Scots, and some of them returned during the Plantation to settle in Ulster. So the present-day Ulster Protestants are not late colonists but the original inhabitants, returning to regain their land from the invading Celts.

This account had a number of appeals to the UDA. First, it offered a convincing riposte to Irish nationalist claims to be engaged in a war against colonialism. It answered the 'Why don't you Brits go home?' question. Secondly, it provided a non-religious

---

[8] S. Bruce, *God Save Ulster!: The Religion and Politics of Paisleyism* (Oxford, 1986).
[9] I. Adamson, *The Identity of Ulster: The Land, the Language and the People* (Belfast, 1982); *The Cruithin: A History of the Ulster Land and People* (Belfast, 1986).

basis for identity and thus might have allowed unionism to escape the thrall of Paisleyism. Thirdly, although it was a counter to Irish nationalist history, it allowed a greater possibility of *rapprochement* with Ulster Catholics than did the evangelical Protestant version, because it was not defined by repeated and recent struggles with Rome and Roman Catholics.

Unfortunately, as the foundation for a plausible Ulster independence movement, Adamson's work was a flop. *Ulster* filled its pages with stories of the Cruithin. Andy Tyrie gave copies of Adamson's *The Identity of Ulster* and *The Cruithin* to visitors to UDA headquarters. John McMichael talked to the press about how much Navan Fort meant to him as an Ulsterman. And the rank and file were not in the least bit interested.

We tried to educate them. We did night classes on history but they weren't fuckin interested. Outward bound and arms training, no bother at all, but getting them to read anything or think, you just couldn't do it. I don't suppose the Provies is any better at getting their operators to learn Irish but our boys were not for it.

Nor was anybody outside the UDA. A lot more could be said about why certain visions of the past become popular and why others, no matter that they are in some sense 'true', fail to excite any interest, but we could note (*a*) that the Cruithin associations were all wrong, and (*b*) that the idea had the wrong sponsors.

Even working-class Protestants who are not evangelicals grow up in a world of late-seventeenth-century symbols: the Orange Order, the Apprentice Boys of Derry, Governor Walker, Enniskillen, Aughrim, and the Boyne. Ideas and images that do not draw on that tradition will have an uphill struggle to acceptance. The additional problem with the Cruithin is that they are pretty well indistinguishable from the Gaels. The artwork on Adamson's books about the Cruithin looks like mock Celt. The protagonists have strange names and do not look like anyone we know. One can associate a lot more easily with King Billy and the Apprentice Boys, who wore trousers, than with long-haired wearers of skins. In talking about his politics, a leading UVF man told me: 'I might have gone for an independence line if Adamson hadn't tried to dress it up with all the Cruithin stuff. A load of Celtic mythology was not going to help anyone here and now.'

The second problem was the UDA itself. A lot of how one feels about an idea or a suggestion depends on how one feels about the person or organization promoting it. German Jews in 1939 were not liable to be easily persuaded of anything by the Nazis. I will return to this problem at the end of the chapter, but the UDA was simply not taken seriously as a source of ideas. Great chaps for vigilante groups, intimidation, and sectarian murder, but not people from whom one takes history lessons.

Common Sense

The next phase in the UDA's politics followed the shock to the loyalist system of the Anglo-Irish accord. In November 1985 Prime Minister Margaret Thatcher and Taoiseach Garret Fitzgerald met at Hillsborough Castle to sign an agreement which repeated the usual bromides about working together for peace and stability in Northern Ireland and then announced a genuinely radical innovation. The agreement established a joint ministerial conference of British and Irish ministers, backed by a permanent secretariat at Maryfield, close to the Stormont estate, to monitor political, security, legal and other issues of concern to the Nationalist minority. Thus, while the agreement was not formally a joint authority, since the UK government had the final word on matters affecting NI, it represented a major change of attitude by the British PM.[10]

Despite the reassuring noises made to them by the British government, unionists saw the granting to the republic of an institutionalized channel for 'interference' in the affairs of Ulster as an unambiguous sign that Northern Ireland was being pushed out of the United Kingdom. Immediately the UUP and DUP formed a coalition to oppose in every way possible the accord.

Protests took a variety of forms. Unionist politicians withdrew from meetings with British government officials. Councils which they dominated suspended business. Unionist members at Westminster resigned their seats to fight by-elections as a referendum on the accord. There were also less constitutional protests. The UDA and UVF issued statements threatening to shoot anyone who collaborated with the new regime. A recruiting leaflet for the UVF which was widely circulated in the Shorts factories said:

[10] W. D. Flackes and S. Elliott, *Northern Ireland: A Political Directory, 1968–88* (Belfast, 1989), 67.

The battle lines are being drawn. We demand the total commitment of all those who oppose republican rule. To those who would contemplate any form of collaboration we issue this solemn and sole warning: If you are not 'for us', then you are certainly 'against us'.[11]

Peter Robinson and other DUP leaders helped form the Ulster Clubs as a new vehicle to co-ordinate grass-roots protest, and McMichael (who was much influenced by Robinson and saw the Clubs as a way of attracting a 'better class' of person to the UDA) was given a place on the steering committee. On 3 March there was a 'Day of Action' which Paisley and James Molyneaux, the leader of the UUP, had promised would be peaceful. However, roads all over the province were barricaded and, despite the UDA and UVF supposedly staying out of the way, there was plenty of intimidation and, unlike the case in 1974, it was given considerable prominence by the local media. Towards the end of March there was serious rioting in Portadown. In McMichael's own fiefdom of Lisburn, eleven Catholic homes were petrol-bombed. When the RUC showed it would police loyalist disorder as firmly as it had done nationalist protests (and in the process killed a young Protestant with a plastic bullet), some loyalists turned against police officers. In Craigavon two RUC homes were attacked. On 8 April loyalists shot at policemen. Police houses in Bangor, Kilkeel, Dungannon, and Lisburn were petrol-bombed. And the loyalist assassins went back to work.

Against this background of political protest, public disorder and sectarian assassination, the UDA in January 1987 published *Common Sense*. Following an interestingly even-handed interpretation of how Northern Ireland had got into its present parlous state, the document suggested a written constitution that could only be changed by a two-thirds majority in a referendum, a bill of rights, and a Supreme Court to safeguard the freedom of the individual. That much was carried over from *Beyond the Religious Divide*. What was new was the clear deal offered to Catholics: they would be given power-sharing under a new name in return for a full commitment to supporting the Northern Ireland state. There would be no return to majority rule but neither would there be the anathema of institutionalized power-sharing. Instead there would be proportionality at every stage of government. Positions would

[11] *Irish Times*, 10 Dec. 1985.

be allocated on the basis of proportion of votes gained. The final paragraphs were stirring:

> The pragmatic alternative to co-determination is to fight a bloody civil war and let the victor dictate the rules by which we will live.
>
> What we propose will probably be described by some as idealistic, ambitious, fraught with difficulties and even dangerous to attempt but so then has anything that was ever worth doing. The most dangerous thing to do, and unfortunately the most politically popular, would be to do NOTHING.

As had been the case with *Beyond*, the proposals were hailed in editorials as 'brave', described by Cardinal Tomas O'Fiaich as 'fresh and constructive', and accepted by the SDLP as a basis for negotiation, but condemned by unionist politicians as power-sharing. Paisley was able to avoid supporting them by pointing out that they involved negotiations with the British government and that was not possible until the hated Anglo-Irish agreement was removed. And the UDA was itself in something of a mess over that issue because, despite *Common Sense*, it was committed to the shared unionist view that there could be no negotiation until the accord was set aside.[12]

What was not spelt out in *Common Sense* was the requirement for an increase rather than a decrease in the UDA's military activity. Despite the denials of his family, 'Big John' was first and foremost a military man. For most of the early 1980s he was the overall military commander of the UDA, or, to put it another way, he was the head of the UFF, a role which was far better suited to his talents than the position of political leader. Among the signatories to the document was 'Cecil Graham', which was the pseudonym of a brigadier with a fearsome reputation. The UFF is important in understanding McMichael and *Common Sense* because he understood that loyalists would only be won over to 'proportionality' if the IRA stopped killing Protestants, and the only way to ensure that was to kill a lot of IRA men. Provided that such killing was followed quickly by political innovation, then Catholics would accept it and there would be no surge of IRA

---

[12] A. Aughey, *Under Siege: Ulster Unionism and the Anglo-Irish Agreement* (Belfast, 1989), has a good discussion of *Common Sense* in the context of the accord.

recruitment. In McMichael's mind there was no conflict between the political and military sides of the UDA.

Were McMichael, 'Cecil Graham', and others genuine in their support for the radical ideas in *Common Sense*? One has to suppose that they were serious; after all, apart from their own boredom, there was no pressure for them to produce any political initiative. They could, as the UVF did, simply leave the two main parties to organize the protests and continue doing what they did best. Some of the impetus undoubtedly came from a belief that, as in 1974, the apparent impotence of the major parties left a vacuum in which the UDA could again find an important role for itself. But even allowing for that, one has again what was seen with Gusty Spence: a willingness of those people who had actually killed, been imprisoned, or risked their lives for their cause to contemplate accommodation with their enemies. One also has McMichael's own ambition. He seriously believed that the Ulster Clubs would provide a vehicle for a new alliance in unionism which would be led by John McMichael.

Whatever the motives behind its production, the impact of *Common Sense* was the same as that of *Beyond the Religious Divide*: very little. However much some people were impressed by the fact of a paramilitary organization producing a reasoned and imaginative policy document, the major parties ignored it, and there was no pressure from the public for them to do otherwise. McMichael's assassination a year after the report's publication put an end to the UDA's political activities, but nobody noticed.

Paramilitary Electoral Performance

Having examined in some detail the political thought of the UDA, we can look at how well its proposals played to the electorate. In contrast to Sinn Fein, which has one Westminster seat and a considerable council presence, the working-class loyalist organizations close to, or fronting for, the UDA and UVF have had very little electoral success. With the exception of Barr, the paramilitary men were the least popular of Craig's Vanguard candidates. The UVF's Volunteer Party was a failure. Although Hughie Smyth built himself a very strong base of support on the Shankill, his Progressive Unionist Party (PUP) did not export very well. Two other candidates in the 1981 local elections polled in the low hundreds where totals of around 1,500 were required to win seats. One of them eventually made it to the Carrickfergus council in 1989.

Despite Barr's reservations about the wisdom of fighting elections, the policies of the NUPRG were put to the test of a local government election in January 1981. A vacancy arose in that part of Protestant west and north Belfast known prosaically in elections as 'Area G'. With only five months before the next scheduled elections, the DUP argued for filling it by nomination. The other parties decided to contest it, but the Official Unionist withdrew, claiming his life had been threatened. Sammy Millar of the UDA and NUPRG was elected on a very low turn-out.

When the full elections came around, the NUPRG added two more candidates. In the predominantly Protestant east Belfast 'Area B', Louis Scott got only 434 first preference votes: less than 3 per cent of the unionist vote. In west Belfast's 'Area E', Sammy Doyle, who would still have been remembered as spokesman for the WDA, recorded 1,135 first preferences: 8 per cent of the unionist vote. He actually began ahead of Hughie Smyth but picked up fewer votes in the transfers and Smyth was elected. The third NUPRG candidate, Sammy Millar, was the only success. His 1,420 first preference votes in 'Area G' were 25 per cent of the unionist vote.[13]

. The IRA showed its commitment to the 'ballot box and Armalite' strategy by attempting to assassinate Millar: win at the ballot box and we use an Armalite to cripple you.

Just three months after the elections, an accidental death produced a vacancy in east Belfast. The UDA canvassed its membership for a popular figure to stand and the job fell to a reluctant Billy Elliott. Elliott was a self-employed plumber who had been in the UDA since its formation (he was one of Herron's bodyguards) and a personable man, but he was not a great political thinker or orator. Standing against Dorothy Dunlop (a leading figure in the UUP who had held the seat before) and with a strong DUP candidate also in the ring, Elliott did well to get just over a thousand votes.

---

[13] This election also saw an attempted comeback by John McKeague, who polled 99 first preference votes in Belfast 'Area A'.

Big Time

Council elections are by and large insignificant affairs. By-elections have minuscule turn-outs, and in major elections there are so many candidates that very few of them attract attention. Personal popularity plays such a large part in the small vote needed to be elected—the success of one Shankill councillor was attributed to him 'attending every funeral on the Road'—that it is difficult to make much of council election results. But in February 1982 the ULDP chose to stand in a contest in which personal popularity would be subordinate to the appeal of the party: a Westminster by-election. Revd Robert Bradford, a Vanguard Unionist and an evangelical Methodist minister, was murdered by the IRA. When his wife declined to be nominated to take his place, the UUP and DUP fielded candidates who were as similar as possible to Bradford: Irish Presbyterian Church minister and Orange Order Grand Master Martin Smyth and the Free Presbyterian Church minister William McCrea.

After he had produced *Beyond the Religious Divide*, Glen Barr was reluctant to stand for election, because failure would have undermined any credibility he had as a political spokesman. John McMichael did not have the sense to appreciate how damaging electoral failure would be for his position and thought he 'had a chance'. Although south Belfast is a predominantly middle-class area, there are several thousand working-class loyalist voters in the Roden Street, Sandy Row, and Village areas and many of them would have been members of the UDA. However, these are the very people with the worst record of turning out to vote, especially when it is an absolute certainty that someone dressed in a Union Jack is going to win. Martin Smyth won with 40 per cent of the vote, the Alliance candidate came second with 27 per cent, and the Paisleyite McCrea came third with 22 per cent. John McMichael gained 576 votes: 2 per cent of the unionist vote.

The 1982 Assembly

The autumn of 1982 saw yet another election for yet another political initiative. Tory Secretary of State James Prior had invented 'rolling devolution'. A regional assembly would be elected and would initially be given only the power to 'scrutinize' Westminster legislation. If the parties elected to it came to agree about forms of devolved government then more and more powers would be delegated to it. In terms of the scale of the contest, such an election should have been ideal for the ULDP, but it fielded only two candidates, both in north Belfast. Between them they gained 5 per cent of the first preference unionist votes. Sammy Doyle was undaunted by this failure and he again stood for the area in the 1985 council elections, when he did little better.

The publication and publicity surrounding *Common Sense* made no difference to the ULDP's political fortunes and could hardly be expected to when the violence in protests against the Anglo-Irish accord had undermined the UDA's claims to be taken seriously as a constitutional political force. However loyalists felt about the accord, those who made a habit of voting were not going to vote for people who petrol-bombed the homes of police officers, and those who liked the notion of burning out 'the SS RUC' did not vote.

Conclusion

The fortunes of Hughie Smyth on the Shankill show that individual working-class loyalists who are close to the paramilitaries can be elected but only when the constituency is so small that personal contacts with voters can win their loyalty, and even then there is a clear reluctance on the part of voters to support someone who is heavily and directly connected. Such reluctance can be indulged because there are always many other staunch unionist candidates. The success of some ex-paramilitaries who have joined the main unionist parties suggests that being involved in the UDA and UVF is not an indelible stain. We can conclude that, while even in the eyes of loyalists there is some stigma in being in the UDA or UVF, it is the structure of Ulster politics that makes it easy for working-class Protestants not to support paramilitaries. That there has not been enough instability to destroy the 'constitutional' parties means that there can be a simple and obvious division of labour. If you want defence or attack, you support your local UVF and UDA. When you want political representation, you can choose from a variety of unionist parties.

The only possibility of successful intervention in a crowded field rested on finding something new to offer the unionist people and there were only two conceivable political innovations: socialism and independence. Most of the paramilitaries I have interviewed have said something to the effect that, were there no border issue, they would be left-of-centre. Before the Troubles, the NILP had four MPs at Stormont, all elected from Belfast (where the party gained almost as many votes as the UUP) and all elected from areas where the paramilitaries recruited strongly. But, once the constitutional issue had been raised again, socialism was not a plausible alternative. Unionism is pure; with so few exceptions that they need not even be mentioned, unionism is supported only by Protestants. But socialism is impure; some of 'them' are socialists. To promote a political position that had any support (no matter how qualified) on the Catholic side of the divide was to lay oneself open to the accusation of treason. Furthermore, socialism was tainted, not only by its Catholic support but also by its own principles. It promoted working-class solidarity, and a large part of the Belfast working class is Catholic. Anything even vaguely left wing was vulnerable to conservative unionists playing the 'red and green card': socialism equals nationalism. In times of relative peace and stability, such as the early 1960s, it was possible for working-class Protestants to support the left-wing unionism of the NILP, but resurgent nationalism removed that option.

As Glen Barr and Harry Chicken rightly perceived, this left only independence as a possible alternative, but the problems were legion. Even if the entire population had favoured it, there would have been misgivings about the economic viability of such a small country on the fringes of Europe (Gibson of the UVF made that point). But even worse, there was no sign that the minority would be any more enthusiastic about an independent Ulster than it was about a British Ulster. Finally, that it was an innovation at all meant that it was suspect. The whole credo of unionism is a journey from Eden to hell. Things were once very good when all of Ireland was British. Then they were good because Ulster was British. Any future is hardly likely to be better than the past and is almost certain to be worse. The most successful unionist politicians are those whose manner and style, as well as politics, are most obviously tied to the past. Even when it is presented as the last chance to hold on to the present, innovation is suspect because it is an admission that something must be given up.

The logic of this argument is that there was and is no obvious political opening for the loyalist paramilitaries. Precisely because they are loyalists there is no possibility of acquiring a position analogous to that of Sinn Fein. When one is fighting to preserve the state from those who would destroy it and to maintain the status quo, one can complain about this or that element of the British government's policies, but one cannot present a radical alternative.

The End of the Ulster Defence Association?

THE years from 1987 to 1991 have not been happy times for the UDA. In August 1987 an edition of the popular television programme *The Cook Report* was devoted to racketeering in the province, and much of it was concerned with the activities of James Pratt Craig. Craig was a Shankill Road loyalist who had been in jail as an 'ordinary decent criminal' when the Troubles began. In 1972 the number of UDA men on remand in Crumlin Road was increasing, and the IRA and UVF were orchestrating claims for the recognition of their imprisoned members as 'special-category' political prisoners. Harding Smith contacted Craig, who was an old friend, and asked him to take charge of the increasing number of UDA men in prison.

This he did, acquiring in the process a reputation as a 'hard bastard'. McKittrick recounts a story told by David Morley, who was IRA commander in the Maze. Morley was comparing notes about how they maintained discipline with Craig and Gusty Spence, who was UVF commander. Craig, according to Morley, said: 'I've got this big fucking hammer and I've told them that if anybody gives me trouble I'll break their fucking fingers.'[1] A prisoner who hit Craig with a broom after an argument narrowly escaped death the next night when his throat was slit. He served the rest of his time in the prison hospital.

When he was released in 1976, Craig became active in the Shankill UDA. Although widely feared, he was not an 'operator'. He is thought to have killed only two men. One was the victim of a hit-and-run accident. The other death was even less deliberate: Craig was examining a gun in a pub on the Road when it accidentally fired, killing a passer-by on the pavement. However, he was involved in planning some of the more successful UFF killings of the period. Although they could never prove it, the

---

[1] *Independent*, 17 Oct. 1988.

RUC tried a number of times to link Craig to the 1976 murder, in the Mater Hospital, of Maire Drumm, the vice-president of Provisional Sinn Fein.

Craig found his forte in 1982 when, with three associates, he discovered that there was an awful lot of money to be made from 'demanding money with menaces'. McKittrick believes that by 1984 Craig was getting money from seventy-two different extortion operations. He was arrested in 1985 and brought to court when a number of businessmen agreed to testify but only under the condition that they could disguise their identities. When the defence successfully argued that such disguises were a denial of the defendants' rights, the case collapsed, and Craig, Artie Fee, and Billy Quee walked. Although again a free man, Craig could not simply return to his old position. In his absence, other UDA men had worked out that there was a major discrepancy between what Craig was extorting and what the UDA was getting.

Craig was put off the Road because we couldn't afford him. When he was in the jail we looked at the books and there was a lot of money that should have been coming to the organization that wasn't. And more than that, he wanted to still keep getting his cut when he was in prison instead of the £12 a week ordinary prisoners get. We told him to fuck off and he offered to settle for £50 a week which gives you some idea of his usual take-home pay!

There was considerable animosity between Craig and other leading west Belfast figures over family and personal relationships. There was also some suspicion that Craig had had 'something to do with' the murder by the INLA of William 'Buckie' McCullough, a YM leader and UDA company commander on the Shankill. Buckie is thought to have been fingered because he was complaining about Craig's fiddles.[2]

When Craig was released, west Belfast UDA told him: 'We don't want yous and we can't afford yous.' However, others in the organization appreciated Craig's services and he went back to work as chief collector for the south Belfast and headquarters

---

[2] M. Dillon, *The Dirty War* (London, 1990), 446–8. Against this must be set the account of a very senior west Belfast man who regarded Craig and McCullough as the best of friends. McCullough was never ignorant of Craig's income and hence, as with the McMichael case, there is no reason why Craig should have wanted him dead.

UDA, supposedly for a fixed percentage of the take.[3] West Belfast agreed, on the condition that he held no other position in the organization. Although unwelcome in the Shankill offices, he was to be found most days in the Sandy Row office of the south Belfast UDA.

Craig's racketeering gave him good reason to keep up the contacts with republicans that he had made while in charge of the loyalist compounds in the Maze. I have already described the problem of extorting money from building sites that bordered loyalist and nationalist areas; both sides wanted their cut. Spheres of influence had to be agreed and criminal deals had to be done. Such deals expanded from the simple carve-up of territory to sharing resources. On one occasion goods stolen in a loyalist area were passed to republicans for sale in their areas.

There is also the suspicion that Craig's contacts extended to passing information. In the early 1980s there was a series of UFF shootings of republican activists which was based on unusually good information. Republicans claimed security-force collusion, but another possibility is that the OIRA was encouraging the UDA to remove some of its rivals by feeding Craig details of suitable targets.

OIRA telling Craig things was fine, but it was rumoured that information was also passing the other way. A number of leading loyalists, all of whom had recently quarrelled with Craig about money, were killed. In addition to Buckie McCullough, there were Lenny Murphy, Frenchie Marchant, and John McMichael. It is extremely difficult to be confident of the truth of any of the stories that surround such killings. It is certain that there was some loyalist assistance in the death of Murphy, and Craig's fear that Lenny was encroaching on his livelihood has been suggested as a motive. However, as in the McCullough case, many people have insisted that there was no ill-feeling between them and that they had even been planning a joint UDA–UVF racket for mutual benefit.

Whatever the truth of those reports, there is no doubt that Craig's racketeering was a propaganda godsend for the RUC,

---

[3] Contrary to Dillon's view, Craig did not make himself the established leader of west Belfast. He was never a brigadier and was heartily disliked by some senior west Belfast men.

which was able to portray the UDA as a bloated parasite on the loyalist community. The exposure in *The Cook Report* was extremely poor publicity for the organization. And it was not only Craig. The programme team laid one trap that made dynamiting fish out the water look sophisticated. Roger Cook posed as a businessmen planning to tender for a very large construction contract in Portadown. He was approached by the UDA and arranged a meeting to discuss 'security'. Concealed cameras filmed Eddie Sayers, the brigadier of mid-Ulster UDA, making unambiguous extortion demands.

At last the leadership began to accept what some sections had been saying for years: that racketeering was undermining the public reputation and standing of the organization. But most of the organization's response to the documentary was a little less than entirely sincere. It announced that Sayers had been dismissed, but nothing about his position changed until he was arrested. The announcement that an internal investigation into racketeering was to be chaired by John McMichael was also thoroughly disingenuous. McMichael, as he had moved up the UDA structure, had gone from being 'an ordinary working bloke', to heading a 'security' firm, owning a pub in Lisburn, and living in an expensive house in a middle-class cul-de-sac. Every senior UDA figure I have interviewed smiled knowingly at my suggestion that McMichael might have acquired the Admiral Benbow by saving from his small salary.

Even if one cannot be sure that extortion money financed McMichael's life-style, there is no doubt that he was perfectly well aware of Craig's activities: Craig was working for him and had been since he had been shifted out of west Belfast. When McMichael's pub got into financial difficulties, Craig gave him £20,000. There was no need for McMichael to investigate Craig or Sayers or any of the other leaders reputed to be on the take, because, even if his own arm was not in the till, he was a very close colleague of these men and knew exactly what they were up to.

The McMichael Murder

According to the line of reasoning of one section of the Inner Council (which is taken up by McKittrick), although most of the

UDA's response to *The Cook Report* was a damage-limiting public relations exercise, Craig was genuinely troubled by McMichael's apparent change of heart. Even if he had no principled objection to extortion, McMichael might still have decided that it had to stop. He was certainly erratic enough for such a change of direction and, although he did not admit what some people suspected—that he had taken a cut out of £250,000 stolen from a bank in Portadown to fund a large arms purchase—he seemed genuinely remorseful about aspects of the distribution of that money.

At a council meeting on 16 December, McMichael talked about clearing things up in the New Year. That supposedly sealed his fate. Six days later he was killed by an IRA bomb placed under his car, outside his house in a quiet cul-de-sac in Lisburn. A week later Sir John Hermon, chief constable of the RUC, used a press conference to give a very large hint that there had been some loyalist involvement in his death. The word which spread quickly through the UDA was that Jimmy Craig had set up McMichael by passing on information about his car (which he changed frequently and had only had for a few days) to the IRA.

We must recognize the difficulty of assessing the many rumours that implicated Craig in various republican killings of leading loyalists. There is a common and understandable tendency to find villains to blame for what may have been simple mistakes, accidents, and coincidences. One also has to be cautious of embellishment. In 1987 the IRA shot and killed William 'Frenchie' Marchant as he stood outside the UVF's offices on the Shankill Road. Craig's critics point out that he was in the area at the time and had argued with Frenchie about money. The first is true and the second may be, but it is probably not true (as the UDA claimed) that Craig had placed Frenchie on the spot by arranging to meet him at that time and place. No such meeting had been planned and Frenchie was often to be found there. A friend of his told me: 'Like a bloody cigar store Indian, he was. Always on the pavement. Having a chat with this and that bloke.' Similar embellishment seems to have gone into the story of the IPLO murder of George Seawright (a leading Shankill loyalist who had been expelled from the DUP for extremism) and the IRA killing of Fred Otley.

On the day George Seawright was murdered, Craig brought two other UDA men to a meeting on Shankill Leisure Centre car park. While they were sitting in the car park, Seawright was shot fifty yards away. Fred Otley was shot in the shop at the corner of Agnes Street and Shankill Road and Craig was sitting twenty yards away in Mikhala's cafe. Others can be the judge of whether these three incidents [Marchant's death is the third] were a coincidence.[4]

The UVF brigade staff, who might be supposed to be well informed and keen to know the truth, questioned Craig and others about the three killings and concluded that he had not been involved.

The McMichael case is even more obscure. The claim that Craig fingered his boss rests on three things: (*a*) the threat that McMichael posed to Craig's rackets; (*b*) Sir Jack Hermon's hint that the murderers had inside assistance; and (*c*) Craig's supposedly unique knowledge of the details of McMichael's new car and his whereabouts. Each of these is contestable. Given his own involvement, it is unlikely McMichael had any intention of doing anything other than asking Craig to go easy on extortion for a while. Someone who was at the 16 December meeting recalls the promise to 'sort things out in the New Year' as something John said in the context of jokingly pointing out that everyone but him was on a salary from the UDA and maybe he should have one; a quite different interpretation of what was said. In his aside at the press conference, Hermon did not actually mention the UDA or even clearly implicate loyalists in the murder. What he said was:

The murder of John McMichael whoever committed it, or whoever orchestrated it regardless of who may have committed it, was designed to cause grievous dissension and disruption and to eliminate a threat to whosoever that threat may have existed. I would not wish to take it further than that. But think of my words very carefully.

The sphinx can hardly have been more guarded. What Hermon actually said was 'this was not just an IRA job'. There is actually a strong candidate (other than Craig) who fits the bill. A person who has since been convicted of serious crimes was supplying McMichael and the IRA with information, and there is suspicion that he had met McMichael that day and passed on the details of

[4] Internal UDA report.

his car to his PIRA contacts. Finally, there is no need for anyone
to have assisted the IRA. Although he was careful and changed his
car frequently, McMichael was not untouchable, and his movements would not have been impossible to follow without inside
assistance.

Whether or not Craig had a hand in all or any of the republican
murders that are now credited to him is probably irrelevant to my
concerns. The important point is that such rumours were widespread within the UDA, and both expressed and caused considerable internal dissension. The rackets, while they were accepted
by many members as necessary to fund the organization, were
embarrassing the UDA. That much of the money was going into
the pockets of some brigadiers was causing considerable resentment. That Craig might have been trading more than was absolutely necessary with republicans was an insult to everything the
organization stood for. The unrest over racketeering gradually
increased and combined with other criticisms to become a rejection
of Andy Tyrie's leadership.

The Ousting of Andy Tyrie

The career of the Supreme Commander represents unusual
longevity in a world where many others have been murdered or
run out of town by their own people, murdered by republicans,
or removed by a long prison term. It was also unusual in that
he came to prominence largely by accident and yet proved a
resourceful and persuasive leader, able to maintain his position
even though he had no 'team' of his own to rival the fire-power of
the brigadiers. He stayed in position so long as he could either
persuade the military commanders that he was the best man for
the job or keep them sufficiently suspicious of each other to
prevent a concerted challenge.

One or two people suspected Tyrie of having something to do
with McMichael's death, but the closeness of the two men prevented that story gaining currency. None the less, McMichael's
death was a double blow to Tyrie's position: it deprived him of an
important supporter and it was yet another 'mistake' to add to too
long a list of mistakes.

What made many of the more 'military-minded' men unhappy

was the lack of killing. After a few good years in the early 1980s, when the UFF killed or wounded a number of leading republicans involved in the hunger-strike protests, the organization had done very little which it could present as a blow to the IRA and its offshoots. Especially after McMichael stood down as overall military commander in March 1987, there was a marked drop in the level of activity at a time when the IRA was continuing to murder, almost at will. The 'military meetings' of senior leaders, previously fortnightly, tailed off.

There was also unhappiness about Tyrie's personnel management. In the early days of the UDA, brigadiers were elected or at least chosen in some manner by their own areas; they were closer to being representatives of their own 'teams' than they were officers in charge of subordinates. Once Tyrie had established himself, he increasingly centralized the organization. In 1985 he backed an unpopular and unsuccessful attempt by McMichael to have the brigade structure replaced by a central command. In later years he took to appointing the brigadiers. When McMichael was killed, Tyrie chose Jackie McDonald as his successor in south Belfast. Whatever virtues McDonald had, he had the great disadvantage of being a close friend of Jimmy Craig and Artie Fee. A number of members profoundly disapproved of the choice of another racketeer and said so, in the local papers and in a BBC *Newsnight* documentary. Their misgivings were fully realized fourteen months later when McDonald was charged with demanding money with menaces and intimidating a witness.

This time the police not only had witnesses willing to testify in court but they also had tape recordings of McDonald, Fee, and two others making demands with menaces. This time the witnesses were not put off by the variety of threats, some of which were quite imaginative. In a nicely macabre touch, one witness's death notice appeared in the *Belfast Telegraph* a week before he was due to give evidence. The evidence of the tapes was so damning that, when confronted with it, the four charged accepted the advice of counsel and changed their pleas to guilty.

Tyrie had previously made other unpopular personnel decisions. When Tommy 'Tucker' Lyttle, the west Belfast brigadier, was in hospital in 1984, Tyrie tried to bring back a previous incumbent who had been pushed out for allegedly enriching himself at the UDA's expense. With support from the east Belfast brigade, the west Belfast men refused to accept Tyrie's appointee and Lyttle retained his position.

The return of Davey Payne was another unpopular appointment. Payne had been involved since the start of the Troubles. He rioted in Divis Street in 1964, he protested against Gusty's trial in 1966, and he became a regular at Ian Paisley's Martyr's Memorial church. He joined the UVF as a YCV, was in Tara, and then took most of his team (which had included some of Lenny Murphy's gang) into the UDA when it was formed. Not for want of police trying, he had never been convicted for a serious offence, but he enjoyed (in both senses of the word) a fearsome reputation. In the early 1970s he was the UDA's main enforcer of internal discipline or Provost-Marshall—a position which made use of his talents and made enemies among his own people. He was interned in 1973 and, when he was released a year later, became brigadier of north Belfast UDA. Although in many senses a successful brigadier—his area did the sorts of things paramilitary organizations do—his fierce temper led him frequently to quarrel with others. After an argument with the west Belfast brigadier, Payne sent some of his men round to his house to kill him. Fortunately for McClatchey, the gunman was reluctant and he was able to escape over the back wall.

Payne left the UDA after allegations about pocketing UDA money and began a successful new career as a manager of community workshops and youth training programmes. One of his enterprises involved training young Protestant and Catholic men who had been injured in the Troubles. He was fêted by Dublin society as a model reformed terrorist. He even made a speech for the Peace People, warning young men against paramilitary activity. This caused a short rupture in his relationship with Tyrie; it also caused some of his old colleagues to visit his house in April 1978 and blast him with a shotgun. He recovered and once again became a close confidant of Tyrie.

Payne's community workshop scheme fell apart when he was investigated by civil servants for financial irregularities.[5] Rather

[5] Officials in the Northern Ireland Office appear to have been enthusiastic in searching for any signs of financial impropriety in projects run by ex-paramilitaries. Glen Barr, who runs a number of extremely successful projects in Londonderry, was also accused of malpractice, but he decided to fight back, was supported by his board, and won the arguments.

than fight the accusations, he resigned and accepted Tyrie's invitation to return to his old post as north Belfast brigadier. The area needed new management. Tyrie did not like the campaign of sectarian murders being organized by a small group in the area, and various UDA businesses were not producing the expected profits. But Payne's return was not welcomed by some companies, and his bullying style of leadership did nothing to endear him to his troops. When Davey Payne was arrested for gun-running, Tyrie tried to appoint his own choice against a clearly expressed local preference, but had to accept the decision of the local volunteers.

It may well be that Tyrie's support for a small group of people who were not widely popular reflects the paucity of choice for senior positions. I will return to this theme in the concluding chapter, but many people in the UDA have commented about the poor quality of their recruits and the difficulty they have had in finding 'good men' to run brigades. There is also no doubt that the running of an organization that spends a lot of its time on activities that are illegal requires a considerable degree of trust among the senior figures and hence there is a strong temptation always to rely on the same small group of people, even if one has doubts about every aspect of their characters. However good Tyrie's reasons for relying on Payne, Craig, and Sayers,[6] trying to bring back McClatchey, and appointing McDonald, to some sections of the membership this was simply cronyism.

Two Hire Cars and an Awful Lot of Rifles

Two weeks after McMichael was killed, an RUC patrol stopped an Austin Maestro and two maroon Ford Granadas outside Portadown and found the second and third to be weighed down with weapons. The load comprised 30 9 mm. Browning pistols, 61 Czech-made Kalashnikov rifles, 150 anti-personnel fragmentation grenades, 124 magazines, and about 11,000 rounds of ammunition. Davey Payne, who was driving the first car, and two other UDA men from north Belfast were arrested.

The arms consignment was the fruit of a bank raid the previous

---

[6] On 9 Dec. 1988 Sayers was sentenced to ten years for his attempt to extort money from Roger Cook.

year. Either £250,000 or £325,000 (depending on which paper one reads) was stolen from a bank in Portadown by a combined UDA–UVF team and was used to finance an unprecedentedly large arms purchase from South Africa. The load was unique in loyalist paramilitary history, not only for its size, but for the co-operative nature of the operation, which involved the UVF and UR.

The UDA's portion was the first to be found and was inter-cepted only a few miles from the Tandragee farmhouse where Payne collected the weapons. The UVF and UR managed to move theirs, but about half of the UVF cache was found less than a month later in an outbuilding behind a house off the upper Crumlin Road on the outskirts of north Belfast. In addition to Kalashnikovs and Browning pistols, the UVF load contained an RPG-7 rocket launcher. In November a small part of the Resistance portion was found. In a report on the Payne arrest the *Irish News* said: 'it is not RUC policy to comment on the source of its information, but it is understood that police were tipped off by a well-placed paramilitary source'.[7]

As usual, the best I can do is to report the various accounts I have been given and comment on their plausibility. At his trial Payne argued that he had been set up by two Inner Council members who wanted to get rid of him for personal reasons. The judge agreed that he had been set up, but rejected the explanation: 'I am quite sure that if the UDA wished to deal with you by way of disciplinary procedures or otherwise, they have shorter and quicker methods.' That is, any brigadier who wanted to get rid of Payne could have had him shot. However, it may have been that Payne was simply too widely feared for assassination to have been an easy option; having him arrested red-handed might have been safer. Against this is the value of the weapons that were lost in the tip-off; no paramilitary leader would willingly hand over such a consignment. Payne could have been set up as easily and more economically with one gun. Unless, and here the options get very tangled, such a paramilitary leader did not want the UDA to enhance its military capabilities. This is the story I have been offered by some UDA men who believe that elements within the leadership (either in the pay or under the influence of the

[7] *Irish News*, 9 Jan. 1988.

Northern Ireland Office) wanted to mute the military side of the organization.

But this version misses the point that, even if a senior UDA man had not wanted to see such weapons used, they remained a valuable and resaleable commodity and would not have been given up lightly.

That the RUC could stop Payne on the Mahon Road only fifteen minutes after he had loaded the car and yet not find the farm suggests that the mole knew only about Payne's plans to collect the weapons and not about their location; that is, that the source was UDA rather than UVF or UR. But again, an alternative surmise is possible. It may well be that the cache was under surveillance and the RUC chose to let it be divided up before swooping so that the 'tout' might be protected and a large number of loyalists might be arrested as they shifted and stored the guns. Enough of the UVF and UR shares was later found to be compatible with the notion that the RUC was on the case before the weapons arrived in Northern Ireland and chose to 'discover' them piecemeal rather than expose the extent of their fore-knowledge.[8] Against that is the fact that a large part of the consignment was not recovered.

Another product of the rumour factory was the claim that Payne had informed on himself; that he was the mole. As soon as he was arrested, the word went out that he would turn 'grass' and be shipped off to Canada or be given a very light sentence. However, Payne's behaviour was, in paramilitary terms, exemplary. He refused to implicate anyone else and, despite the overwhelming forensic evidence against his two companions, insisted that only he had loaded the guns and that the other two had no idea what was in the cars they were driving. Far from getting a light sentence, he was given nineteen years.

I have no idea who fingered Payne and there is a possibility that nobody did. Parts of the UDA leak like a colander. The RUC has all the loyalist paramilitary groups well penetrated and the routine seepage of information to the police may have been enough for

---

[8] This is speculation, but Brian Nelson (for whom see, further, Ch. 10), was involved at an early stage and visited South Africa. As he was then passing information to his minders, the army knew about the operation, but the security forces have a long history of not pooling information.

them to know that Payne was worth watching. If that was the case, why then did the RUC and the trial judge go out of their way to mention an inside informer? We are back to the murkiness of very dirty waters. The claim that there was a tout worked perfectly to set sections of the UDA against each other.

However it came about, the loss of such a large consignment was yet another strike against the UDA's self-confidence and, because he was the Supreme Commander, against Tyrie.

A Bomb and Resignation

On 6 March 1988 Tyrie found a bomb under his car. The IRA denied having anything to do with it, the RUC announced that it was not of any design commonly used by the IRA, and it was claimed by the previously unknown Loyalist People's Action Group, which was taken to be a cover for the anti-Tyrie faction in the UDA. Five days after the bomb attempt, there was a full meeting of the UDA command, at which Tyrie's leadership was roundly criticized. When he failed to get the vote of confidence he asked for, he resigned. In another of those press statements where the distance between rhetoric and reality has to be measured in nautical miles, the Inner Council said: 'We want to place on record our appreciation of Andy Tyrie's services to the organization. The UDA has been and will continue to investigate the attempt on Mr Tyrie's life.'[9]

The Milltown Cemetery Murders

Two weeks later there occurred the first loyalist paramilitary killings to be shown on television. British undercover soldiers shot dead three IRA activists in Gibraltar. The return of the bodies gave republicans an opportunity for making considerable political

[9] The circumstances of the attempt are still a little obscure. Had 'People' been 'Protestant' then PAG would have been one of the UVF's covers, and the two men charged with the murder attempt were also charged with UVF membership, but local sources believe they were in the UDA at the time of the attack and later changed organization. Senior UVF sources deny having anything to do with the bomb and had no obvious reason to want to get rid of Tyrie. Where authorship is obscure, the best way of determining responsibility is to note who wanted the victim out of the way and who benefited. We must assume that Tyrie was pushed by his rivals in the Inner Council.

capital and the route that the bodies took from Dublin was lined with mourners and demonstrators. Nobody expected that loyalists, well pleased with the killings, would want to intervene, and no one was prepared for the actions of Michael 'Flint' Stone, who accompanied mourners to the Republican plot in Milltown cemetery, west Belfast. When the coffins arrived and the speeches began, Stone drew out from a satchel two fragmentation grenades and threw them at the mourners. In the words of the statement Stone made to police:

The grenades went off and it was loud, like a .22 going off. The crowd turned around and looked towards me. I pulled out the Browning pistol. Straight in front of me was women and children. I aimed above them. I wanted to kill the main republicans, not the women and children . . . The crowd was closing in so I left it. I pulled another grenade and threw it at the crowd. I kept walking quick, shooting occasionally at the crowd to keep their heads down. I popped a couple of grenades at the crowd.

Stone and the more adventurous men in the crowd performed a macabre dance for the television cameras—Stone walking towards the M1 motorway, the crowd following and then stopping as Stone fired or threw another grenade. When he ran out of grenades and both guns jammed or emptied, the first men caught up with him.[10]

He was severely beaten and thrown into a car, but, before he could be taken off to be shot, an RUC car blocked the way and rescued Stone from his assailants. The final death toll was three men dead and sixty-eight others injured. When the RUC told him that at least two people were dead, he is said to have replied 'Brilliant. I'm game for anything.'

At first the UDA denied that Stone was a member. Sources in the east Belfast UDA said that he had approached them a number of years before but had been rejected because he was too extreme and unpredictable, a 'head-the-ball'. The denial was genuine. What even the then UDA leadership did not know was that

[10] It is likely that there was supposed to be a driver and a fast car at the bottom of the cemetery. Stone was reported to have said to the police: 'My mate fucked off and left me', but later he insisted he had acted alone. *Sunday World* reported that the job had been planned by a 'senior loyalist paramilitary', although it did not say whether the man was UDA or UVF (*Sunday World*, 5 Mar. 1989). The grenades and Browning were said to have come from the UVF's share of the South African weapons purchase.

Stone's name had been passed on to the mid-Ulster UDA and to John McMichael. McMichael and a very small group in the leadership used Stone as a freelance killer.

Stone claimed the murders of three Catholic men: Kevin McPollin in Lisburn and Dermot Hackett in Omagh in 1985 and Patrick Brady in south Belfast the previous year. He certainly knew a lot about the killings, but a source in the UDA denied that Stone had been the 'shooter': 'He was on such a high when the police questioned him after the Milltown massacre, he'd have confessed to sinking the Titanic if they asked him. That's the sort of character he is.'

Stone also claimed to have been involved in plans to kill John Joseph Davey, Sinn Fein councillor in Magherafelt, Martin McGuinness, the suspected IRA leader in Londonderry, and Owen Carron, the election agent for Bobby Sands.

Certain elements of the UFF operation that were revealed in Stone's trial statements show careful planning. That Stone was not a member of the UFF but a 'freelance' working privately for McMichael and three other members of the Inner Council meant that he was isolated and thus little of a security risk. He did not meet the people running him. In the Brady case, he claims he was sent an envelope containing photographs and information on fifteen IRA suspects and told to pick one. Given the status of the people running him, such distancing was sensible. But generally the Stone case showed the UDA in the poor light. The UDA is a 'military' organization. In addition to preparing for the defence of the loyalist people, it claims the right to assassinate IRA men. Taking out prominent republicans is the part of its operations most popular with its supporters and most easily tolerated by the unionist middle classes. A lot of loyalists were impressed by the UFF, and McMichael's south Belfast people were supposed to be the best team in the UFF. They were responsible for the city-centre attack on Gerry Adams that very nearly succeeded. They were also responsible for the attempted murder of Bernadette McAliskey and her husband. And now this brave, well-oiled fighting machine was shown to revolve around one slightly strange man. Stone's career also shows the UFF's failure to damage the IRA or Sinn Fein. Of his six murders, five attempted murders, and three conspiracies to murder, the attempts on Adams, McGuinness, Morrison, and Davey came to nothing. The three 'successes' were ordinary Roman Catholics who, if they had any connections at all with militant republicanism, were the smallest of small cogs.

The 'Milltown massacre' gave loyalists a new hero. Stone's blood-stained jacket was raffled to raise funds for loyalist prisoners, and Stone tee-shirts proved popular. But his record suggests an organization that was barely functioning 'militarily'.

The New Regime

When Tyrie resigned there was a small but symbolically important change to the furniture in what had been his office. His large 'executive-style' desk was replaced by a round table in the centre of the room. Instead of a 'Supreme Commander' there would now be collective leadership.

The new leadership fared little better than the Tyrie regime. At a 'launch' press conference in March 1988 the Council said that the UDA was 'better armed than at any time in the 1970s' and was ready to direct a military campaign against the IRA, but that 'no innocent Catholic' had anything to fear from them.[11] Yet, of the five UFF murders in 1988 and 1989, two were of Catholics not known to have any republican connections, one was of a man who had served a prison sentence for possession of a rifle, a fourth victim (Free Presbyterian David Dornan) was a complete mistake, and only the fifth could in any sense be regarded in UDA terms as a 'legitimate target'. Pat Finucane was a lawyer who specialized in high-profile republican cases and whose brother was in the IRA.

The one murder sanctioned by the new leadership which did fit its 'reforming' image was that of James Pratt Craig. On 17 October he went to the Castle Inn in east Belfast. As he was playing pool with a 'wee girl', two men in boiler suits burst into the bar, ordered the customers to lie down, and shot Craig a number of times from close range. For good measure they also sprayed the bar and killed a pensioner. Boiler suits, gloves, and a balaclava were later found in a loyalist club just round the corner from the Castle Inn. The UFF said in a statement that Craig had been executed for 'treason'.

[11] *Belfast Telegraph*, 14 Mar. 1988.

The Stevens Enquiry

Some loyalists hate Catholics so much that they think it is proper to kill any Catholic; these people are in a minority. More common is the view that random murder is unfortunate but it should scare Catholics into rejecting the IRA and it is a form of redistributive justice: the community that supports the IRA suffers for that support. But more common yet in loyalist paramilitary circles is the position that only active republicans should be targets.

As we have already seen a number of times, the legitimacy of any particular loyalist murder can be haggled over endlessly. Soldiers and policemen wear uniforms; IRA men are under no such obligation. After most murders, the UDA or UVF will assert that the victim was an IRA or INLA man. Equally predictably the IRA and INLA will deny that the victim was anything other than a random victim of a sectarian murder. In 1979 William Carson was shot dead in north Belfast. At the time he was not claimed by the IRA as a member and the shooting was reported as a 'sectarian' murder. Ten years later his name appeared on the IRA 'roll of honour'.

Accusations of random killing seem finally to have irked the UDA leadership into a serious political mistake. In August 1989, the UFF murdered Loughlin Maginn from Rathfriland in Co. Down. The usual assertions and denials about his IRA involvement followed. Two days after the shooting, the UFF phoned Chris Moore, a BBC reporter in Belfast, and asked him to go to a car park. He was collected and transported to Ballynahinch, Co. Down, where he was introduced to four masked men and shown photocopies of various documents.[12] Most were security-force 'montages' of photographs, names, dates of birth, and other details of IRA suspects, the sort of material used to brief patrols. One paper clearly singled out Maginn. Moore was also shown a video, apparently shot inside a security-force base, which showed a number of photographs of IRA suspects in Co. Down.

The obvious intention of this disclosure was to rebut republican claims that the UFF was engaged in sectarian murder. However, the reaction was far stronger than any previous response to loyalist claims to possessing security-force intelligence. The RUC in-

[12] For Moore's account, see *Irish News*, 14 May 1991.

stituted an enquiry into leaks, headed by John Stevens, deputy chief constable of Cambridgeshire.

In the heat generated by the political responses to the first reports of leaks, classified security-force documents began to fall from the sky. Photocopies of Garda lists of IRA suspects in the Republic were sent to David McKittrick. A sheet of mugshots was sent to the *Sun*. SDLP MP Seamus Mallon was handed a number of sheets. One montage of ten IRA suspects was sent to a nationalist constituent of Mallon with 'We got Maginn—you are next—UFF' written on it. Montages were found to have gone missing from a UDR base at Ballykinler in Co. Down and from an RUC station in Dunmurry. Journalists began to speculate that the UDA was leaking further documents to confuse the enquiry. To press the point about the quantity of information that reached them, UDA men pasted hundreds of photomontages on walls in north and west Belfast and spray-painted 'Stevens. We have hundreds more!' on walls. By the end of October the Stevens teams were investigating eleven separate security leaks involving two hundred alleged IRA suspects.[13]

UDA headquarters in Gawn Street was raided a number of times; documents and a photocopier were removed. On 22 September Tommy Lyttle was arrested. He was interrogated at Gough barracks and released. The editor of *Ulster* was arrested and on 8 December charged with having documents likely to be of use to a terrorist organization.[14] He was actually a very obvious place to start, given *Ulster*'s habit of naming IRA suspects and publishing their photographs. Three UDA men from Derry were arrested for running an 'intelligence factory'.

The Stevens enquiry was supposed to be concerned with the source of leaks, and on 8 October twenty-eight UDR soldiers were arrested in dawn raids involving more than three hundred police officers. Four nights of rioting followed in east Belfast (two off-duty Royal Irish Rifles soldiers were later charged with shoot-

---

[13] *Sunday Life*, 1 Oct. 1988.

[14] For some reason, the *Irish News*, which should know better, kept referring to this man as the editor of the UVF's *Combat*. Figures for the number of documents seized and examined by the Stevens team released at the time (usually in the 1,000s) give a slightly misleading impression of the UDA's intelligence records. Among the 'documents' taken from one house were the selections for a local amateur football team!

ing at the police). Paisley began a 'Hands off the UDR' campaign. Despite the enormous publicity that accompanied these arrests, few serious charges followed from them. Most of the soldiers were released very quickly. Two were convicted of stealing documents from Dunmurry police station and fined. Two were charged with the technical offence of having more than the prescribed amount of ammunition for legally held weapons.[15]

In late January, the Stevens team arrested Brian Nelson of West Circular Crescent in north Belfast. As the senior intelligence officer for the UDA in Belfast, Nelson's job was to collect and collate information on possible targets. Rumours soon spread that Nelson was 'grassing' and a large number of senior UDA officers were arrested: Tucker Lyttle, the west Belfast brigadier; the brigadiers for east Belfast and south-east Antrim; the company commander for A company, west Belfast; and the past brigadier for east Belfast. Nelson, it was claimed, was an army intelligence 'plant'.

In December 1974 Nelson had been sentenced to seven years for kidnapping an educationally sub-normal and registered blind Catholic. The man was lifted in North Queen Street in March 1973 and driven to a UDA club in Wilton Street. He was roughed up and then taken to a car in which he was being driven to what one supposes would have been his death, when it was stopped by soldiers. The victim's diary had been taken from him and returned to his pocket after Nelson had written 'This is the first to go. Two to follow', which was thought to be a reference to the recent murder by the IRA of three soldiers in a 'honey pot' trap in an Antrim Road flat. Despite this record, rumours spread that Nelson had never left the army! He had been sent back to Belfast to infiltrate the UDA. There are two versions of the arrest. According to some people he should never have been on that job. According to others, the kidnapping and the subsequent stopping of the car by soldiers were part of a scam to establish Nelson's credentials. During his three-and-a-half years in prison, he was allegedly taken out for periods of psychiatric treatment; it is now suggested that these were actually 'R and R' and debriefing trips to England![16]

---

[15] *Belfast Telegraph*, 16 Oct. 1989.
[16] *Sunday News*, 21 Oct. 1990.

The official report of the Stevens enquiry was presented in May 1990. In addition to making eighty-three recommendations about tightening up procedures for vetting UDR members and maintaining intelligence files, it noted that ninety-four people had been arrested and fifty-nine of them charged. However, the main gain was imprisoning most of the UDA's leadership. But even this pleasure began to turn sour in October 1990 when charges against the editor of *Ulster*, two brigadiers, and two others were dropped. It appears that the decision had been made not to use Brian Nelson as a witness. But, even without him, it was possible to convict Tucker Lyttle, the most senior UDA brigadier, for intimidation and to force a host of smaller UDA fry into accepting plea bargains on charges of possessing information likely to be of use to terrorists.

During the presentation of the prosecution case against Lyttle (a case so strong he changed his plea to guilty), Nelson's status had to be described, as he was the source of the incriminating documents with Lyttle's fingerprints all over them. An army witness, when pressed, said that Nelson had worked for the army for at least ten years. Quite why that figure was used is not clear, but it might have been to signal that he was not working for the army in 1974 when he was convicted for kidnapping. Few details of Nelson's work as a spy were revealed because he pleaded guilty to a reduced list of charges but it is now clear that Nelson was a UDA man helping the security forces rather than the other way round. His information allowed a large number of UDA plans to be subverted while the UDA gained nothing in return.[17]

A Further Coup

In 1991 there was a further change in the UDA's leadership. The two Inner Council members responsible for the ousting of Tyrie were themselves replaced, which left no one from the pre-1974 leadership in senior positions. The replacement of the old by a new guard that Tyrie had tried to encourage with his Ulster

---

[17] See *Newsletter*, and *Irish News*, 26 June 1991 and *Independent*, 9 January 1992.

Defence Force training schemes has now been achieved, although it was brought about by failure and necessity rather than by planned and orderly succession. Although there has been some talk of inviting back Tyrie and others of his generation, such overtures have either not been pressed or have been declined.

The most interesting act of the new leadership was to agree with the UVF a limiting of 'offensive activity' for the duration of the Peter Brooke-led talks between the political parties about the future government of the province. In part this represents the UDA coming to the view, held by the UVF since 1974, that political progress can only be made by the major unionist parties. The new leaders are coming to terms with the unpopularity of the UDA by trying to clear up the most public and worst excesses of racketeering and by shrinking into the UFF. The end of the 1991 cease-fire was followed by an upsurge of UFF activity and almost complete silence from the rest of the UDA.

Conclusion

The UDA was created by circumstances: the immediate threat of republican violence and the more abstract threat to 'the Protestant way of life' of Irish nationalism. It was initially very popular and successful and it gave the Protestant working class a veto on political developments. The reduction in IRA violence of the mid-1970s removed much of the immediate sense of threat and reduced the salience of the UDA. The desire to add a positive political role to the veto produced the Barr and Chicken political agenda, but, when this failed to excite the province, the UDA was left searching for a purpose.

It could have put all its efforts into a campaign to assassinate republicans, but this would have brought the full weight of the state to bear on it and forced it underground. Tyrie tried to find another role with his training schemes for the Ulster Defence Force. Two ex-Marines in the Derry UDA organized an outward bound-style training camp near Magilligan, but most of the brigadiers and commanders were not interested in spending time and money on the sort of rigorous training programme that would allow the organization to produce hundreds of well-trained NCOs to lead the Ulster people in the event of full civil war. Rather they saw such a cadre as a threat to their own positions. Anyway, the organization was not deluged with applications; most rank-and-file UDA men are happier in the pub than in the hills.

Critics of the UDA have long campaigned to have the organization banned. That it was and still is legal gave the UDA many advantages over the UVF but also caused major problems in sustaining a purpose and an identity. The anomaly of the legal UDA containing within it the murderous UFF may be an offence to constitutionalists, but it is also a problem for the UDA in that the military wing constantly provides loyalist critics with grounds for ignoring or campaigning against the social and political activities of the organization. In an evening-long rumination on the future of the UDA, one ex-brigadier enthusiastically offered the development of the IRA as a model. He wanted the UVF to remain in existence as the parallel to the PIRA (but with greater accuracy in its selection of targets). He thought the UDA should disband the UFF and follow the OIRA strategy of becoming a working-class political party. There are two obvious difficulties with that. The first is that too many UDA men have become too accustomed to using their positions for status and financial rewards. The sort of purge required to cleanse the organization would leave it with no structure at all. Anyway a purely political organization would have little appeal to the very many members who are attracted by the danger, the mystique, the sense of power that comes from being in a paramilitary organization.

The second problem with 'going straight' was mentioned in the previous chapter. These is no gap in the market of unionist politics for a working-class party. To the extent that it was socialist, it would be insufficiently unionist. To the extent that it was unionist, it would not be offering anything new to Ulster Protestants.

The UDA that could have followed the evolution of the OIRA was the UDA of the 1974 strike and it has since lost the trade-union and community leaders who could have made such a transition possible; many of them have gone to the UUP or DUP. Much more likely is that it will try ever less successfully to maintain its dual role. With the departure of first Tyrie and then Lyttle and Elliott, the UDA has now lost the last of the senior men who joined the organization at the start of the Troubles, who relished the public role, and who wanted to create a mass movement. In its range of activities it is now hardly different from the UVF: it arranges assassinations, it runs clubs, and it does welfare work with its prisoners and their families. In terms of its goals, the UDA is now largely indistinguishable from the UVF.

The Nature of Pro-State Terrorism

So far the story of loyalist paramilitarism in Northern Ireland has been told largely in chronological order, with occasional asides to make general analytical observations; that is, as one thing after another. In this final chapter I want to bring these observations together into a general account of loyalist paramilitaries. Such synthesis and summary must involve considerable over-simplification, but a degree of caricature will be worthwhile if it allows us to make sense of the history of the UDA and UVF.

Although the point has not been pressed, much of my thinking about the UDA and UVF has involved an implicit comparison with the IRA. Although my knowledge of republicanism is based entirely on secondary sources, it seems reasonable to suggest that the loyalist paramilitaries differ from the IRA in being awkward terrorists, often unsure about what they are doing and sometimes thoroughly incompetent, and suffering in popularity for their mistakes. In a highly condensed description, one could suggest that the loyalist paramilitary organizations differ from the IRA in being less well organized and less well staffed; less selective and less skilful in their operations; less well funded and less well armed; more vulnerable to the policing of the security forces; more vulnerable to the propaganda work of the government's agencies; less well able to develop an enduring political programme and community base for their activities; more vulnerable to racketeering; and hence less popular with the population they claim to defend. I am not suggesting radical differences between republican and loyalist terrorists, only marginal ones, but, as I will argue, the consequences of those small differences are still very significant. Put simply, I believe these characteristics can be explained by the nature of the project of loyalist paramilitarism.

There is a vast literature on terrorism and much of it is taken up with arguments about definitions: 'one man's terrorist is another man's freedom fighter' and so on.[1] There seems little virtue in

---

[1] There are many typologies of terrorist organizations and types of terrorism, but none seems terribly useful, in that they usually display a lack of conceptual

such arguments. Words do not have 'real' meanings; they are nothing more than conventions and, provided it is abundantly clear what one is saying about whom, one may proceed. To state my conclusion at the start, I believe that many of the differences between the IRA and the UDA and UVF can be traced back to their missions and to the differences between anti-state and pro-state terrorism. Let us assume that a 'state' is relatively stable; there is a government, a security system, a justice system, and so on. Some people are willing to use illegal violence to destroy or radically to change the state. Others are willing to do likewise to protect the state from its enemies. These are anti-state and pro-state terror groups.[2] It is also possible for the agents of the state to engage in terrorism; so we need a notion of 'state terror'. These three terms allow us to say all that we need to say.

The distinction between pro-state and state terror is vital. To return to the theme of Chapter 8, republicans argue that there is no significant difference between the UDA and UVF and the Crown forces; it is all state terror. Nothing in my research leads me to that conclusion. Although they would like to be seen in that light, the UDA and UVF are not branches of the state's security force, as 'the men behind the wire' can testify. Clearly relations between the state's own forces and vigilantes who take it upon themselves to bolster the defences of the state can vary in closeness and warmth. In Guatemala in the 1960s more than twenty right-wing paramilitary organizations were fully supplied with weapons by the army. When Arana was elected president in 1970, many of the terrorists were put on the government pay-roll.[3] But

continuity in the divisions of cases into types. See, for example, F. R. Van Der Mehden, *Comparative Political Violence* (Englewood Cliffs, NJ, 1973), 7. Wilkinson distinguishes revolutionary, sub-revolutionary, and repressive terrorism but talks about the IRA, UVF, and UDA in the same category (P. Wilkinson, *Political Terrorism* (London, 1974)). For a good summary of many definitions and typologies, see A. P. Schmid, *Political Terrorism* (New Brunswick, 1983).

[2] Of course, most groups are neither entirely uncritical of the state nor critical of every aspect. The Israeli terror organization Gush Enunim in paradigmatic pro-state fashion was critical of the government's apparent lack of resolve in combating Palestinian attacks on the state but was also critical of many aspects of government policy; see E. Sprinzak, 'From Messianic Pioneering to Vigilante Terrorism: The Case of Gush Enunim', in D. C. Rapoport (ed.), *Inside Terrorist Organizations* (London, 1988), 194–216. In contrast, the loyalist paramilitaries have been relatively uncritical both of the British government and of their local unionist leaders.

[3] There is a voluminous literature on right-wing paramilitary groups in Latin

such co-option is not the only possibility. If the state encourages and tolerates the pro-state group, then the latter has many of the advantages of the former, but, if the government feels that its own agencies are capable of dealing with the threats to the state, then the pro-state terror group is in competition with the state, and, except in the extreme circumstance where the state itself collapses, is bound to lose in that contest. And it loses in a manner quite different from the defeat of the anti-state terror group. It is not overcome but eroded; eaten from within rather than destroyed from outside. The extent to which the state accepts the claims of the vigilante group to be acting on its behalf is clearly a variable matter. To assume that governments generally approve of or tolerate terrorist groups of the same political complexion is a major mistake that would make the history of the UDA and UVF incomprehensible.

We can see the problems which the UDA and UVF have had in competing with the state in a number of arenas.

Recruitment

At some point in almost all my interviews, the person I was talking to generalized from some particular mistake or organizational weakness to a general problem of the narrow base from which the UDA and UVF recruited. The following from a senior UVF man, who had been in the UPV and Tara, can represent all of those comments:

Loyalists fell down because the middle classes didn't give us the leadership they did in 1912. The potential was there for a good organization but in 1969, when certain people made noises and insinuated that it was 1912, the leadership wasn't forthcoming.

We can see why the middle classes were not flocking to paramilitary organizations. The state had not yet collapsed. They were far less directly affected by competition with Catholics and they were not being burnt out and shot at. Business life continued

America. On Guatemala, see N. Gall, 'Slaughter in Guatemala', *New York Review of Books*, 20 May 1971, pp. 13–17, and K. F. Johnson, 'Guatemala from Terrorism to Terror', *Conflict Studies*, 23 (1974), 1–19. See also M. Morley and B. Petras, 'Chile: Terror for Capital's Sake', *New Politics*, 1 (1974), 36–50, and J. B. Treaster, 'Argentina: A State of Fear', *Atlantic Monthly*, 240 (1977), 16–26.

much as usual. Furthermore, even major changes to the Northern Ireland state are less of a problem for the middle classes than for the working classes or for farmers. They are more cosmopolitan and draw their sense of identity far more from Britain and Europe than from Ulster. Their unionism is much more like that of Terence O'Neill in deriving from their sense of being 'British' rather than from strong attachment to the land and sacred history of Ulster.[4]

The reluctance of the middle classes to get involved is also clear (but less severe) on the Catholic side, but there is a major difference between loyalist and republican ability to recruit from the working class. Any pro-state terrorist organization has the problem that it competes with the government's security forces for personnel. In theory the IRA, because it competes only with the SDLP and not with the institutions of the state, can draw from all circles of nationalists. Although it recruits primarily from the working class, it has access to all sections of that constituency. The UDA and UVF are more restricted. A working-class Protestant who wishes to do something positive to combat IRA terrorism, safeguard his family, or defend Ulster can do those things in a variety of high status, well-rewarded channels. He can join the RUC or the UDR. If he wants to combine such a commitment with a full-time job, he could join the RUC Reserve or become a part-time UDR soldier. Boyle, Hadden, and Hillyard come to the same conclusion:

The pattern of paramilitary activity on the Loyalist side is also affected by the fact that there are a number of legitimate outlets for those members of the Protestant community who wish to play their part in the fight against the IRA. Many committed loyalists, who on the Catholic side might be members of the IRA, join the RUC Reserve or the UDR.[5]

Although his search for an outlet for his patriotism was unusual in its persistence, one senior UDA man exemplified the process. He had tried to join the RUC in the 1950s but been rejected because he was too short.

[4] The differences in attachments of various social groups to 'British' and 'Ulster' identity are explored in R. Wallis, S. Bruce, and D. Taylor, 'Ethnicity and Evangelicalism: Ian Paisley and Protestant Politics in Ulster', *Comparative Studies in Society and History*, 29/2 (1987), 293–313.

[5] K. Boyle, T. Hadden, and P. Hillyard, *Ten Years On in Northern Ireland: The Legal Control of Political Violence* (London, 1980), 22.

When things started to get bad, I tried to join the Specials but they were being stood down. I put my name down for the UDR but for some reason—they never tell you the reason—I was rejected. So I had to look elsewhere. I got involved with my local vigilantes and just went on from there.

Compared with loyalist paramilitary organizations, the police and the army are selective. Many of the people who in only slightly altered circumstances might have become competent terrorist 'operators' have been siphoned off, and the UDA and UVF are left to recruit from the least competent sections of their population. Despite deliberate attempts by the UDA and UVF to attract and retain older, more respectable men, many loyalist paramilitaries had previous records. In 1975, 61 per cent of convicted loyalists (but only 45 per cent of republicans) had previous records. In 1979, the figures were 86 per cent and 57 per cent.[6]

The state and the pro-state terror group recruit from the same population. The Crown forces have the advantages of being legal, respectable, and paying well. That they come from the same backgrounds and may be motivated by similar values does not mean that those who serve the state officially will aid those who do the same in a private capacity. Even if the initial motivation was the same, and often it is not, the Crown forces are organizations which thoroughly socialize their new recruits so that loyalty to the force or the regiment replaces loyalty to the kids one went to school with who are now in the UDA. Those who stay in the security forces for more than a few years and enjoy rewarding careers put their own organization first. Even if they were pursuing identical goals (which they are not), the Crown forces would not be 'in bed' with the paramilitaries; they compete for the prestige of first or most completely attaining those goals. The security-force and ex-security-force personnel who do assist the paramilitaries are usually of low rank and of short service, and their unsuccessful careers suggest personality problems. With rare exception, they are marginal characters, people who left or were forced to resign because, for a variety of reasons, they were not very good soldiers or policemen. Albert Baker, who led a UDA murder group in east Belfast in the early 1970s, was a deserter from the Royal Irish Rangers. Michael Stone, a hero for his Milltown cemetery killings,

[6] *Fortnight*, 7 May 1977, pp. 6–8.

joined the Royal Irish Rangers in November 1979 and was discharged three months later.

To sum up in an exaggerated way to make the point, some competent and committed loyalists sublimate their politics in their careers as policemen or soldiers. The second most competent strata join the RUC or UDR but are unsuccessful and leave, are forced out, or are not promoted. A very small number of these people actively assist loyalist organizations or become activists themselves. Finally there are the loyalists who are not accepted by the RUC or UDR.

We can ask what sorts of people are attracted to the UDA and UVF. There is no doubt that many recruits are well-meaning people motivated only by a spirit of patriotism and social responsibility. There is also no doubt that many are drawn primarily by the opportunities for easy money, excitement, and vicious thrills. The two types compete to define the ethos of the organizations; the more the second sort come to the fore, the more the respectable are squeezed out.

These observations can be summarized simply: the appeal of any terrorist organization will depend in part on the existence of alternative expressions of the values which that organization purports to embody. An east Antrim Protestant who feels moved to 'do something about the IRA' can join the UDR or RUC; a west Belfast Catholic who wishes to drive out the colonial oppressors has only republican terrorism. The pro-state terror group has to compete with legitimate state agencies; the anti-state terror group does not.

State Penetration

The RUC and the British army have managed to insert their own personnel into the IRA and have turned IRA activists. They have also been able to use various trawl methods of intelligence-gathering to build up very detailed profiles of republican areas. With far less effort, the security forces know what is going on in loyalist circles and can thus bring perpetrators into their net. Once that contact is made, once the first two or three people are pulled in, then the consequences outlined below in the discussion of loyalist responses to interrogation follow.

Of course, the extent to which close ties to members of state security forces will be detrimental to pro-state terror groups depends on the attitude of the state to those groups. Through either an unwillingness to believe that Protestants did that sort of thing or an unwillingness to fight a war on two fronts, the security forces have at times been reluctant to act against loyalist para-militaries. The first year of sectarian murders and the lack of a response to them anything like as vigorous as the army's Falls Road curfew is an example, as is the inertia of the security forces during the 1974 strike. However, when the state does turn its attention to pro-state terror groups, it can pursue them with far

TABLE 11.1. *Policing efficacy, 1981–7*

Year	Republican		Loyalist	
	Political murders	Persons charged with murder	Political murders	Persons charged with murder
1981	69	27	12	21
1982	71	32	13	18
1983	54	23	7	52
1984	40	36	7	5
1985	42	17	5	7
1986	41	5	14	7
1987	69	8	11	20
TOTAL	386	148	69	130

Source: RUC Information Office.

more success and far less effort than anti-state groups. If one compares the success of internment, one can see the point. Most of the Catholics interned, especially in the first swoop, were not active IRA men. When the state decided to intern loyalists, it almost always interned the right people (although often for not quite the right offence).

One can also see a stark difference in the ability of the police to make persons 'amenable' for serious crimes. Table 11.1 lists under the headings 'republican' and 'loyalist' the number of murders committed by each side in 1981–7, and the number of people charged with murder (although these figures generally relate to the murders of previous years). There are weaknesses with this presentation—it would be more useful to know what percentage of murders by each side was cleared up—but the contrast between the two sets of figures is so great that it is very unlikely to be much changed by using conviction rates rather than numbers of people charged. In all but two of the eight years, the number of loyalists charged with murder was greater than the number of victims, and, in those two, the totals were close. In the same period, the number of IRA personnel charged with murder was considerably smaller than (often less than half) the total of the IRA's victims. Or, to describe the same data in another way: very similar numbers of loyalists and republicans were charged with murder but the republicans killed 386 people while loyalists killed only 69. To cite a non-police source, Ed. Moloney in early 1982 wrote that the RUC's conviction rate for republican murders was between 50 and 60 per cent while that for loyalist murders was between 90 and 100 per cent.[7] To put it simply, the RUC finds it a lot easier to catch loyalist killers.

There can be no better anecdotal example of police penetration than the clearing-up of the murder of Catholic businessman Jack Kielty in Dundrum. A young police constable was having an affair with a Protestant woman. After a sexual encounter one night, she told him that her brother had been the driver for the murderers. The constable got dressed and went off to tell his divisional commander. Four of the people involved in the killing (including the policeman's girlfriend) were arrested, charged, and convicted.

Northern Ireland is such a small place that a great deal is known about the 'operators' on both sides. It is often said that the problem is not knowing who killed whom but proving it in court. The paramilitary organizations are not quite that transparent, although well-informed journalists and policemen do know a great deal. However, loyalists do seem a little more transparent than republicans, and this is related to the nature of their mission. The anti-state terror group often represents a minority people with a long history of subordination; people who see themselves as oppressed and persecuted underdogs are not likely to boast and brag about their achievements, except in the very tight circles of their own people. Often the anti-state group will have had a long history in which it has learnt the value of secrecy. The position of the pro-state terrorist is very different. He believes he is defending the status quo, the state, the government, and he is much more open about his activities. Republican and loyalist killers are equally

[7] E. Moloney, *Irish Times*, 20 Nov. 1982.

proud of what they do, but the latter are much more likely to boast openly about it because they expect (or at least feel they are due) the congratulations of the general public.

To summarize, because the pro-state terror group recruits from the same population as the state's security forces, it sometimes has the advantage of being able to 'tap' the expertise and resources of the state (as in the case of UDA–UVF men who join the UDR). The cost is that the security forces have the pro-state terror groups well penetrated and are able, when they wish, to police the pro-state groups much more easily than the anti-state groups.

Organization and Planning

While they may do other things, paramilitaries are fundamentally concerned with killing people. The bottom line is violence or the threat of violence (which is only convincing if the threat is sometimes carried out). In contrast to most IRA actions, which show a great deal of planning, many loyalist 'moves', especially in the early days, were haphazard and spontaneous, involving little more organization than a few people drinking in a pub and deciding to go and do something. In contrast to IRA actions, a very high proportion of loyalist killings were committed by people who had been drinking.

As we have seen, a very large proportion of loyalist victims were Catholics who were not active republicans. In terms of their own claims about what they were doing, the loyalist organizations were incompetent; instead of killing leading IRA men and Sinn Feiners, they killed 'any oul Taig' who had the misfortune to fall into the hands of a team out for a kill. There will obviously be arguments about the classification of some murders, but we can accept the general outline of the data from the Irish Information Partnership in Table 11.2.

Loyalist paramilitaries have been responsible for 705 (25.3 per cent) of the deaths between 1969 and 1989 and about three-quarters of these—when one adds those Protestant civilians mistaken for Catholics (as distinct from those shot as 'touts') to the Catholic civilian total—have been of uninvolved civilians. While there has been a marked increase in selectivity since the 1970s,

TABLE 11.2. *Victims of republican and loyalist paramilitaries, 1969–89*

Status of victim	Republican		Loyalist	
	No.	%	No.	%
Security forces	847	52.7	10	1.4
Republican paramilitaries	146	9.1	21	3.0
Loyalist paramilitaries	18	1.1	40	5.7
Civilians				
Catholic	173	10.8	506	71.8
Protestant	379	23.6	14	16.2
Other	22	1.4	12	1.7
Prison officers	23	1.4	2	0.3
TOTAL	1,608	100.1	605	100.1

Source: Adapted from Irish Information Partnership, *Agenda: Information Service on Northern Ireland and Anglo-Irish Relations* (6th edn., London, 1990), 295.

nationalist paramilitaries remain a very small proportion of the total.[8]

If a loyalist was to be cold blooded about this, he could describe the sectarian murder campaign as successful in that it frightened a lot of Catholics and 'made the fuckers appreciate the cost of not getting rid of the IRA'. If the purpose was simply to terrorize the minority community or to exact communal revenge, then it succeeded. However, very few loyalist paramilitary leaders have defined their goal in those terms and for good reasons. It would be quite at odds with their self-image as decent law-abiding and reluctant 'soldiers'. The IRA also fails to live up to its self-image. A large proportion of its victims do not fall into its own categories of 'legitimate' targets. None the less, the IRA proportionately kills more members of the security forces and representatives of the British state than the UDA and UVF do leading republicans: about half its victims have been members of the security forces. But one needs to be careful of the contrast. If we say that the IRA is better at killing the targets it has selected, this could mean (*a*) that it is more skilled, or (*b*) that it can choose from a wider range of targets which are easier to hit. Both of these seem to be the case.

Taking the second point first, the anti-state terrorist organiza-

[8] It is worth noting that there has been a marked increase of the 'accuracy' of loyalist murders in recent years as the total has gone down. This almost certainly has a lot to do with the electoral success of Sinn Fein, which has given loyalists a variety of more accessible targets.

tion has a relatively easy job in finding its targets. The agents of the state—the police and the army—must be identified by their uniforms. Indeed, far from being able to merge into the background, their role requires that they stand out and be visible; a large part of their purpose is not so much to do anything as to be seen. They represent, in their visible persons, the continuity and security of the state. Although small units can disguise themselves (the RUC's E4a units or the SAS, for example), the bulk of the security forces have to be seen in order to be doing their jobs.

Furthermore, the range of people who can be defined by an anti-state organization as 'legitimate' targets is extremely wide. Not only the security forces but anyone who assists them can, with varying degrees of acceptance by the supporting population, be described as legitimate. Where, as in the Ulster case, one has a majority population who are not just acquiescent but active supporters of the status quo, there is a huge population of legitimate targets. First it is policemen who are killed when their station is mortared. Then it is the builders who accept the contracts to rebuild those stations. Then it is public utility engineers who repair services to the stations. Finally, the IRA adds the men who deliver the bread and the milk. When one includes those who do not refuse to serve members of the security forces (the owners of the Dropping Well pub in Ballykelly, for example), then one has defined almost all Protestants (with the possible general exception of women and children) as legitimate targets. Even old age does not exclude someone who has earlier been in one of these categories.

The pro-state terrorist group has a much smaller target to aim at. In theory it must confine itself to attacking anti-state terrorists and those who actively support them, and such people are hard to find. Unlike the targets of the IRA, who have to put themselves on show, the people the UDA and UVF most want to kill—IRA gunmen—keep themselves hidden. Even the public fronts—Sinn Fein politicians, for example—are better hidden than people playing a similar role in the majority community. Even without them taking active steps to avoid loyalist assassins, such people are harder to find because they generally stay in the bosom of the minority (and hence small, introverted, and secretive) population.

The response of many loyalist gunmen in such a situation is to engage in random sectarian killings. To an extent (although to less of an extent than is commonly supposed) this reduces the popularity of the UDA and UVF within their own communities and exacerbates the problems of morale, fund-raising, and recruitment. That this is seen as a problem by the paramilitaries is clear from the frequent apologies for the mistakes of the past and promises to do better next time. What makes loyalist random anti-Catholic violence damaging to their public standing is the contrast between those actions and the martial rhetoric which is so important a part of their claims to legitimate descent from the 1912 UVF. The men who followed Craig and Carson and who fought at the Somme as the 36th (Ulster) Division did not have romper rooms, Lenny Murphy, or the east Belfast gang which dumped bodies by the Connswater River.

Here we need to add an important general sociological principle. People do not respond to the objective reality of a situation; they respond to their perceptions of that reality, and perceptions can be shaped. Whether a particular action is the proper execution of a traitor, a justified attack on an oppressor, a tragic mistake, or the act of blood-crazed gangsters is, in the end, a matter of competing rhetorics. Each side tries to persuade its public to accept its definition of the situation. Thus we come back to the competition with the state. Large parts of the Catholic population are not receptive to government propaganda. Although far from uncritical of their 'defenders,' their general disposition is to be more favourable towards the IRA's own interpretations of its actions than to the government's interpretations. The UDA and UVF compete with the agencies of the state they claim to defend and their constituency is more receptive to the views of the government. The IRA finds it easier than do the UDA and UVF to persuade its people that racketeering, sectarian assassination campaigns, and intimidation are necessary evils of a just war. Or, more exactly, it does a better job of persuading its people that what may look like gangsterism and mindless violence is no such thing.

Resilience under Arrest

The lack of selectivity in the murder campaign has a small but important consequence for the UDA and UVF. When the RUC has any lead at all to a loyalist killing, the group in question often falls like a house of cards, and this is undoubtedly a large part of the explanation for the RUC's greater success against loyalists than nationalists. It only needs one or two members in custody for the police to be told about the whole operation.

Good interrogators will find a gap in the defences of most prisoners, but there are two reasons why it is easier to persuade loyalists to talk. First, the frequent 'mistakes' can be used to play on an incipient sense of shame and guilt. It is easier to remain silent when one feels justified, and it is easier to feel justified about 'legitimate' targets than it is about accidents and errors. A young man who follows orders to eliminate a 'dangerous informer' and later discovers that he has been used to settle a personal quarrel, and a teenager who blows up an 'IRA pub' and finds that he has killed a harmless old man who was a friend of his father, will be a lot more susceptible to the police officer's encouragements to 'come clean' than will a man who murders an IRA activist.

Secondly, there is the problem of boastfulness. IRA men see the RUC as enemies and not as people who either ought or actually do share their values and hence as a worthy audience for their bragging. Loyalists can expect a certain degree of sympathy and even at some subconscious level expect to be rewarded for killing the people who kill policemen. Thus, after they rescued him from a republican mob, Michael Stone could brag to the police: 'I'm game for anything!'

Individual behaviour is shaped by contexts, and an important context for resilience after arrest is the general relationship between the community and the paramilitary organization. The more close-knit the community and the more committed it is to the support of the terrorist organization, the less likely people are to plead guilty or implicate others. Communal support (or at least toleration) for the IRA is a major source of reinforcement for the arrested terrorist; it is the raw material for building and sustaining a self-image of heroism. But even when the suspect lacks the 'right stuff', the community is liable to provide a little stiffening for the backbone, because the potential talker will be aware that the future of his family will be related to his behaviour. If he is seen to act as a model terrorist—saying nothing, refusing to recognize the court, doing his time as a good organization man—then his family will be rewarded with financial support and approval. If he does not, they may be ostracized, which can vary from simply not being given any money to being themselves terrorized out of their neighbourhood. Although the dislike for 'touts' is probably similar on both sides, there is a significant difference in response to co-operation with the police that falls short of 'grassing'. Except in the most deprived loyalist areas there is not the same blanket hostility to the police and the courts that one finds in many Catholic areas. How could there be when the police and the courts represent the state that the UDA and UVF are defending?

It is no part of my argument that there are no similarities between republican and loyalist terrorists. It is enough to establish that what pro-state terrorists may gain on the swings of recruiting from the same people as do the state's security forces and sharing some of the goals of the government, they amply lose on the roundabout of being more accessible to state policing.

Politics and Social Work

The republican movement has benefited from the active involvement of a large number of university-educated and potentially upwardly mobile people. It has an intellectual cadre which has been skilled at presenting its violence in the best possible light and which has been able to broaden the appeal of the organization by promoting various social campaigns. A journalist who has spent many years reporting in Northern Ireland said that when he was interviewing IRA men he had trouble keeping up with their thinking; when he was interviewing loyalists he had trouble finding any. An exaggeration, no doubt, but the history of the Volunteer Party and the fact that John McMichael became the UDA's political spokesman show the difficulty the loyalists have had in finding credible spokesmen for a credible political and social programme.

In part this is a problem of personnel, but it is also a problem of project. However slim the chances of the IRA succeeding in its mission, it has a goal which is clear and which is minimally consistent with its actions. It has to compete with constitutional nationalism and it loses in that competition, but its cause remains clear enough to serve as a focus for political action. There is almost no room for loyalist paramilitaries to develop a clear political programme, because straightforward unionism is well catered for by major political parties and, albeit grudgingly, is supported by the state. For loyalists to be simply unionists means that they cannot develop a distinct politics. This was recognized by Barr and those who pushed the UDA towards negotiated independence, which was a novel but unpopular programme.

A similar principle of competition with the state allows us to see why the loyalist paramilitaries have been less successful than the IRA in using various forms of community action as a way of building a solid base of popular support. The only times the UDA and UVF have been obviously good at community action were when civil unrest prevented Protestant people using the state's agencies: for example, when the 'no-go' areas or the UWC strike temporarily disrupted social services. The Catholic areas that most strongly support the IRA are peopled by men and women who are almost permanently disaffected from the state and hence who are available to participate in a variety of 'community' activities (such as founding Irish-language schools) which are at root minor forms of rejection of the state. Many residents of Ballymurphy and the Divis flats are unwilling to call on the RUC to police hooliganism and anti-social behaviour; there is, therefore, a space for the IRA to take on that role. The anti-state group can set itself up as an alternative 'state' in its base communities and, in so far as it provides for their needs, it acquires additional support and legitimacy. The pro-state group is competing with the state itself. The UDA cannot set up 'loyalist' schools.

When loyalist paramilitaries do offer themselves to the electorate on fairly conventional platforms (either as members of mainstream parties or as independent local councillors), they are not generally well supported. As one UDA man who stood for Belfast council a number of times put it:

When the Taigs was running up the streets with guns, then I was the boy. Just the ticket. Come and save us. But when it settles down, its thank you and goodbye. It comes to voting and the Protestant people would rather elect some respectable wanker.

Loyalists could always vote for some 'respectable wanker' because there is no shortage of legitimate parties supporting the ends (if not the means) of the paramilitaries.

There is another small point in the difference between Protestant and Catholic attitudes to the government that is significant for understanding the failure of loyalist paramilitary organizations to match the IRA in developing political and social work. As it has done in other inner city areas where there is widespread alienation and disaffection, the government in Northern Ireland has created a large number of quasi-governmental agencies to promote improved housing, training for the unemployed, small business start-up schemes, healthy leisure activities, and the like. Naturally, it wants such agencies to have the secondary function of domesticating the disaffected. In both loyalist and republican areas this has led to arguments about the influence of paramilitary organizations, and funding has been withdrawn from government-sponsored work creation schemes in both Catholic and Protestant areas.[9] However, because they are pro-state organizations, it is much more often the case with the UDA and UVF than with the IRA that people who were or might easily have become leading figures have been 'neutralized' by being incorporated by the state: 'You want to know where our leaders went? Look at [. . .] and [. . .]. Working for the bloody government.'

Funding

Paramilitary organizations do not come cheap, and financial support for a pro-state terror group is always costly. One either gives money or sees some other principle (such as 'thou shalt not rob banks') compromised. When the survival of one's own people or of the state (and the pro-state population sees the two as the same) is threatened, such costs are reasonable sacrifices. When the immediate threat recedes, the costs are seen as unreasonable, and 'voluntary' funding has to be replaced with various forms of illegality and coercion. If money is no longer coming in from membership dues or gifts, then it has to be stolen or extorted, and neither of these is good for public image, the morale of the organization, the quality of recruits, or the sense of self-worth of activists.

The funding problems of the pro-state terrorist organization go further back than the problems with general popularity. Popularity

[9] See *Newsletter*, 28 Nov. 1989, and *Sunday World*, 10 Dec. 1989, for stories on an ACE scheme in the loyalist Glencairn estate that had its government funding withdrawn. See *Irish News*, 4 Dec. 1989, for SDLP questioning of government funding for a cross-community project led by Gusty Spence.

within one's own population may not be important if there is some outside agency—another nation-state or a sub-population of the same ethnos—who are willing to supply money. The IRA has the Irish-American community in the United States to support it; it also had Libyan and East German aid. The loyalists do not receive any significant amount of funding from outside agencies because those nation-states or pressure groups which feel a pressing urge to help maintain the United Kingdom will support the government and not the UDA or UVF.

There are four problems of racketeering.

Public image.   Bank robbing and extortion have made it very easy for the government to portray the UDA and UVF as unprincipled gangsters, and, back to the pro-state problem, the unionist people are more responsive to the views of the state than are nationalists.

Organizational morale.   Although it need not follow, it also seems to be the case that such activities exacerbate tensions within the loyalist organizations. Numerous arguments within the UDA and UVF have resulted from rumours and suspicions about the arrival and departure of money. Legal fund-raising allows good accounting procedures. When money is being raised from hijacked drinks lorries, bank robberies, extortion, prostitution, pornography, and drugs, one cannot have respectable accountants. One has a cash economy and the constant possibility of sticky fingers.

Quality of personnel.   The quality of recruits also suffers. The more principled loyalists did not become paramilitaries in order to rob banks, threaten building contractors, and sell pornography. Those people who like that sort of thing and are good at it are disliked by the more respectable (usually older) members who withdraw, leaving the hoodlums as a greater proportion of the members.

Personal morale.   Some loyalists are willing to go along with the necessary fund-raising activities but clearly have personal problems with their self-image as a result and hence become susceptible to RUC blandishments when they are arrested and questioned.

However, I want to draw back slightly from the common perception of gangsterism that one finds in the media. It is widely assumed that gangsterism and sectarian murders reduce support for the UDA and UVF. They do, but perhaps not to the extent that is imagined. In understanding the complaints that working-class loyalists make about 'wee bastards with new cars', it is important to allow for the general expressions of resentment, envy, and disparagement that people often make of their neighbours who seem to have more than they deserve. Such complaints do not mean that they do not support the 'wee bastards'. One also has to be cautious in interpreting attitudes to sectarian murder. Loyalists are no more heartless monsters than are republicans. On both sides one finds the same ambivalence: sympathy for individuals who are perceived as 'innocent' victims alternates with something close to indifference and even pleasure that 'they are getting it now'. Dislike of some aspect of terrorism is always entered into an equation. How much racketeering or sectarian murder count against the paramilitaries depends on how good a job they are doing on other fronts and on the amount of republican activity.

Internal Cohesion and Discipline

Finally I would like to draw together a number of points about organizational cohesion. It is hard not to be struck by the weak and often irrational internal discipline of the loyalist paramilitaries. Disagreements might lead to someone being shot in the head, but, as often as not, serious breaches of discipline would go unpunished. In the 1970s UDA brigadiers went accompanied by bodyguards to protect them, not from the IRA but from other brigadiers. When one company commander was released from prison, he found two cars waiting for him; one from west Belfast and one from east. With a serious expectation of being shot by one or other group of his own people, and not being sure which he should fear most, he had to gamble on which car to join.

Discipline is a product of commitment and popularity. Where everyone is strongly committed to a common cause, the discipline is self-imposed. The IRA certainly gets greater commitment from its members. There may be many reasons for this. Apart from anything else, the 'physical-force' tradition of nationalist struggle has a very long history, and many Catholics are well socialized into its demands.[10] The pro-state group will always be less certain of its actions because its shared past is too closely mixed with the history of the state and support for the Crown forces.

There is also a cohesion imposed on the anti-state group by the common circumstances of its people. Although the extent and sense of 'oppression' varies within the Catholic population, republicans can better play on shared circumstances to create a common cause. A major impetus to pro-state terrorism is the sense of being under threat, and this varies considerably from area to area and class to class. Although within each community there are vast differences of circumstance, their status as the minority population gives Catholics more in common with each other than have loyalists. It seems no accident that the UDA and UVF have never managed to centralize their organizations. They remain local area groups only loosely affiliated to a central structure. Although it has now been a company of the UDA for twenty years, the WDA still uses its own name first and UDA second on floral tributes.

Where discipline within an organization is not produced automatically by all the members agreeing about what ought to be done, there needs to be some mechanism for resolving conflicts. In the paramilitary world, that comes down in the end to shooting dissidents. If the UVF declares a cease-fire, wishes it to hold, and wishes to retain its credibility, it must be in a position to punish any UVF man who breaks ranks. Such exercises of power will always provoke ill-feeling among friends, relatives, and comrades of the punished offender, but where there are widespread community support for the goals of the organization, no other organizations working towards those goals, and considerable confidence that the leadership of the organization is doing a good job, such disciplining of dissidents will be accepted. The IRA's brigade staff can order the killing of its renegades without endangering the future of the IRA. The brigade staff of the UVF have far less freedom to act to maintain discipline because the UVF enjoys far

---

[10] Republican movements are not immune to fragmentation, as the existence of the INLA and IPLO demonstrates. However, it is worth noting that, while loyalist feuding occurred between and within the UDA and UVF, on the republican side it is the INLA and IPLO which have suffered most from internal strife. See appropriate entries in W. D. Flackes and S. Elliott, *Northern Ireland: A Political Directory, 1968–88* (Belfast, 1989).

lower levels of member commitment and community support than does the IRA. And the explanation for that is again the competition between the pro-state terror organization and the state.

Conclusion

In the main body of the text I have tried to record and explain the details of the history of loyalist paramilitarism. In this final chapter I have tried to show that there is a common thread running through the apparently contingent and accidental features of the UDA and UVF. If one is looking for the most economical description of the last twenty-five years of loyalist paramilitarism, one can find it in the general problems of pro-state terrorism.

The modern state claims for itself a monopoly of coercion. The anti-state group has a relatively simple and sensible task. The power of the state is such that it is very unlikely to win, but, provided enough members of the subordinate population are sufficiently alienated from the state, an organization using violence to destroy that state can prosper; hope can be found in the history of successful coups, rebellions, and anti-colonial wars. In contrast, the project of pro-state terrorism is far less simple and far from sensible. This is not an assertion that one sort of terror is right or reasonable while another is wrong or irrational. It is not a moral but an empirical proposition. If the government does a little blind-eye turning, the pro-state terror group is advantaged, but if the government insists on maintaining its monopoly of coercion, the pro-state organization is in the position of a corner store competing with a multinational. So long as the state itself is not in complete disarray (as in the Lebanon, for example), then its security forces will be better able and better legitimated than any private vigilante group to protect the state.

To explain the recent past is difficult enough and to predict the future is foolish, but the reader might reasonably expect such a lengthy study as this now to 'put up' and follow retrospect with prospect. What is the future of loyalist paramilitarism? Although the book was never conceived as an evaluation of the UDA and UVF, the story can be read as one of decline, from a high point of popularity and influence in the early 1970s to a period of stagnation and retrenchment in the early 1990s. One reader ruefully commented that the text 'was like some catalogue of mistakes—

fifty things the Prods did wrong'. Other versions would have been possible. One could have begun by observing that, despite the lack of the sort of professional, well-educated and well-trained leadership the UVF enjoyed in 1912, the loyalist paramilitaries have remained in business for twenty-five years, which is considerably longer than many would have predicted at the start of the Troubles. One could have argued that their terror campaign and mass mobilization of working-class Protestants prevented the British government from the sort of 'sell out' that looked possible at the start of the Troubles when William Whitelaw was holding secret talks with IRA leaders. One could note that, with the decline in the number of loyalist murders, the proportion of attacks on leading republicans has increased. It could have been stressed that the last decade has not seen anything like the Shankill Butchers and the romper rooms. The story has not been told in the positive way those still active would have liked because I have tried to explain what the world looks like to those whose actions I have been describing, and what I heard from most of those I interviewed—even some who still command the organizations—was weariness and distaste. Even those who stress the good 'military operations' still find it hard to identify a purpose, a direction, or a programme in what they are now doing. The novelty has gone. The notion that a few killings would make any difference to anything has gone. Too much of what their organizations are now doing is just more of the same. Even the best 'hits' disrupt the IRA's structure for only a few weeks before new leaders fill the vacancies. A very detailed audit of the paramilitary organizations could point to slightly greater certainty and direction in the UVF, which has never really had ambitions beyond killing IRA men, but the overall impression is one of men treading water rather than swimming.

The talks between the Northern Ireland political parties that stumbled into life in the summer of 1991 and quickly petered out were always unlikely to find a solution to Ulster's crisis. There is no 'Northern Ireland problem' for which there is a solution. There is only a conflict in which there must be winners and losers. The fundamental fact that even the most constitutional nationalists and even the most liberal unionists have incompatible desires combines with a lack of consensus within each camp to make substantial agreement seem an insubstantial hope. For unionists who dare to face it, the future looks bleak because it is clear that the British government is far more concerned about good relations with Dublin and a good press abroad than it is with the interests of Ulster Protestants. There will be no diminution of the Republic of Ireland's part in the running of the North and, although change is slow, Northern Catholics are becoming more numerous and more influential. Some unionist politicians conclude that the deal should be cut now, while they still have something to deal, but those who advocate active compromise face as yet insuperable obstacles in selling a 'sell-out' to their own people. However, that unionists are not yet ready to volunteer for accommodation with Northern Catholics and the Republic's government does not mean that they will put up much of a fight when such accommodation is slowly insinuated into the daily life of the province. That remains the first big question for the future of the UDA and UVF: to what extent are Protestants prepared to fight against the British government's policy? Contrary to the views of a UDA spokesman,[11] I would say 'not very much'. In comparison to the opposition to the 1974 power-sharing executive, response to the Anglo-Irish accord was distinctly muted. The second big question is this: even if Ulster Protestants were prepared to fight, would they do so under the aegis of the UDA or UVF? Again, my answer has to be quite different from that hoped for by the UDA and UVF: no, they would not. Even in 1974 the poor opinion of the paramilitaries forced them to operate behind a 'front' of the UWC and the coalition of politicians, and little that has happened since has enhanced the reputation and popularity of the UDA and UVF. A close examination of the murders and attempted murders committed by loyalists in 1990 and 1991 shows that many of their victims could be more 'legitimate' as targets than the media suggested.[12] But that is not the point. The point is that even unionists are happy to believe these are sectarian attacks, and there are enough murders that are indefensible even in UDA and UVF terms to confirm that impression. Thus the mid-Ulster UVF interspersed the murders of active republicans with what were simply tit-for-tat killings. When the IRA killed an off-duty UDR

[11] *Irish News*, 10 June 1991.
[12] The libel laws prevent me from reporting the details of what might form an alternative version.

man in a car park on the shores of Lough Neagh, the UVF murdered a young Catholic in similar circumstances. When the IRA killed Protestant businessmen whose companies worked for the security forces, the UVF shot dead two young girls and a young man in a shop on a Catholic estate. The gruesome arithmetic of good and bad hits makes no impact on the general unionist perception that, whatever the UDA and UVF may think of themselves, they are not Carson's Volunteers, defending the realm.

This suggests that, whatever the UDA's and UVF's capacity for continuing their present levels of activity, they are unlikely to flourish again. Not enough people are persuaded of their usefulness to overlook their defects. However, we cannot assume that the option of armed resistance to political change has been entirely exhausted. One is back to the terrible equation of fear of death and loss of political power. Since the 'Ulsterization' of the security forces, the call for 'troops out' has become something of a red herring. A starker but more realistic way of describing the Ulster Protestant nightmare is expulsion from the United Kingdom. If Britain expels its troublesome province, if whatever regime is established fails to retain the confidence of the local security forces, and if republican violence increases (as it would be sure to), then one will have a return to the circumstances that brought the loyalist paramilitaries into existence in the first place. The record of the UDA and UVF over the last twenty-five years has created a legacy of distaste and distrust that means that the security situation will have to deteriorate far more next time for there to be the same response, but sadly such deterioration is not unimaginable. The final word can be left to a retired UDA brigadier:

We've had our go and blown it. If the people wanted me back, I might do it again, but I can't see it, not with the reputation the UDA has now. But if the politicians can't sort it out and the British ever pull out, the Ulster Protestant people are not going to lie down. So long as the Provies keep picking us off, we'll kill them and, if there's ever a straight fight or it gets like the Mau-Mau, we'll be back or something like us and you can bet on that.

STATISTICAL APPENDIX

THE following tables and figure present in convenient form some of the statistical material that has informed the text.

Characteristics of Loyalist Terrorists

TABLE A.1. *Age and previous criminal records of Diplock defendants, 1975 and 1979* (%)

	Republicans		Loyalists	
	1975	1979	1975	1979
Age				
14–16	7	8	14	2
17–20	63	45	42	13
21–24	13	19	11	28
25–29	8	13	16	22
30–40	4	7	8	21
Over 40	1	4	4	4
Not known	4	4	5	9
Record				
None	55	43	39	14
Non-scheduled	31	33	49	52
Scheduled	7	11	5	13
Not known	7	13	8	20

Source: adapted from K. Boyle, T. Hadden, and P. Hillyard, *Ten Years On in Northern Ireland: The Legal Control of Political Violence* (London, 1980), 23.

'Scheduled offences' are basically those that are Troubles-related. Although the differences should not be exaggerated, the comparison does illustrate the point about paramilitary personnel made in Chapter 11. Loyalists are more likely than republicans to have previous records for 'ordinary' crimes, and members of the 1979 loyalist cohort are more likely to have previous records for non-political crimes than the 1975 cohort, a change that might be explained by the gradual withdrawal from loyalist paramilitary organizations of the more 'respectable' trade-union and community-leadership element.

TABLE A.2. *Socio-economic status of Diplock defendants, 1975* (%)

Occupational group	Protestant		No data	Catholic		No data
	Employed	Unemployed		Employed	Unemployed	
I	—	—		1	—	
II	3	—		2	—	
III—Skilled non-manual	1	—		8	1	
III—Skilled manual	27	7		17	5	
IV	14	2		15	4	
V	16	17		9	24	
Student/ schoolboy	8			7		
Housewife	1			2		
No data			4			4
Number	(123)	(48)	(8)	(178)	(98)	(12)

Source: *Fortnight*, 7 May, 1976.

The number of cases is too small to draw much from comparisons between loyalists and republicans, but the concentrated class base of loyalist paramilitarism is clear; only 4 per cent of loyalist defendants were not working class.

TABLE A.3. *Summary of Fatal Casualties in Northern Ireland, 1969–1989*

Status of victim	Agency responsible					
	Security forces	Republican paramilit- aries	Loyalist paramilit- aries	Other and unidentified	Total	Percent- age of total
Security forces	15	847	10	4	876	31.44
Republican paramilitaries	123	146	21	6	296	10.62
Loyalist paramilitaries	13	18	40	2	73	2.62
Civilians						
Catholic	149	173	506	74	902	32.38
Protestant	25	379	114	57	575	20.64
Other	4	22	12	1	39	1.40
Total	178	574	632	132	1,516	54.41
Prison officers	0	23	2	0	25	0.90
TOTAL	329	1,608	705	144	2,786	
Percentage of Total	11.81	57.72	25.31	5.17	100.00	

Source: adapted from Irish Information Partnership, *Agenda*, 295.

As I have argued at various places in the text, the classifications of many victims around the paramilitary/civilian divide can be contested. However, the big picture is reasonably informative and it shows a number of things: the very large number of civilian victims, the record of both sides in killing their own civilians, and the record of both sides in killing large numbers of their own members. Probably because republican groups have been more willing to administer the 'death penalty' to their own wayward members, they have actually killed more republican than loyalist paramilitaries.

Comparing Republican and Loyalist Terrorism

In many senses the relationship between republican and loyalist violence is of interest. Loyalists argue that their violence is a reaction to republican violence and Figure A.1 would appear to offer strong evidence for that claim, at least for the first decade of the Troubles. Statistical analysis of such data cannot prove which causes which, but it is possible to measure 'correlation'—the degree to which the two lines move together and are thus in some way associated—and it is extremely high. The Pearson's 'r' measure of correlation between republican and loyalist rates of murder was 0.74 at $p < 0.001$ for the year totals and, using the most exacting measure of monthly totals, it was 0.58 at $p < 0.001$, both of which are highly significant correlations.

Indices of Political Violence

TABLE A.4. *Indices of political violence, 1970–1986*

Year	Type of activity			Estimated weight of explosives (lb)		Armed robberies	
	Shooting incidents	Explosions	Bombs neutralized	Explosions	Neutralized	Number of robberies	Total stolen (£000)
1970	213	153	17	746	59	—	304
1971	1,756	1,022	493	10,972	3,001	437	791
1972	10,628	1,382	471	47,462	19,978	1,931	612
1973	5,018	978	542	47,472	32,450	1,215	573
1974	3,206	685	428	46,435	27,094	1,231	572
1975	1,803	399	236	13,753	11,159	1,201	545
1976	1,908	766	426	17,596	16,252	813	447
1977	1,081	366	169	2,839	2,188	591	233
1978	755	455	178	5,343	5,860	442	855
1979	728	422	142	11,180	4,530	434	497
1980	642	280	120	9,059	6,405	412	555
1981	1,142	398	131	9,621	9,168	587	1,392
1982	547	219	113	11,199	7,300	580	830
1983	424	266	101	6,923	7,503	622	702
1984	334	193	55	8,545	6,114	627	656
1985	237	148	67	11,711	7,715	459	a
1986	392	254		a	a	—	
1987	674	384				969	
1988	537	458				805	
1989	566	420				663	

a Figures no longer reported.

Source: Northern Ireland Annual Abstract of Statistics; RUC Chief Constable's Report; B. Rowthorn and N. Wayne, *Northern Ireland: The Political Economy*

Security-Force Establishment

TABLE A.5. *Strength of security forces on 31 December each year since 1969*

Year	RUC Full-time[a]	RUC Reservists full-time	RUC Reservists part-time	RUC Total[a]	UDR Part-time	UDR Full-time	UDR Total	Total 'Ulsterized' security forces	British army[b]	Total security forces
1969[c]	3,061	0	0	3,061				3,061	2,693	5,737
1969	3,044	0	0	3,044				3,044	7,952	14,489
1970	3,809	0	436	4,245	2,243	49	2,292	6,537	7,662	17,146
1971	4,086	0	1,284	5,370	3,880	234	4,114	9,484	14,258	29,411
1972	4,257	153	1,981	6,391	8,111	645	8,762	15,153	17,183	32,365
1973	4,391	290	2,224	6,905	7,444	833	8,277	15,182	15,848	32,096
1974	4,564	510	3,350	8,424	6,934	890	7,824	16,248	14,550	31,925
1975	4,902	661	4,158	9,721	6,227	1,427	7,654	17,375	14,441	34,902
1976	5,253	870	3,827	9,950	6,214	1,524	7,738	17,688	14,245	35,172
1977	5,692	1,002	3,684	10,378	5,951	1,693	7,644	18,022	14,147	35,599
1978	6,110	1,188	3,417	10,715	5,670	2,192	7,862	18,577	13,124	34,795
1979	6,642	1,305	3,209	11,156	5,154	2,469	7,623	18,779	12,976	35,420
1980	6,943	1,685	3,067	11,695	5,179	2,554	7,733	19,428	11,271	34,128
1981	7,334	2,060	2,810	12,204	4,741	2,738	7,479	19,683	11,040	33,931
1982	7,718	2,174	2,666	12,558	4,391	2,739	7,130	19,688	9,516	32,613
1983	8,003	2,295	2,198	12,496	4,342	2,793	7,135	19,631	9,110	32,012
1984	8,127	2,532	1,987	12,646	4,094	2,683	6,777	19,423	9,014	31,738
1985[d]	8,259	2,755	1,753	12,767	3,713	2,765	6,478	19,245	9,920	32,822
1986	8,234	2,754	1,660	12,648	3,751	2,784	6,535	19,183	9,645	28,828
1987	8,236	2,987	1,657	12,880	n.a.	n.a.	6,364	19,244	9,695	32,633
1988	8,247	3,016	1,652	12,915	n.a.	n.a.	6,312	19,227	9,658	28,841
1989	8,264	3,018	1,607	12,889	n.a.	n.a.	6,342	19,231		

[a] Excluding Ulster Special Constabulary. [b] Excluding Territorial Army. [c] As at 30 June 1969.
[d] Figures as at 30 Nov. 1985 for UDR, BA, and TA.

Source: adapted from Irish Information Partnership, *Agenda*, 316.

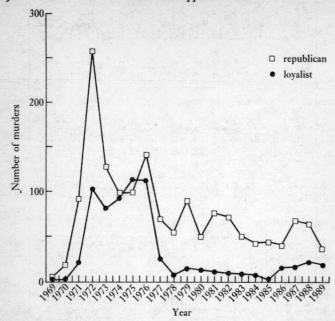

FIGURE A.1. Comparison of number of murders committed by Republicans and loyalists

Source: Data provided by Irish Information Partnership.

Sentencing of Paramilitaries

Table A.6, in conjunction with the different rates of terrorist activity for republican and loyalist organizations shown in Table A.3 and Figure A.1, clearly illustrates the greater success of the security forces in apprehending loyalist killers.

TABLE A.6. *Affiliations of prisoners sentenced to life since 1974 and still imprisoned, February 1990*

Republican		Loyalist		No affiliation
OIRA	—	UDA	64	
PIRA	136	UFF	5	
INLA	15	UVF	107	
Other republican	—	RHC	1	
		Other loyalist	14	
TOTAL	151		191	37

Source: adapted from Irish Information Partnership, *Agenda*, 321.

SELECT BIBLIOGRAPHY

ADAMS, J., *The Financing of Terror* (London: Hodder and Stoughton, 1988).

ADAMSON, I., *The Identity of Ulster: The Land, the Language and the People* (Belfast: Pretani Press, 1982).

—— *The Cruithin: A History of the Ulster Land and People* (Belfast: Pretani Press, 1986).

ALEXANDER, Y., and GLEASON, J. M. (eds.), *Behavioral and Quantitative Perspectives on Terrorism* (London: Pergamon, 1981).

ARTHUR, M., *Northern Ireland: Soldiers Talking* (London: Sidgwick and Jackson, 1988).

ARTHUR, P., *The People's Democracy, 1968–1973* (Belfast: Blackstaff Press, 1974).

—— and JEFFERY, K., *Northern Ireland since 1968* (Oxford: Basil Blackwell, 1988).

AUGHEY, A., 'Sectarian Conflict, 1972–77', in K. Jeffery (ed.), *The Divided Province: The Troubles in Northern Ireland, 1969–1985* (London: Orbis, 1985), 70–86.

—— *Under Siege: Ulster Unionism and the Anglo-Irish Agreement* (Belfast: Blackstaff Press, 1989).

—— and McILHENEY, C., 'The Ulster Defence Association: Paramilitaries and Politics', *Conflict Quarterly*, 11/2 (1981), 32–45.

BARZILAY, D., *The British Army in Ulster* (Belfast: Century Books, 1973–81), ii–iv.

BELL, G., *The Protestants of Ulster* (London: Pluto Press, 1978).

BEW, P., GIBBON, P., and PATTERSON, H., *The State in Northern Ireland, 1921–72: Political Forces and Social Classes* (Manchester: Manchester University Press, 1979).

BISHOP, P., and MALLIE, E., *The Provisional IRA* (London: Corgi, 1988).

BOULTON, D., *The UVF, 1966–73: An Anatomy of Loyalist Rebellion* (Dublin: Gill and Macmillan, 1973).

BOYD, A., *Brian Faulkner and the Crisis of Ulster Unionism* (Tralee, Co. Kerry: Anvil, 1972).

—— *Holy War in Belfast: A History of the Troubles in Northern Ireland* (New York: Grove Press, 1972).

BOYLE, J., *A Sense of Freedom* (London: Pan, 1977).

BOYLE, K., HADDEN, T., and HILLYARD, P., *Law and State: The Case of Northern Ireland* (London: Martin Robertson, 1975).

—— —— —— *Ten Years On in Northern Ireland: The Legal Control of Political Violence* (London: Cobden Trust, 1980).

BRADFORD, N., *A Sword Bathed in Heaven: The Life, Faith and Cruel Death of Robert Bradford MP* (Basingstoke: Marshall Pickens, 1984).

BREWER, J. D., GUELKE, A., HUME, I., MOXON-BROWNE, E., and WILFORD, R., *The Police, Public Order and the State* (London: Macmillan, 1988).

BRUCE, S., *No Pope of Rome: Militant Protestantism in Modern Scotland* (Edinburgh: Mainstream, 1985).

—— *God Save Ulster!: The Religion and Politics of Paisleyism* (Oxford: Oxford University Press, 1986).

—— 'Protestantism and Terrorism in Northern Ireland', in A. O'Day and Y. Alexander (eds.), *Ireland's Terrorist Trauma: Interdisciplinary Perspectives* (Brighton: Harvester Wheatsheaf, 1989), 13–33.

—— 'The Ulster Connection', in G. Walker and T. Gallagher (eds.), *Sermons and Battle Hymns: Protestant Popular Culture in Modern Scotland* (Edinburgh: Edinburgh University Press, 1991), 231–55.

BUCKLAND, P., *The Factory of Grievances: Devolved Government in Northern Ireland, 1921–39* (Dublin: Gill and Macmillan, 1979).

—— *James Craig: Lord Craigavon* (Dublin: Gill and Macmillan, 1980).

CAMERON COMMISSION, *Disturbances in Northern Ireland*, Cmnd 532 (Belfast: HMSO, 1969).

CLARKE, A. F. N., *Contact* (London: Pan, 1983).

COLLINS, R., 'Three Faces of Cruelty: Toward a Comparative Sociology of Violence', *Theory and Society*, 1 (1974), 415–40.

COMMUNITY RELATIONS COMMISSION RESEARCH UNIT, *Flight: A Report on Population Movement in Belfast during August 1971* (Belfast: Community Relations Commission, 1971).

COOGAN, T. P., *The IRA* (London: Fontana, 1980).

CROZIER, B., *The Rebels: A Study of Post-War Insurrections* (London: Chatto and Windus, 1960).

DARBY, J., *Intimidation and the Control of Conflict in Northern Ireland* (New York: Syracuse University Press, 1986).

DE BARÓID, C., *Ballymurphy and the Irish War* (Dublin: Aisling, 1989).

DEUTSCH, R., and MAGOWAN, V., *Northern Ireland, 1968–74: A Chronology of Events* (3 vols.; Belfast: Blackstaff, 1973–5).

DILLON, M., *The Shankill Butchers: A Case Study of Mass Murder* (London: Hutchinson, 1989).

—— *The Dirty War* (London: Hutchinson, 1990).

—— and LEHANE, D., *Political Murder in Northern Ireland* (Harmondsworth, Middlesex: Penguin, 1973).

DUGARD, J., 'International Terrorism: Problems of Definition', *International Affairs*, 50 (1974), 67–81.

EGAN, B., and MCCORMACK, V., *Burntollet* (London: LRS Publishers, 1969).

ELLIOTT, S., *Northern Ireland: The First Election to the European Parliament* (Belfast: Queen's University, 1980).

—— *Northern Ireland: The Second Election to the European Parliament* (Belfast: Queen's University, 1985).

—— and SMITH, F. J., *Northern Ireland: Local Government Elections of 1977* (Belfast: Queen's University, 1977).

—— —— *Northern Ireland: The District Council Elections of 1981* (Belfast: Queen's University, 1981).

ENLOE, C. H., 'Police and Military in Ulster: Peacekeeping or Peace-Subverting Forces?', *Journal of Peace Research*, 25 (1978), 243–58.

—— *Ethnic Soldiers: State Security in a Divided Society* (Harmondsworth, Middlesex: Penguin, 1980).

FARRELL, M., *Northern Ireland: The Orange State* (London: Pluto, 1980).

—— *Arming the Protestants: The Formation of the Ulster Special Constabulary and the Royal Ulster Constabulary, 1920–27* (London: Pluto, 1983).

—— *Twenty Years On* (Dingle: Brandon Books, 1988).

FISK, R., *The Point of No Return: The Strike which Broke the British in Ulster* (London: André Deutsch, 1975).

FLACKES, W. D., and ELLIOTT, S., *Northern Ireland: A Political Directory, 1968–88* (Belfast: Blackstaff Press, 1989).

FOOT, P., *Who Framed Colin Wallace?* (London: Pan, 1990).

GALL, N., 'Slaughter in Guatemala', *New York Review of Books*, 20 May 1971, pp. 13–17.

GALLIHER, J. F., and DeGREGORY, J. L., *Violence in Northern Ireland: Understanding Protestant Perspectives* (Dublin: Gill and Macmillan, 1985).

GIBBON, P., *The Origins of Ulster Unionism: The Formation of Popular Protestant Politics and Ideology in Nineteenth-Century Ireland* (Manchester: Manchester University Press, 1975).

GREER, S., 'The Supergrass System', in A. Jennings (ed.), *Justice under Fire: The Abuse of Civil Liberties in Northern Ireland* (London: Pluto, 1988), 73–103.

HALL, M., *20 Years: A Concise Chronology of Events in Northern Ireland 1968–1988* (Newtownabbey, Co. Antrim: Island Publications, 1988).

HAMILL, D., *Pig in the Middle: The Army in Northern Ireland, 1969–1984* (London: Methuen, 1985).

HENDERSON, R., *George Wise of Liverpool* (Liverpool: Protestant Reformers' Memorial Church, 1967).

—— *Seventy-Five Years of Protestant Witness* (Liverpool: Protestant Reformers' Memorial Church, 1973).

HESKIN, K., *Northern Ireland: A Psychological Analysis* (Dublin: Gill and Macmillan, 1980).

HEZLET, A., *The 'B' Specials: A History of the Ulster Special Constabulary* (London: Tom Stacey, 1972).

HOGAN, G., and WALKER, C., *Political Violence and the Law in Northern Ireland* (Manchester: Manchester University Press, 1989).

HOLROYD, F., and BURBRIDGE, N., *War Without Honour* (Hull: Medium, 1989).

IRISH INFORMATION PARTNERSHIP, *Agenda: Information Service on Northern Ireland and Anglo-Irish Relations* (6th edn., London: Irish Information Partnership, 1990).

JENNINGS, A. (ed.), *Justice under Fire: The Abuse of Civil Liberties in Northern Ireland* (London: Pluto, 1988).

JOHNSON, K. F., 'Guatemala from Terrorism to Terror', *Conflict Studies*, 23 (1974), 1–19.

KELLEY, K. J., *The Longest War: Northern Ireland and the IRA* (London: Zed, 1988).

KELLY, H., *How Stormont Fell* (Dublin: Gill and Macmillan, 1972).

KENDRICK, S., BECHOFER, F., and McCRONE, D., 'Recent Trends in Fertility Differentials in Scotland', in H. Jones (ed.), *Population Change in Contemporary Scotland* (Norwich: Geo Books, 1984), 33–52.

KINGSLEY, P., *Londonderry Revisited: A Loyalist Analysis of the Civil Rights Controversy* (Belfast: Belfast Publications, 1989).

LACQUER, W., 'Interpretations of Terrorism: Fact, Fiction and Political Science', *Journal of Contemporary History*, 12 (1977), 1–42.

LEBOW, N., 'The Origins of Sectarian Assassination: The Case of Belfast', in A. D. Buckley and D. D. Olson (eds.), *International Terrorism* (Wayne, NJ: Avery Publishing, 1980), 41–53.

LINDSAY, K., *Ambush at Tully-West: The British Intelligence Services in Action* (Dundalk: Dundrod, 1979).

LUCY, G., *The Ulster Covenant: A Pictorial History of the 1912 Home Rule Crisis* (Lurgan: The Ulster Society, 1989).

LYONS, H. A., 'Violence in Belfast: A Review of Psychological Effects', *Community Health*, 5 (1973), 163–8.

McFARLAND, E., *Protestants First: Orangeism in 19th Century Scotland* (Edinburgh: Edinburgh University Press, 1990).

McGUFFIN, J., *Internment* (Tralee, Co. Kerry: Anvil, 1973).

McKEOWN, C., *The Passion of Peace* (Belfast: Blackstaff Press, 1984).

McKEOWN, M., *Two Seven Six Three: An Analysis of Fatalities Attributable to Civil Disturbances in Northern Ireland in the Twenty Years between July 13, 1969 and July 12, 1989* (Lucan, Co. Dublin: Murlough Press, 1989).

McKITTRICK, D., *Despatches from Belfast* (Belfast: Blackstaff Press, 1989).

McNAMEE, P., and LOVETT, T., *Working-Class Community in Northern Ireland* (Belfast: Ulster People's College, 1987).

MARRINAN, P., *Paisley: Man of Wrath* (Tralee, Co. Kerry: Anvil, 1973).

MATZA, D., *Delinquency and Drift* (New York: John Wiley, 1964).

MOLONEY, E., and POLLAK, A., *Paisley* (Swords, Co. Dublin: Poolbeg Press, 1986).

MOODIE, M., 'The Patriot Game: The Politics of Violence in Northern Ireland', in M. H. Livingston (ed.), *International Terrorism in the Contemporary World* (Westport, Conn.: Greenwood Press, 1978).

MORLEY, M., and PETRAS, B., 'Chile: Terror for Capital's Sake', *New Politics*, 1 (1974) 36–50.

MOXON-BROWNE, E. P., *Nation, Class and Creed in Northern Ireland* (Aldershot, Hants: Gower, 1983).

MURRAY, R., *The SAS in Ireland* (Cork: Mercier Press, 1990).

NEAL, F., *Sectarian Violence: The Liverpool Experience, 1819–1914* (Manchester: Manchester University Press, 1980).

NELSON, S., *Ulster's Uncertain Defenders: Loyalists and the Northern Ireland Conflict* (Belfast: Appletree Press, 1984).

NORRIS, J., *Serial Killers: The Growing Menace* (London: Arrow, 1988).

O'DAY, A., and ALEXANDER, Y. (eds.), *Ireland's Terrorist Trauma: Interdisciplinary Perspectives* (Brighton: Harvester Wheatsheaf, 1989).

O'DOWD, L., ROLSTON, B., and TOMLINSON, M., *Northern Ireland: Between Civil Rights and Civil War* (London: CSE Books, 1980).

O'MALLEY, P., *The Uncivil Wars: Ireland Today* (Belfast: Blackstaff Press, 1983).

O'NEILL, T., *The Autobiography of Terence O'Neill* (London: Rupert Hart-Davis, 1972).

ORR, P., *The Road to the Somme: Men of the Ulster Division Tell their Story* (Belfast: Blackstaff Press, 1987).

PAISLEY, I., jun., *The Case of the UDR Four* (Cork: Mercier Press, 1991).

PATTERSON, H., *Class Conflict and Sectarianism* (Belfast: Blackstaff Press, 1980).

PEARSON, J., *The Profession of Violence: The Rise and Fall of the Kray Twins* (London: Grafton, 1985).

PROBERT, B., *Beyond Orange and Green: The Political Economy of the Northern Ireland Crisis* (Dublin: Academy Press, 1978).

PURDIE, B., *Politics in the Streets: The Origins of the Civil Rights Movement in Northern Ireland* (Belfast: Blackstaff Press, 1990).

ROSE, R., *Governing Without Consensus: An Irish Perspective* (London: Faber and Faber, 1971).

—— *Northern Ireland: A Time of Choice* (London: Macmillan, 1976).

ROSENBAUM, J. H., and SEDERBERG, P. C., 'Vigilantism: An analysis of establishment violence', *Comparative Politics*, 6 (1974), 187–224.

ROUCEK, J. S., 'Sociological Elements of a Theory of Terror and Violence', *American Journal of Economics and Sociology*, 21 (1962), 165–72.

ROWTHORN, B., and WAYNE, N., *Northern Ireland: The Political Economy of Conflict* (London: Polity Press, 1988).

RYDER, C., *The RUC: A Force under Fire* (London: Octopus, 1990).
—— *The UDR* (London: Methuen, 1991).
SCARMAN TRIBUNAL, *Violence and Civil Disturbances in Northern Ireland in 1969*, Cmd 566 (2 vols.; Belfast: HMSO, 1972).
SCHMID, A. P., *Political Terrorism: A Research Guide to Concepts, Theories, Data Bases and Literature* (New Brunswick: Transaction Books, 1983).
SMYTH, C., *Ian Paisley: Voice of Protestant Ulster* (Edinburgh: Scottish Academic Press, 1987).
SNYDER, D., 'Theoretical and Methodological Problems in the Analysis of Governmental Coercion and Collective Violence', *Journal of Political and Military Sociology*, 4 (1976), 277–93.
SPRINZAK, E., 'From Messianic Pioneering to Vigilante Terrorism: The Case of Gush Enumim', in D. C. Rapoport (ed.), *Inside Terrorist Organizations* (London: Frank Cass, 1988), 194–216.
STORR, A., 'The Patriot Game: The Politics of Violence in Northern Ireland', in M. H. Livingston (ed.), *International Terrorism in the Contemporary World* (Westport, Conn.: Greenwood Press, 1978), 231–7.
STYLES, G., *Bombs Have No Pity: My War Against Terrorism* (London: William Luscombe, 1975).
TAYLOR, P., *Beating the Terrorists? Interrogation in Omagh, Gough and Castlereagh* (Harmondsworth, Middlesex: Penguin, 1980).
THORNTON, T. P., 'Terror as a Weapon of Political Agitation', in H. Eckstein (ed.), *Internal War* (New York: Free Press, 1964), 71–99.
TREASTER, J. B., 'Argentina: A State of Fear', *Atlantic Monthly*, 240 (1977), 16–26.
VAN DER MEHDEN, F. R., *Comparative Political Violence* (Englewood Cliffs, NJ: Prentice-Hall, 1973).
WALLER, P. J., *Democracy and Sectarianism: A Political and Social History of Liverpool, 1868–1939* (Liverpool: Liverpool University Press, 1981).
WALLIS, R., BRUCE, S., and TAYLOR, D., 'Ethnicity and Evangelicalism: Ian Paisley and Protestant Politics in Ulster', *Comparative Studies in Society and History*, 29/2 (1987), 293–313.
WARDLAW, G., *Political Terrorism: Theory, Tactics, and Counter-Measures* (Cambridge: Cambridge University Press, 1989).
WIENER, R., *The Rape and Plunder of the Shankill: Community Action: The Belfast Experience* (Belfast: Farset Co-operative Press, 1980).
WILKINSON, P., *Political Terrorism* (London: Macmillan, 1974).
—— *Terrorism and the Liberal State* (London: Macmillan, 1986).
WILLIAMS, T. D. (ed.), *Secret Societies in Ireland* (Dublin: Gill and Macmillan, 1973).
WOODS, I. S., 'Boys of the Boyne', *Scotland on Sunday*, 1 July 1990.
WRIGHT, F., *Northern Ireland: A Comparative Analysis* (Dublin: Gill and Macmillan, 1987).

WRIGHT, S., 'A Multivariate Time Series Analysis of the Northern Irish Conflict, 1969–76', in Y. Alexander and J. M. Gleason (eds.), *Behavioral and Quantitative Perspectives on Terrorism* (London: Pergamon, 1981), 283–328.

INDEX

OXFORD

MORE OXFORD PAPERBACKS

This book is just one of nearly 1000 Oxford Paperbacks currently in print. If you would like details of other Oxford Paperbacks, including titles in the World's Classics, Oxford Reference, Oxford Books, OPUS, Past Masters, Oxford Authors, and Oxford Shakespeare series, please write to:

UK and Europe: Oxford Paperbacks Publicity Manager, Arts and Reference Publicity Department, Oxford University Press, Walton Street, Oxford OX2 6DP.

Customers in UK and Europe will find Oxford Paperbacks available in all good bookshops. But in case of difficulty please send orders to the Cash-with-Order Department, Oxford University Press Distribution Services, Saxon Way West, Corby, Northants NN18 9ES. Tel: 0536 741519; Fax: 0536 746337. Please send a cheque for the total cost of the books, plus £1.75 postage and packing for orders under £20; £2.75 for orders over £20. Customers outside the UK should add 10% of the cost of the books for postage and packing.

USA: Oxford Paperbacks Marketing Manager, Oxford University Press, Inc., 200 Madison Avenue, New York, N.Y. 10016.

Canada: Trade Department, Oxford University Press, 70 Wynford Drive, Don Mills, Ontario M3C 1J9.

Australia: Trade Marketing Manager, Oxford University Press, G.P.O. Box 2784Y, Melbourne 3001, Victoria.

South Africa: Oxford University Press, P.O. Box 1141, Cape Town 8000.

OXFORD BOOKS

THE NEW OXFORD BOOK OF
IRISH VERSE

Edited, with Translations, by Thomas Kinsella

Verse in Irish, especially from the early and medieval periods, has long been felt to be the preserve of linguists and specialists, while Anglo-Irish poetry is usually seen as an adjunct to the English tradition. This original anthology approaches the Irish poetic tradition as a unity and presents a relationship between two major bodies of poetry that reflects a shared and painful history.

'the first coherent attempt to present the entire range of Irish poetry in both languages to an English-speaking readership' *Irish Times*

'a very satisfying and moving introduction to Irish poetry' *Listener*

PHILOSOPHY IN OXFORD PAPERBACKS
THE GREAT PHILOSOPHERS

Bryan Magee

Beginning with the death of Socrates in 399, and following the story through the centuries to recent figures such as Bertrand Russell and Wittgenstein, Bryan Magee and fifteen contemporary writers and philosophers provide an accessible and exciting introduction to Western philosophy and its greatest thinkers.

Bryan Magee in conversation with:

A. J. Ayer	John Passmore
Michael Ayers	Anthony Quinton
Miles Burnyeat	John Searle
Frederick Copleston	Peter Singer
Hubert Dreyfus	J. P. Stern
Anthony Kenny	Geoffrey Warnock
Sidney Morgenbesser	Bernard Williams
Martha Nussbaum	

'Magee is to be congratulated . . . anyone who sees the programmes or reads the book will be left in no danger of believing philosophical thinking is unpractical and uninteresting.' Ronald Hayman, *Times Educational Supplement*

'one of the liveliest, fast-paced introductions to philosophy, ancient and modern that one could wish for' *Universe*

LAW FROM OXFORD PAPERBACKS

INTRODUCTION TO ENGLISH LAW
Tenth Edition

William Geldart

Edited by D. C. M. Yardley

'Geldart' has over the years established itself as a standard account of English law, expounding the body of modern law as set in its historical context. Regularly updated since its first publication, it remains indispensable to student and layman alike as a concise, reliable guide.

Since publication of the ninth edition in 1984 there have been important court decisions and a great deal of relevant new legislation. D. C. M. Yardley, Chairman of the Commission for Local Administration in England, has taken account of all these developments and the result has been a considerable rewriting of several parts of the book. These include the sections dealing with the contractual liability of minors, the abolition of the concept of illegitimacy, the liability of a trade union in tort for inducing a person to break his/her contract of employment, the new public order offences, and the intent necessary for a conviction of murder.

THE OXFORD AUTHORS

General Editor: Frank Kermode

THE OXFORD AUTHORS is a series of authoritative editions of major English writers. Aimed at both students and general readers, each volume contains a generous selection of the best writings—poetry, prose, and letters—to give the essence of a writer's work and thinking. All the texts are complemented by essential notes, an introduction, chronology, and suggestions for further reading.

Matthew Arnold
William Blake
Lord Byron
John Clare
Samuel Taylor Coleridge
John Donne
John Dryden
Ralph Waldo Emerson
Thomas Hardy
George Herbert and Henry Vaughan
Gerard Manley Hopkins
Samuel Johnson
Ben Jonson
John Keats
Andrew Marvell
John Milton
Alexander Pope
Sir Philip Sidney
Oscar Wilde
William Wordsworth

Oxford Reference

The Oxford Reference series offers authoritative and up-to-date reference books in paperback across a wide range of topics.

POLITICS IN OXFORD PAPERBACKS
GOD SAVE ULSTER!
The Religion and Politics of Paisleyism

Steve Bruce

Ian Paisley is the only modern Western leader to have founded his own Church and political party, and his enduring popularity and success mirror the complicated issues which continue to plague Northern Ireland. This book is the first serious analysis of his religious and political careers and a unique insight into Unionist politics and religion in Northern Ireland today.

Since it was founded in 1951, the Free Presbyterian Church of Ulster has grown steadily; it now comprises some 14,000 members in fifty congregations in Ulster and ten branches overseas. The Democratic Unionist Party, formed in 1971, now speaks for about half of the Unionist voters in Northern Ireland, and the personal standing of the man who leads both these movements was confirmed in 1979 when Ian R. K. Paisley received more votes than any other member of the European Parliament. While not neglecting Paisley's 'charismatic' qualities, Steve Bruce argues that the key to his success has been his ability to embody and represent traditional evangelical Protestantism and traditional Ulster Unionism.

'original and profound . . . I cannot praise this book too highly.' Bernard Crick, *New Society*

HISTORY IN OXFORD PAPERBACKS

THE STRUGGLE FOR
THE MASTERY OF EUROPE 1848–1918

A. J. P. Taylor

The fall of Metternich in the revolutions of 1848 heralded an era of unprecedented nationalism in Europe, culminating in the collapse of the Hapsburg, Romanov, and Hohenzollern dynasties at the end of the First World War. In the intervening seventy years the boundaries of Europe changed dramatically from those established at Vienna in 1815. Cavour championed the cause of *Risorgimento* in Italy; Bismarck's three wars brought about the unification of Germany; Serbia and Bulgaria gained their independence courtesy of the decline of Turkey—'the sick man of Europe'; while the great powers scrambled for places in the sun in Africa. However, with America's entry into the war and President Wilson's adherence to idealistic internationalist principles, Europe ceased to be the centre of the world, although its problems, still primarily revolving around nationalist aspirations, were to smash the Treaty of Versailles and plunge the world into war once more.

A. J. P. Taylor has drawn the material for his account of this turbulent period from the many volumes of diplomatic documents which have been published in the five major European languages. By using vivid language and forceful characterization, he has produced a book that is as much a work of literature as a contribution to scientific history.

'One of the glories of twentieth-century writing.'
Observer

RELIGION AND THEOLOGY
IN OXFORD PAPERBACKS

A HISTORY OF HERESY

David Christie-Murray

'Heresy, a cynic might say, is the opinion held by a minority of men which the majority declares unacceptable and is strong enough to punish.'

What is heresy? Who were the great heretics and what did they believe? Why might those originally condemned as heretics come to be regarded as martyrs and cherished as saints?

Heretics, those who dissent from orthodox Christian belief, have existed at all times since the Christian Church was founded and the first Christians became themselves heretics within Judaism. From earliest times too, politics, orthodoxy, and heresy have been inextricably entwined—to be a heretic was often to be a traitor and punishable by death at the stake—and heresy deserves to be placed against the background of political and social developments which shaped it.

This book is a vivid combination of narrative and comment which succeeds in both re-creating historical events and elucidating the most important—and most disputed—doctrines and philosophies.

OXFORD REFERENCE

THE CONCISE OXFORD COMPANION TO ENGLISH LITERATURE

Edited by Margaret Drabble and Jenny Stringer

Based on the immensely popular fifth edition of the *Oxford Companion to English Literature* this is an indispensable, compact guide to the central matter of English literature.

There are more than 5,000 entries on the lives and works of authors, poets, playwrights, essayists, philosophers, and historians; plot summaries of novels and plays; literary movements; fictional characters; legends; theatres; periodicals; and much more.

The book's sharpened focus on the English literature of the British Isles makes it especially convenient to use, but there is still generous coverage of the literature of other countries and of other disciplines which have influenced or been influenced by English literature.

From reviews of *The Oxford Companion to English Literature*:

'a book which one turns to with constant pleasure . . . a book with much style and little prejudice' Iain Gilchrist, *TLS*

'it is quite difficult to imagine, in this genre, a more useful publication' Frank Kermode, *London Review of Books*

'incarnates a living sense of tradition . . . sensitive not to fashion merely but to the spirit of the age' Christopher Ricks, *Sunday Times*